A Way Out of No Way

A Way Out of No Way

A MEMOIR OF TRUTH, TRANSFORMATION,
AND THE NEW AMERICAN STORY

Raphael G. Warnock

PENGUIN PRESS · *New York* · 2022

PENGUIN PRESS
An imprint of Penguin Random House LLC
penguinrandomhouse.com

Insert Image Credits: pp. 1–7, courtesy of the author and the Warnock
family; pg. 8, (top) AP Photo / John Bazemore, (bottom) Barry Williams
via Getty Images; pp. 9–12 courtesy of Richard A. DuCree;
pg. 13 (top) courtesy of Warnock for Georgia, (bottom) courtesy of
Dasheika Ruffin; pg. 14 courtesy of Warnock for Georgia;
pg. 15 (top) courtesy of Richard A. DuCree, (bottom) courtesy of
the Warnock family; pg. 16 courtesy of the Warnock family.

LIBRARY OF CONGRESS CATALOGING-IN-PUBLICATION DATA
Names: Warnock, Raphael G., author.
Title: A way out of no way : a memoir of truth, transformation, and the new
American story / Raphael G. Warnock.
Description: New York : Penguin Press, [2022] | Includes index.
Identifiers: LCCN 2022001968 (print) | LCCN 2022001969 (ebook) |
ISBN 9780593491546 (hardcover) | ISBN 9780593491553 (ebook)
Subjects: LCSH: Warnock, Raphael G. | United States. Congress.
Senate—Biography. | African American legislators—United
States—Biography. | Legislators—United States—Biography. |
Legislators—Georgia—Biography. | African American
Baptists—Clergy—Biography. | African American political
activists—Georgia—Biography.
Classification: LCC E901.1 .W367 2022 (print) | LCC E901.1 (ebook) |
DDC 328.73/092 [B]—dc23/eng/20220201
LC record available at https://lccn.loc.gov/2022001968
LC ebook record available at https://lccn.loc.gov/2022001969

Printed in the United States of America
1st Printing

Set in SabonLTPro
Designed by Cassandra Garruzzo Mueller

For Chloé Ndieme and Caleb Babacar,
With all my love and prayers for your future,
and with profound gratitude for the best title ever!
—Dad

Do not get lost in a sea of despair. Do not become bitter or hostile. Be hopeful, be optimistic. Never, ever be afraid to make some noise and get in good trouble, necessary trouble. We will find a way to make a way out of no way.

CONGRESSMAN JOHN LEWIS

Contents

CHAPTER ONE

Boys Like Us   1

CHAPTER TWO

Close yet So Far   21

CHAPTER THREE

Becoming a Morehouse Man   49

CHAPTER FOUR

New York State of Mind   73

CHAPTER FIVE

Stepping Out on My Own   99

CHAPTER SIX

Spirit of the Kings   119

CHAPTER SEVEN
Putting On My Own Shoes   143

CHAPTER EIGHT
Making History   173

CHAPTER NINE
Fighting for Our Lives   207

Acknowledgments   231

Appendix 1: Let My People Go, William Belden Noble Lecture,
Harvard Memorial Church   235

Appendix 2: Maiden Speech on the Senate Floor   251

Notes   261

Index   269

A Way Out of No Way

CHAPTER 1

Boys Like Us

I could tell by the sound of my mother's voice. Something was wrong.

"Ray," she said, taking a deep sigh before finishing her voice-mail message that day in September 1997. "I need to talk to you about something."

My mother, Verlene, then fifty-nine years old, is a proud Georgian, having spent nearly all her days in the 110 miles between the towns of Waycross, where she was born, and Savannah, where she eventually landed and raised her own family. Mom is a preacher with a God-given sense of spiritual discernment, or what some might call a sixth sense, and she could read people and situations better than anyone I've ever known. So, when she said she needed to talk, I was always inclined to listen carefully.

When she called me that day, I was living in New York City,

pursuing a doctoral degree at Union Theological Seminary, and working as an assistant pastor at Harlem's iconic Abyssinian Baptist Church. As the eleventh of twelve siblings in our big family, I was the first to graduate from college, and my parents and siblings were protective of me. They tried hard not to distract me with bad news from home, which usually meant I was the last to know if something was wrong.

"So, Mom, what's going on?" I asked when I reached her later that day at home in Savannah.

"Keith got arrested," she said finally, referring to the brother one step above me in birth order, though we are five years apart. She sounded sad and exhausted. I was stunned. Hurt. Confused. *My* big brother, the proud police officer?

"Arrested?" I said. "For what?"

There was a long pause.

"Drugs," she replied.

He was charged with aiding and abetting the distribution of cocaine by providing security for drug dealers. He had been caught in an FBI sting that implicated eleven officers—ten current and former officers of the Savannah Police Department, and one from Chatham County.

This was incomprehensible. There must have been some kind of mistake. Not Keith, my stocky, clean-cut older brother, the high school football player who was so in love with the Dallas Cowboys that his friends nicknamed him Dorsett, after the team's celebrity running back of the 1980s. My mind flashed back to those joyful, carefree days.

• • •

Keith was the athlete of the family. He ran track and played foot-ball at Johnson High School, which first opened in 1959 on the east side of town as a laboratory school for Savannah State College (now Savannah State University), a historically Black college. The high school was named in honor of Solomon "Sol" C. Johnson, a prominent businessman who in 1889 became the second editor and ultimately the owner of *The Savannah Tribune*, one of the coun-try's oldest Black-owned newspapers. In our day, the school was better known for the uniqueness of its mascot, the Atom Smashers, than for the prowess of its football team. Despite Keith's famous nickname and his pretty good skills on the field as a running back, Johnson High went almost two years straight during his time there without winning even a single game. That didn't stop the fans from showing up each week, though, hoping for a miracle.

I played in the Myers Middle School band at the time. I'd switched from the trumpet to the baritone horn to fill a need in the brass section of our band. One special Friday night we got to per-form during halftime with the Johnson High School band on the football field at Savannah State. The Atom Smashers were ahead, and I will never forget the thrill of counting down the last seconds of that game. The miracle we all had been anticipating finally hap-pened. The team broke its long losing streak, and the crowd went wild, as if our boys had just won the state championship. Students rushed from the stands onto the field, and I joined the flow, with my eyes darting around, searching for my big brother. When I spotted his jersey, I dashed across the field and wrapped him in the biggest hug. And for a moment, the two of us—me in my band uniform and Keith in his dirty football gear—stood there under the glare of the Friday night lights, feeling like stars.

The Herbert Kayton Homes public housing project, where my family lived, sat in the school attendance zone for Johnson High. I was about nine years old when we moved there. My oldest siblings were grown and living on their own by then, which left six of us kids living in the four-bedroom apartment with our parents, and we all shared one bathroom. Occasionally, one of the older siblings would move back home for a short while, making our tight space even tighter. But we always made room. We were taught that next to God family trumped all else.

My father, Jonathan Warnock, had served in the U.S. Army during World War II and was self-employed. He hauled junk, mostly abandoned cars, salvaging their metal at the local steelyard in exchange for cash. In my youngest years, he also served as pastor of a small Pentecostal Holiness church. Mom stayed at home to take care of our big family.

I mostly remember Kayton Homes as a nurturing village, even in the 1980s when the crack epidemic and the deadly HIV/AIDS virus swept into and devastated poor communities like ours throughout the country. But in a place where there were too many missing fathers, I had two devoted parents at home, and they kept church at the center of our lives. On Sundays, there were two services, the first in the morning with a short afternoon break before the evening service. A few Sundays a year were designated as "Youth Sunday," and the young people of the congregation under eighteen years old conducted the entire program, sometimes even the sermon. One such Sunday night, Keith volunteered to deliver the sermon, and as I sat there, listening to him express his faith, I thought, "Well, I can do that!" Not long afterward, I took a turn in the pulpit, expressing my faith, to be sure, while also trying to one-up my big brother.

Keith and I, the two youngest boys in the family, shared a room. He slept on the bottom bunk, and I slept on the top. But, as I said, there were five years between us, and when you're a kid, that can feel like a generation. So he and my five other big brothers were my silent protectors, and they helped buffer me from the potential dangers of our neighborhood. God only knows how many times I might have been spared from being a target when a neighborhood troublemaker learned, "Oh, that's Keith's baby brother!" There was plenty of trouble around, but despite my surroundings I never felt unsafe or threatened. I don't even recall ever getting into any fights. The love, support, and validation I got from my family shaped how I saw myself and the world around me.

Keith and I were among the last to leave our crowded house. He proudly enlisted in the U.S. Army right out of high school in 1983. In a neighborhood where many kids did not even finish high school and those who did tended to go straight into the job market with no special skills, Keith was going to make something of himself. I was so proud. We all were. Going into the army would give him a chance to serve his country and a path forward, out of generational poverty. He would acquire skills, perhaps even a college degree, for the changing job market and enter safely into the middle-class life we imagined for ourselves.

Before Keith even left for the army, I was practicing the role of big brother. One Sunday afternoon, when my sister Valencia was eleven and I was twelve, we joined some friends—all pastors' kids (affectionately called PKs)—at their house for dinner, a ritual deep in the culture of the Black church, the soul food that always follows the food for the soul. Their parents and our parents were friends. Their dad, the Reverend Maurice Rouché, was the pastor of the church that we were by then attending as a family and where I had preached my first sermon about a year earlier. For all of us, Sundays were typically dedicated to church, except for the afternoon break. After our meal, we kids piled into a car and headed to a nearby grocery store.

Jheri curls were a very popular hairstyle at the time, and some of the girls were busy looking for their Care Free Curl activator and other products. I had a habit back then of walking with my hands in my pockets, which was just adolescent awkwardness. But as we moved about the store, a man, dressed in army fatigues, quickly approached us.

"Come with me!" he said authoritatively.

Instinctively, my sister started to move. I stopped her, reminding her that we were not to go anywhere with a stranger.

"Who are you?" I asked the man.

"Security," came the response.

I asked to see his badge, and he flashed one, responding sarcastically, "Is this good enough for you?"

As the security officer marched us through the store, I noticed the judgmental eyes of shoppers on us. The walk of shame seemed to take forever. Down the aisle. Past the cashiers. And up a flight of stairs to an observation room. He and other officers had been watching us. He informed us that we needed to be frisked. It was obvious what he suspected, but what good would it do to protest our innocence? He would see soon enough. Seeing that no female officer was present, I requested one to handle my sister. We were just children, but I felt protective of her. They searched each of us and of course found nothing. We had taken nothing. We were not shoplifters. With that, we were casually dismissed without an apology or even an acknowledgment of the humiliation we had just experienced. Instead, the officers lectured me to keep my hands out of my pockets while walking through a store. One of them even joked that the next time I entered the store I should just look up at the mirrored observation room from which they had watched us, smile, and wave. It was my first brush with the myriad ways in which Black people experience hurtful and demeaning racial stereotyping and discrimination in everyday life.

By the 1980s, America's booming, post–World War II industrial era was fading, and old rust belt towns and inner-city communities, like the one around Kayton Homes, were suffering badly from what the Harvard University sociologist William Julius Wilson would describe as "the disappearance of work" with all of its attendant consequences. It was a historical inflection point that cried out for historic investments in skills training for a new kind of industrial era: the emerging digital age of personal computers, information technology, and increasing automation. Instead, the country made heavy investments in a different kind of industry: a massive, increasingly privatized prison-industrial complex that would over a couple decades make the land of the free the incarceration capital of the world.

In the news reports I caught back then, Black boys, particularly those in low-income neighborhoods in the nation's cities, were discussed mostly as statistics. Numbers without names or faces. Or faces to be feared. The crack epidemic brought a lot of deadly weapons and gang warfare to a lot of streets. That warfare was met with more. They called it the war on drugs. And it devastated and hollowed out whole communities. The instructions given to boys like us were more about avoidance than aspiration: Young man, do not end up dead. Or in prison.

My brother was one of the lucky ones. He managed to escape the street war and entered into another. He would serve in Operation Desert Shield during the first Gulf War, in 1990, and survive it, too. A few years later, he returned home, worked for a while, and eventually joined the Savannah Police Department. We had stayed in touch through the years as I attended college and moved to New York City for seminary. As far as I knew, he loved his job. With a strong athletic build, my brother looked good in uniform. His army uniform and his police uniform. He had been a police officer less than two years when my mother called me in New York to tell me about his arrest.

The headline screamed, BUSTED TRUST. I couldn't make sense of the news story I was reading online about his arrest. I called my brothers and sisters. Had we missed something? Had something gone awry in the military? Had Keith seen things during the war that messed up his mental health? My siblings were all as baffled and heartbroken as I was. We'd grown up under the same roof and the same rules. Though Keith's father, my mother's first husband, had been largely absent from his life, my dad provided us all with an upstanding example. People today would call us a blended family, but we never thought of ourselves as half- or step-anything. We were one family. Together, our parents instilled good Christian values. Honesty. Humility. Hard work.

Exasperated, I uttered, "He wasn't raised like this."

I soon flew home to Savannah to help the family find an attorney, and the news was even worse than I thought. There were many hours of police surveillance tape, an attorney we hoped to hire told me. "Your brother is in a world of trouble," he said.

A magistrate judge had set Keith's bond at $50,000. Dad used a small piece of property he owned as collateral to post the required 10 percent of the bond. Dad didn't have to come up with actual cash, but his property would be forfeited if Keith did not show up for trial. This enabled Keith to wait for his day in court under house arrest with an electronic monitoring device attached to his ankle.

Ultimately, my family could not raise the attorney's $20,000 retainer fee. That was nearly more than my parents brought home all year, and everybody around us was not much better off. It quickly became obvious that we would not be able to afford a decent lawyer. As I got in the car alone and headed to the airport for my flight back to New York, the harsh reality of it all burned like hot coals in my chest. First a warm trickle, then a tear, and soon a flood poured down my face. His life—our lives—were about to change forever.

As I learned more about my brother's case, my disappointment in him was matched by my anger at the criminal justice system. All the defendants were Black. In a police force that was dominated by white officers, the FBI had targeted only African American officers. In my brother's case, the FBI controlled the entire operation, including the amount of drugs that were supposedly being transported—enough to meet the mandatory minimum sentencing guidelines and guarantee long prison terms. The operation had used a convicted felon to lure the rookie officers into a fabricated drug operation with the opportunity to make some easy cash.

I didn't dismiss my brother's behavior. In fact, it made me angry. He had allowed himself to be enticed into a criminal scheme that might have landed drugs in poor Black communities, the kinds of communities I've always fought to protect—except that none of it was real. The felon who set the deal up was an FBI informant, and the drugs belonged to the FBI. It seemed clear to me that the federal government had taken full advantage of a rookie cop who used very bad judgment. And no matter what my brother's role might have been, he deserved fair treatment in a system with a long history of racism.

At the opening statements, when one of the defense lawyers raised the selective prosecution issue, the incensed judge admonished him: The race card will not be played in these proceedings. And if anyone does, punishment for using it will be swift in coming and painful upon arrival.

The race card was a direct reference to the O. J. Simpson trial two years earlier, which revealed the deep racial divide in experience and perspective between white and Black citizens, owing to their respective encounters with the criminal justice system. For white America, the "not guilty" verdict for Simpson, rendered by a predominantly Black Los Angeles County jury, was a gut punch, deeply biased and unbelievably unfair. On the other hand, Black people, in public spaces from coast to coast, cheered. But they were not necessarily cheering for O. J., who had long cut any real ties to the African American community. And they certainly were not cheering the tragic and violent deaths of Nicole Brown Simpson and Ron Goldman. Too many of them knew that pain in their own families. Rather, they were cheering for Johnnie Cochran, Simpson's incredibly talented lawyer who, with his brilliance, had bested a system that meted out deep injustice in courtrooms and police brutality on streets in South Central Los Angeles and in Black and brown communities across America. A thousand times a thousand. Every single day. They remembered the deep pain of the Rodney King verdict, just a few years earlier, by a mostly white jury, after seeing his brutalization on tape; knew all too well the presumption of guilt laid upon their own bodies just for entering a store; and heard through the dark tunnel of that experience the resonating voice of a lawyer who spoke with the rhythm of a poet and the righteous indignation of a preacher: "If it doesn't fit, you must acquit."

But there would be none of that in the federal courtroom of Judge B. Avant Edenfield. The attorneys had been warned: keep race out of it, no matter if it were true, or the consequences would be severe.

Nonetheless, I put together a fact sheet detailing everything I knew about the case and contacted some pastors in Savannah to find out if they would be willing to protest the selective prosecution that targeted African Americans. There were a number of meetings, including one with the Reverend Joseph Lowery, then president of the Southern Christian Leadership Conference (SCLC), who happened to be in town. I also had a conversation with the Reverend Jesse Jackson, whose local point person, Joe Beasley, connected me with clergy in Savannah at the state meeting of the General Missionary Baptist Convention of Georgia. Days later, I organized a press conference in Savannah with some of the ministers to ask questions about the case. The ministers called on the presiding judge, who had already shown his hand of bias, to recuse himself.

The usually sluggish pace of the criminal justice system seemed to operate on steroids in Keith's case. He was arrested in September 1997, and he went to trial in November, just two months later. The entire trial lasted about five days. I got to testify as a character witness for about five minutes, recalling my brother's strict upbringing in the church, his athleticism, and his trouble-free teen years. When court adjourned for the jury to deliberate, we all exited the courtroom, and my siblings and I gathered, along with our parents, under a big oak tree, dripping with Spanish moss, in the adjoining town square. Savannah's historic antebellum architecture has always given the city a certain southern charm. But its monuments to Confederate soldiers and celebration of Civil War history also harbor the story of a time that was anything but charming for African Americans. Nevertheless, my hometown's beauty and character are undeniable—verdant town squares with cobblestone streets, and oak trees that have been growing for hundreds of years. Beneath the vast canopy of one of those old oaks and with the thick, humid air of Savannah pushing against our lungs like a heavy burden, my family joined hands in a circle and breathed out prayers to God for mercy.

The jury returned quickly—within hours. We filed back into that federal courtroom as a family—waiting, worrying, hoping that somehow, no matter how tense the room felt in that moment, our prayers would be answered. I searched the jurors' faces for clues about their decision, but they seemed to avoid looking our way. That was not a good sign. The clerk read the verdict: guilty. There was a loud, collective gasp among my family members, and the tears flowed as we held one another in disappointment and disbelief.

"Don't let them take him away!" Valencia cried, wailing for her big brother.

I saw pain, shock, and fear in Keith's eyes, and I felt completely helpless, as the U.S. marshals pushed him against a wall, hand-cuffed him, and led him away. Our hearts broke.

I was back in New York a few weeks later as Keith appeared before the same judge for sentencing. Once again, my mother called with the news: life in prison. *Life?* Nobody had died. Nobody had gotten physically hurt. Nobody even got high. Yet my brother, then a thirty-three-year-old man and army veteran with no prior criminal history, was sent to prison for the rest of his life without the possibility of parole. This was a stunning lesson about the unevenness of the criminal justice system and the racist implications of 1980s and 1990s federal drug laws that put in place the mandatory minimum sentencing guidelines, making such harsh sentences possible and rendering too many Black and brown lives disposable.

To this point, I had been a student preparing myself for ministry, studying at the feet of giants, mostly following their lead—at Morehouse College in Atlanta, at Union Theological Seminary in New York, and at two historically significant Baptist churches, Sixth Avenue Baptist Church in Birmingham, Alabama, and Abyssinian Baptist Church in Harlem. But the spiritual meets the practical in the lives of hurting people who are facing systemic injustice. This is where ministry moves beyond the pulpit, where the church becomes a site for human transformation and the preacher actually becomes a sermon, embodying through example the gospel ethic of love and justice.

I learned how to advocate for my brother, how to articulate the larger human rights issue, and how to rally people around it. I learned, too, how to stay the course, no matter how bleak the outlook. I drew strength from the great examples of leaders like the Reverend Dr. Martin Luther King Jr., who told the white establishment poetically but unapologetically that Black people were no longer willing to wait for their freedom and then inspired an entire, multiracial movement of freedom fighters to march until the walls of legal segregation came tumbling down; the Reverend Dr. Lowery, among Dr. King's closest confidants and one of the founders of the SCLC and its longest-serving president, who stayed in that role from 1977 to 1997, during which time the movement to free South Africa was afoot; the Reverend Dr. Otis Moss Jr., a preacher's preacher and movement foot soldier who turned words into poetry and poetry into power in the pulpit and in the public square; the Reverend Dr. Prathia Hall, a fiery preacher who blazed new trails for women as one of the first female field organizers for the Student Nonviolent Coordinating Committee in the early 1960s; Marian

Wright Edelman, a Spelman valedictorian and Yale Law School graduate who put her brilliance and passion to work speaking up and fighting for poor, voiceless children through the Children's Defense Fund; the Reverend Dr. Calvin O. Butts III, the activist, university president, and pastor of Abyssinian, possibly New York's most influential Black congregation, where he had mentored me personally and directed the church's resources into economic ventures that helped to lift the city's poor and working class; and his pastoral predecessor the great Samuel DeWitt Proctor, also a past college president, scholar, leader of the Peace Corps in Africa, and mentor to many students who matriculated at North Carolina A&T, including a young Reverend Jesse Jackson. Growing up, I thought of Reverend Jackson as a larger-than-life civil rights superhero who channeled the liberationist vision of the civil rights movement into two presidential runs, situating political issues in a moral frame and laying the groundwork for candidates of color and women to run and win high political offices presumed out of reach for them. These and many other courageous souls whom I admired showed me that to be effective, you have to be willing to put your body in the game—show up, give what you have (your time, your money, your skills), and do what you're asking of others.

Over the next two-plus decades, I did all I knew to do for my brother. I wrote letters, accepted calls, encouraged him, visited him, and never stopped trying to find a strong, competent attorney who would help our family fight for justice on his behalf. I even met with the famed attorney Johnnie Cochran and some of his associates in New York. Meanwhile, Keith was transferred across the country from one federal prison to another, making it more difficult for our family to visit him regularly. At one point he was sent to a federal prison in Leavenworth, Kansas, which has a large U.S. Army base that trains young privates, as Keith once was. My visits with Keith, though far-flung and infrequent, were essential to our brotherly bond. To touch him, laugh with him face-to-face, and see the passage of time in each other helped us to feel connected. In those moments, the prison walls and everyone else in the visiting room faded away, and we were just two brothers spending time together, catching up on news about family and friends, feeling a bit of normalcy in a situation that was anything but that.

The years were passing, loved ones were growing older, and the dreams that my brother had dreamed as a young man in his prime—what he could become, what he could have, what he could do with his life—were slowly evaporating. When Keith first went to prison, he had been married just a year or two. Around the time of the trial, he and his wife, Robin, conceived a child. Keith was in prison by the time Zoé, his beautiful baby girl, was born, and each year he spent behind bars marked another birthday for his young daughter. Five. Twelve. Sixteen, not so sweet. I was in awe of Keith's strength and how he managed to keep a positive outlook, but occasionally when I asked how he was doing, he couldn't hide the sadness.

"I'm tired," he'd say.

His exhaustion was mental, yet he was unwilling to let the depression overtake him. He fought the urge to feel hopeless and hung on to the belief that he would get out of prison someday. It was the biggest dream he could manage. For both of us, saying goodbye was the toughest part. The thought of him there without easy access to family, especially on holidays like Christmas and Thanksgiving, when our family had big, raucous traditional gatherings, never ceased to sadden me. Yet we never lost faith that he would join us again at our mom's kitchen table someday. And we never stopped fighting to make it happen.

The lessons I learned while advocating for my brother would inform my ministry work in the years ahead in the pulpit, in the community, and even now as a U.S. senator in service to the state of Georgia and my country. I've seen up close the scourge on the American soul that is mass incarceration, particularly of Black and brown men, like my brother. Mass incarceration is one of the pressing civil rights issues of the day, and my push for more than two decades to free my brother is a steady source of fuel that fires my fight for real change, for transformation.

In my brother's case, a federal judge, nominated by the president of the United States and confirmed by the U.S. Senate, had issued that unjustly harsh sentence. Keith's experience underscores the importance of one of the democratic values that I hold most dear: voting rights. The right to vote is at the core of a well-functioning democracy. The president and senators are elected by the people, exercising their right to vote. A vote is sacred. It avows the worth of every human being. It is in essence a prayer for the kind of world we desire for ourselves and our children.

On election night in January 2021, when I learned that a record number of Georgia voters had chosen to make me the state's first African American U.S. senator and only the eleventh Black senator in the entire history of the institution, I was overjoyed and deeply humbled. My dad had not lived long enough to see this day. Neither had my older brother Terry, who died in August 2012, nearly two years after my father. I desperately wanted to share this life-changing moment with my eighty-two-year-old mother, who I had insisted remain quarantined at home in Savannah because of the pandemic. My sister Joyce had the same thought, pulled out her cell phone, and punched in Mom's number.

"Mom," I said when she answered. "This is your son, *Senator Raphael Warnock!*"

She laughed. I could hear such joy in her laughter. I've learned to read her voice—a skill picked up over decades of trying to figure out a strong woman who keeps her sorrows buried deep. It was the sound of her voice that gave a hint of her pain all those years ago when she called to tell me about my brother's arrest.

My mother embodies the pain and the promise of America. She spent many days as a teenager in the 1950s bent over in scorching heat and in the cotton fields of Waycross, Georgia. But those now-wrinkled hands that once picked somebody else's cotton had picked her baby boy to be a U.S. senator. She endured the degradation of Jim Crow in the land of her birth yet experienced her country's compassion as it helped to provide housing, food, and student loans for my college debt when my father's hard work was not enough. She'd felt the heartbreaking injustice of racism in an American criminal justice system that had sent her second-youngest son, a soldier and first-time offender, to prison for the rest of his life. Yet, here in this same America, Georgia voters were sending her baby boy to represent them in the U.S. Senate.

And just maybe in this fractured moment in history, he'd get to help live out the meaning of his name, Raphael: "the Lord heals." To help our nation make a way out of no way.

But in our time on the phone that election night, Mom was having none of the serious talk. With a sense of humor that can bring levity to even the grandest moment, she wanted to make sure I wasn't getting a big head.

"Great!" she said, responding to my pronouncement that I'd won the Senate race.

She liked the sound of it, her son, a *U.S. senator.* But just in case there was any doubt who was the boss, she added, "I'm still Mama!"

We burst into laughter.

CHAPTER 2

Close yet So Far

In 2009, Keith had been transferred to a small federal prison in Estill, South Carolina, then a majority-Black town of roughly two thousand people. Named for a Confederate officer, Estill sits about fifty-two miles north of Savannah. This was the closest my brother had been to home in the decade since his incarceration, and our family was grateful that we could at least see him regularly. It had been tough enough that he was in prison. But his incarceration in places so far from home made the pain even more excruciating, especially for our parents. No phone calls or second-hand reports, even from a sibling's occasional visit, could ever equate to a mother and father laying their own eyes on their child.

By the time my parents got to see Keith in Estill, my father was ninety-one years old and needed a cane to steady his steps. But he was determined to see for himself how Keith was faring, so my brother Jeffrey drove our parents to the prison for a visit. They all sat in the visitors' room with several other families, gathered around individual tables with their imprisoned loved ones. Dad seemed impressed by how healthy Keith appeared under the circumstances.

"Your eyes look bright," Dad told him. "Looks like you've been taking care of yourself."

Mom kept the conversation flowing, but Dad was mostly quiet, even more contemplative than usual. By nature, Dad was a deep thinker, sage and reflective. He often spoke in parables. Even when we got into trouble with him as children, he was more likely to use lessons from the missteps and wrong turns in his own life to correct us. By the time he finished what felt like a sermon, we almost would have preferred the spanking.

Dad wasn't the kind of man who wasted time on small talk or frivolity. I don't recall him ever taking time out for recreation or a vacation. Even though he once fished to earn money, he never took us kids fishing for fun. The beach was just a half-hour drive away from home, but he never took us there either. He was cut from that generational cloth where father primarily meant two things: provider and protector. He felt no obligation to befriend his children, yet he was kindhearted and warm. We always knew he was there for us, and we felt his love, though he rarely spoke of it. Sometimes, he would regale us and later the grandchildren with magic tricks, like pulling a coin from behind our ears. He even created a puzzle, using two wire hangers that he twisted into two flawless rectangles, connected by what he called a key. He would challenge us to use the "key" to disconnect the pieces, and despite our best efforts we never could. He'd then turn his back, disassemble it in seconds, leaving us with our mouths agape. My older siblings called him Rock for all the traits the moniker implied: strong and dependable, but also stubborn and immovable. So I can imagine the bit of unspoken awkwardness Dad must have felt that day—this man of such strong character and faith, who had preached to his children all our lives about making good choices to avoid places like this, sitting inside that place, contemplating how a boy he'd raised had wound up here, close yet so far from home.

Born in 1917, Jonathan Warnock was the youngest of Samuel and Carrie Warnock's four children. He was the baby of the family, yet his two older brothers and sister nicknamed him Father because he always seemed older than his years. He was just four years old when his family left their home in rural Burke County, Georgia, and relocated to Savannah. His paternal grandfather, Madison Warnock, owned a farm in Burke County, and Samuel and Carrie lived and worked on the farm. At Carrie's insistence, they left for Savannah, a city that seemed to offer more autonomy and the opportunity for a better life.

As a young man, Dad was drafted in the U.S. Army during World War II and served about a year, all Stateside. He experienced firsthand the indignities of that era's Black military men, who served their country dutifully at a defining time in its history yet were treated as second-class citizens, particularly in the segregated South. Dad headed back home to Savannah on a public bus. He was dressed proudly in his army uniform as the bus rolled through town, pulled to a stop, and began filling with new passengers. The white bus driver pointed at my father and ordered him to get up and move farther back so a white teenager could sit. To the white driver and passengers, the skin he was wearing was more consequential than the U.S. Army uniform he was wearing. Dad knew the grave consequences a Black man could face if he dared to disobey. Black men and boys had been dragged from their homes and lynched for less. He obliged but never forgot.

Inspired in part by his own internal entrepreneurial drive but also by his refusal to suffer the everyday indignities and economic vulnerabilities of working for people who refused to acknowledge his humanity in the Jim Crow South, Dad always worked for himself. He had a fierce work ethic, and his hauling business sometimes transported produce—peaches, apples, watermelons—or a load of glass or junk cars to area markets or factories. By the early 1960s, he was divorced with a teenage son, Jonathan Emmanuel, who was old enough to help in the business. The two of them were transporting a load of glass in the truck late one rainy evening with two other teen boys, whom Dad had enlisted to assist. Suddenly a car appeared out of nowhere on the rural Georgia highway and rear-ended Dad's truck. The car slammed hard into the truck and skidded partly underneath its chassis. When Dad and his stunned passengers climbed out of their vehicle, they saw blood and glass everywhere. They also saw a horrific scene inside the car, where the driver, a young white man, had been decapitated. The passenger, another young white man, had been thrown from the vehicle but miraculously survived the crash. White residents of the area heard the commotion and began gathering at the dreadful scene. Shattered lives and shards of glass spilled all over that rural Georgia highway. Within minutes, the sheriff, also white, arrived, lights flashing and sirens blaring.

As Dad looked into the sea of white faces, a sense of foreboding filled him. Saddened by what had just happened and terrified by what appeared on the verge of happening, Dad inched close to his boys and whispered that they had to stick together. They might have to fight for their lives. Dad began to pray. Not the long or eloquent prayer of a Sunday morning preacher, but the hushed sounds and urgent pleas of a man in trouble. As they would sometimes do in those late-night prayer services in the Holiness Church tradition, in which I was raised, Dad simply called on the name of Jesus—repeatedly, silently, passionately. The sheriff approached and in his thick Georgia drawl questioned Dad and his passengers about the accident. Then, after taking his time to survey the scene, the sheriff turned to Dad with an unexpected question: "You boys need a ride home?"

In shock, Dad and the teenagers glanced back and forth at one another. The sheriff added that he'd warned the young men in the car multiple times about driving drunk and flying so recklessly up and down those rural back roads. This wasn't the reaction Dad expected in this era with a group of Black men left to explain the death of a young white man and the injury of another. But Dad and his helpers all lived to tell the story. And tell it, Dad did—over and over in his sermons, recounting God's grace and mercy. After recounting the story, he would often recite the scripture that says, "The name of the Lord is a strong tower: the righteous run into it and are safe" (Proverbs 18:10).

Dad had entered parish ministry in his forties, eventually becoming the senior pastor of Triumph the Church and Kingdom of God in Christ. My mother joined the congregation when she returned to Savannah after a failed marriage. She had been about eighteen years old when she first made her way to Savannah and lived with an aunt who was a Holiness preacher. In time, Mom got married, moved for a few years to Florida, and started her own family. But the marriage didn't last, and when she moved back to Savannah, her new pastor was divorced with four children (a son and three daughters). Mom was twenty-one years younger, also divorced, and the mother of six children (five sons and a daughter).

One evening after service, one of the church mothers, a position of authority and reverence that is bestowed on the most senior women of the congregation, told my father that a young lady from church needed a ride home. The young lady was my mom. The two of them talked during the ride and realized that they had much in common, despite the obvious age difference. A friendship began blossoming, and on one occasion when the pastor drove his new friend home, she invited him inside. He marveled over how this single mother managed to keep her home so spotless, well organized, and orderly while raising six children there.

He had an idea and politely excused himself.

"I'll be right back," he said and left briefly.

He returned a short while later with a take-out dinner for Mom and her children. The thoughtful gesture immediately won over the children, especially Jeffrey, the big eater of the family. That was the first of many dates, often with all six of the young mother's children in tow. The pastor would come by in his burgundy station wagon, and they'd all climb in for a ride to River Street, a walk down its cobblestone way lined by little shops, then a stop on the way back home at the local Dairy Queen. The couple soon fell in love and got married, blending their families into one.

I entered the world on July 23, 1969, the eleventh child in our big family. My father was thrilled that God had blessed him with another son at fifty-two years old. He believed in the power of words and put much thought into my name. He chose Raphael, whom people of faith believe was an archangel and healer—thus, the Hebrew meaning, "the Lord heals." For my middle name, he picked Gamaliel, a wise Jewish teacher of the law who mentored the apostle Paul and in a critical moment defended the apostles against persecution. The name means "gift from God."

I was the baby of the family for less than a year when, just ten days short of that mark, my sister Valencia Reneé, number 12, came along. The two of us were raised as close as twins, and in everybody else's eyes we were a unit, nicknamed Ray and Nay, "the babies." We were post-civil-rights-movement babies, born in the years following the assassinations of Dr. King and Robert Kennedy, and the killing of three Black students at South Carolina State in Orangeburg. We were born amid the chaos of Vietnam War protests, a burgeoning Black Power movement, and a nation still reckoning with the complexity of its own self-understanding, conceived in liberty, expanded through genocide, built by slaves.

There was still so far to go, but we reaped the benefits of the movement, of paths cleared, doors kicked open, and a country that was coming to grips with the ugliest parts of its past and deciding that "we the people" could be better. Jim Crow with its discriminatory policies and practices was receding to the Dream—the Beloved Community that recognizes the intrinsic worth of every human being, values love over hate, and defends the right of every American to justice and equality. A backlash against the social justice demands of the civil rights movement was also already afoot and the fight to realize the dream continues today.

I never drank from a colored water fountain, used a colored restroom, or attended a school assigned by the color of my skin. I was never forced to give up my seat on the bus to a white passenger, as my father had been while dressed in his military uniform on that shameful day. While he told his children the story, Dad never seemed bitter. It was at his church that I learned to recite the Pledge of Allegiance. In Dad, I saw a true patriot who loved his country, despite its flaws, a man who never lost faith that his country someday would find a way to live up to its ideals.

America's story has always been complicated.

I grew up watching Dad work to the point of exhaustion every day and still fall short of the ability to provide fully for our family. But, thanks to the assistance of the federal government, my family never lived outdoors, we never went hungry, and I never missed out on an opportunity to learn. As a preschooler, I attended Head Start, a program aimed at helping to prepare children from low-income families for school. In high school, I was accepted into the Upward Bound program and spent Saturday mornings and six weeks during the summer on the campus of Savannah State College for enrichment in mathematics, English, and science. When it came time for college, I received Pell Grants and low-interest student loans that helped to pay my way. These were all good, federally financed programs that have given America's poor children a chance and lifted poor Black children from the sunken places caused by generations of willful racism.

I was a happy kid, and everyone in the family figured I was born to be a preacher, just like my dad. My older sister Joyce even playfully nicknamed me the Joseph of the family, a biblical reference to the dreamer who was favored by his father and ultimately rose to become a powerful ruler of Egypt, second in charge under Pharaoh. But as far as I know, my siblings never plotted to kill me or sell me, as Joseph's did. And I certainly was not spared from teasing. One could not survive growing up in the big Warnock household with a thin skin. We children grew up playing a game called the dozens, during which participants try to outwit one another with the best insult. And we played it about as much as we prayed. Everybody got teased, mercilessly. So I learned to dish it out as well as I could take it and even became somewhat of a master of the "yo' mama" jokes.

Our sense of humor must have come from our mother, whose own mother, Lucinda Armstrong Brooks, had a raucous humor that reminded me a bit of Moms Mabley, the trailblazing Black comedian who rose to stardom in the 1960s, telling slightly raunchy jokes, dressed as a toothless old lady in a housedress and floppy hat. My grandmother mostly kept it clean, but she was always trying to make us laugh. My maternal grandfather, James Alfonso Brooks, was the more serious of the two. He was a tall, burly man with big hands and feet at least a size 13. He had to lean way over just to get through the door of the family's little house on Vernon Street in

Waycross. He was sharp, articulate, and very well read, though he had no formal post-secondary education. Stacks of books surrounded him in his bedroom, and they were all in Braille. My grandfather was blind, and he navigated the double darkness of blindness and life as a Black man in the South with his big brown hands. He served as chairman of the Deacon Board at Friendship Baptist Church and with a distinctive bass voice sang in a quartet there. Everybody in town knew and respected Deacon Brooks.

Once, a pair of white police officers knocked on his door after being called by my grandparents' neighbors. The officers explained that the neighbors were upset about a disagreement that had occurred between their daughter and my mother's older sister. An imposing figure, my grandfather explained in his deep voice with perfect diction that it seemed to him that this was a dispute between teenagers and that the neighbors ought to discipline their teenage daughter and he surely would discipline his. The officers agreed and were about to walk away when my grandfather posed a question: "Which way are you boys going? Can you drop me off at the church?" Grandpa got to church that day in the back of a police car.

My grandfather called my grandmother Doll, and when my mother was growing up, the family owned a popular Laundromat. My mother and her siblings pitched in to help their parents operate the place. But by the time I came along, the building had been lost to fire, and all that remained was its concrete slab, which became a sort of playground for us kids. When Mom took us to visit her parents, I noticed that my grandfather's artificial eyes always peered up, seemingly locked on the ceiling. But when we entered his room, he stretched out those big hands to feel the shapes of our heads, which enabled him to tell his grandchildren apart. He also made a living with those hands, creating beautiful wicker furniture for sale. Grandma fed our sweet tooth with her delicious homemade cakes and, of course, kept us entertained.

My paternal grandfather, Samuel, had died by the time I was born, but I recall my father's mother, Carrie, as a strong, stern, and independent woman. After all, it was she who in the 1920s had left the family's farm in Burke County for Savannah on her own, staying there until Samuel realized that this was the direction the family would take in search of a new start. Carrie, or Lil' Mama, as we called her, saved her money and managed the family's affairs on her own terms. For a while, the family owned a fish market. And at the age of fifty-eight, the woman, born in 1892, learned to drive. Her grandchildren might have been a primary motivation as she carted them from place to place.

My brother and older cousins tell me that she took them on a surprise visit one day to the local Chevrolet dealer. When she told the salesclerk that she would like to take a look at the pretty green station wagon on the sales floor, he informed her that she could not afford that car but he would gladly show her their used cars out back. She responded that she would actually like to see the price on the car that had caught her eye. Again, he insisted that she walk with him to see the used cars she could probably afford. Losing her patience, Lil' Mama said, "I didn't ask about the damn cars outside. I asked you about THAT one!" With a condescending smirk on his face, he finally relented and told her the price: $3,000. My grandmother sat down, reached into her purse and pulled out a roll of bills. And then another. And another. She rolled back her stockings and retrieved another. After that day, the grandkids all enjoyed riding around in Grandma's brand-new 1952 Chevrolet, paid for in cash. Perhaps my grandmother, like some others from her generation, never quite overcame the trauma of the 1929 stock market crash and the run on the banks. When she died in 1985 and family members were cleaning out the house, they found about $11,000, a large sum for my family, in rolls of cash stashed away in paper bags bound in rubber bands, in Eight O'Clock Coffee canisters, under mattresses, in cabinets, and in various crannies of her home, where she lived alone until the ripe old age of ninety-three.

I was fifteen when she died, and at her funeral I led the choir, singing the solo part of a song recorded by the gospel artist Keith Pringle titled "I Feel Like Going On." My godmother, Mable Butler, was a musician who sang and played the piano, and from the time I was about five years old, she began putting me before our small church congregation to sing. I can't help but laugh when I picture myself then, a skinny kid, standing there with precious little life experience, earnestly belting out hymns like "He Touched Me" and intoning with considerable pathos heavy gospel lyrics like James Cleveland's "Lord, help me to hold out until my change comes."

Throughout my childhood, there was usually so much laughter in our house. We couldn't afford cable, and seldom did we go to the movies. So we spent much time trying to figure out how to prank a sibling or catch one another off guard. I was still in elementary school when I used my skills as a budding young preacher to trick

Jeffrey. The Pentecostal and Holiness churches of my childhood were places brewing with a passionate and palpable spirituality that manifested itself in song, sermons, and shouts of praise. Worship often culminated in an altar call or prayer lines where the preacher would speak directly to the individual concerns of members, exalting and encouraging them, offering prayers of faith and affirmation, including the "laying on of hands," as modeled by the apostles of the early church. So it wasn't too unusual when I approached Jeffrey and laid my right hand on his forehead, as if I were about to pray for him. Unsure what to think but careful not to reject a blessing from above, he closed his eyes.

"In the name of Jesus," I said slowly in my best revivalist voice. "God is going to give you . . ."

I paused for effect and then bellowed, "A new face!"

My brother's eyes popped open as he realized he'd been had. One for baby boy. My parents, who had been watching the whole time, fell out laughing. And I dashed away to avoid my comeuppance.

We kids made our own fun, and among our favorite family pastimes was an activity we jokingly called ghetto skiing, considering it was as close as we would get to a ski slope at the time. Interstate 16 ran high behind our public housing development, and a smooth, grassy hill sloped from the side of the highway ramp down to our neighborhood. We'd walk to a nearby furniture store and take big empty appliance boxes that had been set out for trash and mash them down into cardboard sleds. We'd proceed up to the ramp, then stand, sit, or lie on our makeshift sleds and slide down the slope. We were so confident in our skills that my sister even slid down the hill a time or two with our one-year-old niece in her arms. I'm so thankful that, as the church people always said, God looks out for children and fools.

We were a traditional religious family with Mom as the primary caretaker for the children. Mom cooked, cleaned, and washed never-ending loads of laundry at a time when she had to hang each piece on a clothesline to dry. She was, too, our prayer warrior. As a boy, I sometimes awakened late at night or in the wee hours of morning to use the only bathroom in the house and would find the door locked. As I stood there, restlessly waiting my turn, I could hear my mother's voice, calling out to God in prayer for her children, at times by name.

We looked to Dad as the head of the household. All the boys helped in some way in Dad's junk business (though my older brothers always claimed I wasn't required to work as much as they had been). By the time I was old enough to assist, Dad's business focused mostly on abandoned cars, salvaging their metal at the local steelyard in exchange for cash. Dad would leave his business cards, with his telephone number and the message "We Buy Junk Cars" in large letters, on old cars. A brilliant, self-educated man, my father even devised his own pulley system to load the cars onto the truck and stack them atop one another. How Dad designed and built different versions of these pulley systems—welding together spare parts of steel on the back of an old Mack truck, safely lifting, loading, stacking, and hauling cars—all without any formal training in engineering or physics and without incident, baffles my mind to this day. He took the old vehicles to a small piece of property he owned off the beaten path, next to a railroad track. He then salvaged the metal parts and took them to Chatham Steel Corporation in town for cash.

It was grueling work, and sometimes he was so tired when he made it home that his eyes closed while he was chewing at the dinner table. And that was just the exhaustion from his day job. For many years he also served as a pastor, which had its own time demands and responsibilities. Both my parents were dedicated to their work in the church and made sure we attended Sunday school, sang in the choir, and participated in youth activities. At home, my parents made the Bible as real to us as family history by telling us stories about the people and events in the scriptures in a way that we could understand, like the story of twelve-year-old Jesus getting lost in Jerusalem. I was four or five years old, riding in the car with Mom at Christmastime one year, when she began telling me about how Jesus was accidentally left behind in Jerusalem as his parents returned from their annual pilgrimage to the Festival of the Passover. Assuming he was within the company of travelers, they went a day's journey before realizing he was missing. Not finding him among relatives or friends, they returned to Jerusalem, where they found him after searching for a terrifying three days, my mother explained. They finally found him in the temple, discussing the faith among the teachers and elders, who were all amazed by the boy's brilliance. When his parents told him of their frantic search, Jesus responded, "Did you not know that I must be about my Father's business?" That sounded a bit sassy to my young ears, especially after Jesus had caused his parents so much worry. So I looked up at my mom with my characteristically big, almond eyes and said earnestly, "Mary should've gotten a big ol' switch and tore Jesus up!" Mom could do nothing but laugh.

Years later, when a bit of sibling rivalry inspired me to preach my first sermon at age eleven, I harked back to that biblical story with a sermon, titled "It's Time I Be About My Father's Business," encouraging young people to get involved in the work of faith and service. My mom helped me to write it. From that moment through my twenties, I'd talk through my sermons with my parents after a simple question, "What do you think about this?"

I admired my father's preaching style and wanted to be just like him. A preacher in the Holiness Church tradition, he preached with clarity, passion, and fire. Often using vivid illustrations and recalling the challenges, near misses, and miraculous survival stories of his own life, Dad spoke of a God who walks beside you through life's dark moments and dangerous valleys. One who never abandons us, especially those who feel forgotten, discarded, and lost in a mean, cold world. The junkman who lifted abandoned junk cars on weekdays, seeing their value, lifted broken people on weekends, convincing them of theirs.

I so wanted to be like my dad that at times I practiced being him.

One summer day, when I was about six years old, I was preaching in my empty room. I hit my stride and slipped into that preachsing rhythm, modeling some of the revival preachers I had heard on the radio or seen at our church, inhaling one long breath after another, sounding between phrases as if I were on the verge of hyperventilating. Sweat poured down my face. Unbeknownst to me, my mother stood watching and listening just outside my door. With keen discernment, Mom sensed that this was indeed child's play—yet perhaps something more. I was imitating the highly animated expressions of a faith she hoped would become my own. She smiled and summoned my brothers. "Somebody go and rescue that boy," she said calmly. One of my brothers, most likely Keith because we shared a room, entered our room, put his arm around my shoulder, and cooled me down.

With the age gap between my older brothers and me, I never attended school with them, and I was too young to really hang out with any of them. So I had my own friends. When I was in the fifth grade, a guy named Gary McCoy moved with his family next door. Gary loved science and books, like me, and we became the best of friends, and remain so to this day. One summer, the two of us read all the books in the Kayton Homes' little resource library. Another time, we decided we would create our own pesticide and get rich selling it. We raided our parents' cleaning supplies and mixed everything we could find—409, Mr. Clean, bleach, and more—in an old spray bottle. When we sprayed it on a couple of bugs and they died, we knew we had hit the jackpot. But before we could figure out how to mass-produce our concoction and make money, our plan blew up—literally. Gary had taken the bottle home one evening, and that night a small explosion blasted the cap off.

Gary and I soon advanced to building things. We sometimes took the bus to the local mall and spent the day at Radio Shack, which at the time sold science kits with pieces that could be assembled into various projects. Once each of us built a crystal radio, a simple radio receiver, assembled on a wooden board with a ground wire that enabled it to operate without batteries or an electrical cord. For the junior high science fair in seventh grade, I read a book that described how to build an electric quiz game and came up with the hypothesis for my project: Can you build an electric quiz game using school supplies? With Gary's help, I assembled the supplies, and we walked across the street to B&B's, a hardware and paint store. We were explaining to an employee what we were trying to do when a bespectacled, sandy-haired older guy overheard us and offered a suggestion.

"You need a soldering gun," he said, walking toward us. He explained that the soldering gun is a pistol-shaped tool that would help us attach our pieces for the desired result, and he talked us through the steps of how to do it. Gary helped me put the game system together, complete with a buzzer, using typical school supplies, like paper clips, for the school science fair. I was ecstatic when my project won a blue ribbon at both the local and the regional levels. I was even invited to the state fair, but my family couldn't afford the trip to Atlanta, which would have required that we drive there and cover the costs of lodging and meals. But from then on, Gary and I considered Tom, the clerk at B&B's, a new friend, and we often stopped at the store counter to chat with him when we came up with a new crazy scheme.

I never learned anything more personal about Tom than his name, but I never forgot his kindness. He was just a random white salesclerk who saw two young Black boys in the hardware store as we were: smart, creative, and ambitious. He didn't stereotype us, make assumptions about our purpose in the store, or dismiss our ambitions. He chose instead to affirm our humanity, to be kind, a gesture that left a lasting impression on a couple of boys in their formative years.

Around the time that Gary and I were building things, I began thinking of a career as an electrical engineer. While I loved preaching, I saw how hard my father struggled to make a living and knew he never would have been able to survive on his pastor's salary alone. From what I saw, parish ministry was not the kind of full-time career that would enable me to make a decent living. My favorite hobby was building things or taking them apart, studying their inner pieces, and then figuring out how to put them back together. I even kept two shoeboxes, filled with random wires, batteries, and other small spare parts, underneath Keith's bottom bunk in our room. I'd carefully collected the items, knew exactly what was in each box, and didn't want anything to disappear. That led to one of my favorite creations: an alarm to keep my baby sister, Valencia, out of my room. I put the alarm together, primarily using wires, aluminum foil, and a horn that sounded when she tried to open the door. It worked hilariously well.

Gary and I were both good students, and as high school sophomores we were recruited by the local health department to work as peer counselors. We worked for a program that aimed to flip peer pressure on its head by using teens to influence other teens to abstain from sex or at least protect themselves. The goal was to reduce teen pregnancy. The teen counselors were trained to talk about abstinence, as well as various methods of birth control. I could hardly believe we got paid for doing this. It was a rare office job that teens could get before age sixteen, and I kept it throughout high school. During the summer, my position was financed by the federal Job Training Partnership Act, which, in part, provided federal subsidies to companies that hired kids from low-income families. Programs like this took some of the burden off poor parents by enabling their children to help provide for themselves. The programs also kept impressionable teens engaged in productive, skills-building work and off the streets. Where else could a poor teenager from the projects get training in a professional office environment, like the one where Gary and I worked? As part of that work, we also served at a teen runaway shelter called the Bridge, where we helped to operate the crisis hotline. At one point, I was promoted to office manager and drafted a letter inviting churches to be part of our network by allowing the teen counselors to visit and talk to youths in the congregations. I knew the church community, and the campaign was well received as invitations from churches and community groups began to pour in. One of our public presentations was covered by WTOC, the local CBS affiliate, and I was interviewed for the story. After watching my interview, Doug Weathers, a popular anchor for the station, reached out to his sister, Norma Weathers, a teacher at my high school, to inquire about me. She happened to be my civics teacher. The next thing I knew I was the new teen reporter at WTOC, delivering stories related to teenagers every Friday on the 5:30 p.m. news.

Still, there was another form of communication that most captured my imagination and interest. I'd decided to pursue a career in preaching and parish ministry. I sometimes talked to Dad, who was a very thoughtful exegete of scripture and thought about its practical implications in the lives of ordinary people. Long before my introduction to theologies of liberation in seminary, it was my non-seminary-trained dad who suggested to us that Jesus found himself on the wrong side of the powers that be because, as Luke 4:18 suggests, he sided with the poor. Dad also fully supported my mother when she later felt called to preach. Many churches and denominations, including Pentecostals and Baptists, to this day use the scriptures to justify their exclusion of women from the pulpit. Throughout much of my childhood, women could give exhortations from the floor of the sanctuary. But the raised pulpit was reserved for pastors, and all of the pastors were men. I was in high school when Mom started her own at-home Bible study with a few friends who wanted to spend more time examining the scriptures. About a dozen people met in our living room in the Kayton Homes on Tuesdays, about 7:00 p.m. Often, I made it home in time to enjoy some of the punch and cookies afterward. Occasionally, I walked into the kitchen during the day and found Mom seemingly in another world, with her back to the door as she washed dishes. I could hear her preaching in a whisper, working out sermonic ideas in her head, trying to find her voice as a minister. Mom's Bible studies eventually grew into a small Holiness church, where she served as pastor. Dad had retired as a pastor by then, and their roles flipped; she became his pastor until his death.

In high school, another preacher increasingly captured my attention and focus: the Reverend Dr. Martin Luther King Jr. At the Bull Street public library, which I could freely visit, unlike Black people in the generation right before me, I found old LP recordings of some of the mass meetings during the civil rights movement. I repeatedly played one of Dr. King's key sermons, "A Knock at Midnight," which he had delivered on a number of occasions. Through the recording, I could feel the power in the room so many years ago as King turned one of Jesus's parables on prayer into a call for the church to pray with its feet—to reject racism, classism, and blind emotionalism so that the faithful could answer the knock of desperate people seeking hope in desperate times. His eloquent manner of speaking and powerful message deeply moved me. He preached a different kind of gospel from what I'd typically heard in most churches. Not only did he focus on the personal salvation of followers of Christ, but he used the lens of the scriptures to examine and speak out against racial injustice and oppression. In doing so, he had motivated masses of people to speak up for themselves and change racist systems.

I took the further step and began imagining myself in that space as the preacher. I even began trying to sound like Dr. King. There is a musical quality to King's preaching, a kind of singing it while saying it. The son, grandson, and great-grandson of preachers, he had a style steeped in the "whooping" tradition of folk religion but refined in elocution by his training at Morehouse College, Crozer Theological Seminary, and Boston University. I loved the way his preaching to the head and heart caused both the person with a PhD and the person with little education at all to feel he was speaking directly to them.

After my first sermon at Calvary Temple, my home church, word spread quickly around parts of Savannah about the precocious young preacher who sounded a bit like King. Like my church, many of those churches held services that were led largely by the youth once or several times each year. This created opportunities for me, and eventually I began getting invitations to speak at Youth Day programs in churches across the city. By the time I was seventeen, I spoke with the cadence of a seasoned Baptist preacher, standing in pulpits across Savannah, leaning slowly and authoritatively into each syllable, as if eternity itself were contained in every word. Channeling King's voice, I began the journey toward finding my own.

I felt at home in the pulpit. I loved the exhilaration of studying the Bible and finding fresh new ways to explain the scriptures. I loved the ability to move people, encourage them, get them to act. I'm not one of those preachers with a dramatic testimony of "running from the call" to do God's bidding, initially rejecting the responsibility that comes with it, only later to experience a monumental moment of reckoning. Instead, I moved steadily toward the call with the belief that if I did my best to be faithful, I would end up where I'm supposed to be. Most of the churches that were inviting me were Baptist. Until then, I had not ventured far beyond my family's Pentecostal Holiness faith, which like most churches, regardless of denomination, focused on helping people live chaste, holy lives. Most churches tended to concentrate on the side of faith that emphasizes one's personal walk with God. Few of them saw social justice issues as central to their Christian identity or the church's mission. Their occasional engagement in the political and social justice arenas was tangential at best.

To my surprise, though, an assignment for an eleventh-grade English literature class would take my religious awakening to a new level. The class had been studying literary devices like metaphors, symbolism, and imagery, and as the teacher described each term, I thought, "That sounds like Black preaching to me." I'd heard my father and other Black preachers all my life use words in their sermons to compare like things and paint vivid pictures of heaven and hell, trials and tribulations, to drive home their point. So, when the teacher assigned the class to write a paper about the use of those literary devices in a work of our choosing, having already written several papers on the Euro American classics, this time I chose symbolism and imagery in Black sermons and spirituals.

While searching in the library for source material, I stumbled across a book called *The Spirituals and the Blues* by the theologian James H. Cone, who made the case for how slaves and their descendants used music, particularly the old spirituals and the blues, to express themselves, communicate subversively, and survive the harsh conditions of slavery and oppression. I also discovered his book titled *For My People: Black Theology and the Black Church* and encountered therein the term "black theology," a perspective that ties the gospel to the fight against the oppression of Black people in America. Dr. Cone was a primary voice in this field, starting that conversation in the late 1960s with an argument that God identifies with the struggles of the poor and in the American context that had to mean the liberation struggle of Black people.

My spiritual awareness broadened even more in my senior year of high school when my job supervisor, the Reverend Marvin Lloyd, a local minister, gave me a small anthology called *Best Black Sermons*. He knew that I was a preacher and would be heading off to college soon, and he wanted me to have the book, which included riveting sermons from many of the giants in the Black activist Baptist preaching tradition, including King, Benjamin Elijah Mays, Otis Moss Jr., Kelly Miller Smith, and Samuel Berry McKinney. As King had earlier, they astounded me with the power and relevance of their messages. Their words seemed to lift right off the pages.

Their eloquent, powerful call for people to stand up for themselves pricked my soul and removed the scales from my eyes.

I was maturing enough to see that the culture of injustice is still embedded in the soul of this nation, as deep as the southern roots of the centuries-old, moss-draped oak trees that grow like canopies over the cobblestone streets of my hometown. It is a culture that marks a group of African American preachers' kids who stop in the grocery store for snacks between church services on a Sunday afternoon as criminal suspects, based solely on the color of their skin. A culture that turns a blind eye as tens of thousands of people begin dying in an AIDS epidemic, in its earliest days primarily white gay men, followed by a disproportionate share of Black and brown victims. A culture that considers Black lives disposable in a federal war on drugs that targets them and throws them away in prisons with disparately long sentences. Rooting out this lingering culture of bigotry and injustice is part of the movement's unfinished work.

It wasn't lost on me that practically all the preachers I was gravitating toward were Baptist. Many of them, including King, were also Morehouse men. In the years ahead, both institutions would transform my life.

By the time my parents were finally able to visit Keith at the federal prison in Estill, the years were showing on Dad's frail body. Keith could see it. He got up from the table in the visitors' room and fetched crackers from a big vending machine for Dad with hope that a bite to eat could sustain our father's strength. But Dad kept saying that he was cold. Always a small, strong man, he seemed that day just small. Dad had seen what he had come there to see: his boy was holding up well. And Keith, seeing Dad's discomfort, didn't want to keep him there much longer. So, as difficult as it was to part from his family after so many years, Keith stood to say goodbye. They hugged and left hopeful that, with the distance gap closed, their visits would become regular.

That was not to be.

On September 27, 2010, Mom summoned all the children to the hospital, where Dad had been admitted after suffering from complications caused by pneumonia. We gathered in the waiting room outside the intensive care unit and prayed. My sister Joyce, who also is a pastor, and I spoke words of comfort, reminding our family that if Dad was indeed transitioning from us, as the doctors predicted, it was sad but not tragic. At ninety-three, he had lived a full life, surrounded by the love of his wife, children, extended family, and church family, and he was moving in that grand, beautiful procession from life on this side to eternal life.

"At this point, all we can do is wait on God," I told my family.

The youngest, Valencia, always a "daddy's girl," went back into Dad's room for a final, tearful goodbye. Mom had made her way to Dad's side as well. Moments later, I heard the doors swing open and Valencia screaming my name: "Ray, come here!"

My sister redirected our mother back to the waiting room as a swirl of young doctors pushed and pulled on Dad's frail body to resuscitate him. Resuscitation can seem like such a violent ritual. Dad was by then skin and bones, his body whittled down to less than one hundred pounds. It appeared the tremendous measures needed to save him first might break him. The family had discussed this very scenario and decided that we didn't want him to suffer like this; we wanted him to go in peace. I hadn't known that I would be the one to deliver the family's wishes in that final moment. But then one of the doctors looked up at me and said, "Sir, we can keep doing this, but is this really what you want?"

No, it was not, I uttered. The frenetic atmosphere grew suddenly silent and still, and the realization crept all over me that my first hero, my first example, my first teacher, was gone. I stood silently, tears sliding down my face, knowing my life was forever changed.

I summoned the strength to make my way back to the waiting room to break the news to my family. My eyes met my mother's first, and I knew she already knew. The earthly journey was complete for the man who had been her pastor (and she his), best friend, life partner, and father in their beautiful, blended family. As I stood there on wobbly legs, I spoke the only words I knew that could bring a bit of comfort to Mom and the rest of my hurting family at such a time: "The Lord has spoken."

A few days later, I was honored to preach my father's eulogy. The message was titled "The Extraordinary Epitaph of an Ordinary Man," and I opened with a poem by the nineteenth-century English poet Percy Shelley, which I learned in that eleventh-grade literature class. It is a famous poem that underscores the foolishness and the folly of thinking of oneself too highly. The poem focuses on the epitaph of an Egyptian pharaoh whose tombstone boasted of his greatness, beginning, "My name is Ozymandias, king of kings." But Shelley used the sharp contradiction of the former king's near-buried tomb and the decay surrounding it to show that all powerful rulers and their empires come to an end. I contrasted that poem with the biblical story of Enoch, a humble man whose story is barely told in the scriptures. We learn simply in Genesis 5:22 and 5:24 that "Enoch walked with God." There is little else. But then in Hebrews, when great heroes of the Bible are cited for the kind of exemplary faith that pleased God, Enoch is mentioned among them. He might not have commanded the attention of the scribes, but he was seen by the one who mattered and thus gained the reward of eternal life.

"His story, though it should, will not tonight make the CBS Evening News," I said of my father. "In the eyes of the world, my daddy was an ordinary man. But that's all right. Because Enoch was an ordinary man. But he had an extraordinary epitaph."

My father represents the salt of the earth, blue-collar brother, brilliant with no college degree or prestigious credentials, innovative enough to create miracles with his hands, the kind of Black man whose life doesn't make the headlines for either shooting hoops or shooting bullets, for breaking out or breaking in. So, like most among us, he remains unseen. He loved his wife. He took care of his family. He shepherded the people in his church. He endured racism without becoming bitter. And he loved his country. He was a walking sermon.

We laid Dad to rest in a veterans' cemetery in South Carolina, not far from our home in Savannah. And the inscription on his tombstone is how he would want to be remembered.

"Private Jonathan Warnock. He walked with God."

CHAPTER 3

Becoming a Morehouse Man

Although no one in my very large immediate family had ever graduated from a four-year college or university, I always knew that I would. My older siblings worked in various trades that mostly required vocational school and on-the-job training. Like my dad, my older brothers pursued good and honorable work that involved working with their hands. Emmanuel and Jeffrey became truck drivers, Leon became a carpenter, and Terry and Frank were painters. Keith joined the army and later law enforcement. My sisters, Aunetta and Wandetta, were unionized telecom workers, and Joyce, a respiratory therapist. Together, they and my parents were a part of the village that protected and nurtured me and Valencia, the youngest. They believed in me, and that made it easy for me to believe in myself.

It was the Upward Bound program, though, that strengthened that confidence and provided a path for the pursuit of my dreams.

Upward Bound is a federal program from Lyndon B. Johnson's Great Society era. The program identifies high school students from low-income communities and/or those who would be among the first generation in their family to graduate from college and coaches them for academic success. For a kid growing up in a neighborhood where, as far as I know, nobody had a bachelor's degree, it demystified the idea of college and gave me a clear vision of what was possible.

I will forever remember with gratitude my Johnson High School principal, Gwendolyn P. Goodman, who selected me for the program. Mrs. Goodman was a diminutive African American woman with real gravitas. She was among my earliest examples of what strong leadership looks like. Each morning, she stood, arms folded across her chest, in the hallway of the school to greet her students. Her countenance and composure said, "I love you, but don't try me." And if you had good sense, you didn't. Mrs. Goodman was not only our principal but also for many a mentor and a mother. There were about a thousand of us students; roughly 55 percent of the student population was white and 40 percent or so Black and, reflective of the larger community, a handful of Asian and Latino students. Honestly, I was shocked, when I later moved to Atlanta and then to New York and traveled the country, to discover how racially segregated most American public schools were then and still are today, nearly seventy years after the Supreme Court in *Brown v. Board of Education* declared segregation unconstitutional.

If she didn't know the names of all one thousand students, in the ways that really matter Mrs. Goodman knew us and our families. A Savannah State graduate and lifelong educator, she had taught some of our parents as a biology teacher in the same school in her earlier days. I was drawn to her poise and powerful presence, and from the moment I first heard her on the intercom giving the morning school announcements, I felt a connection to her. She had the most impressive, polysyllabic vocabulary of anyone I knew. Like me, she loved big, pretty-sounding words. On the day she summoned me to her office and told me that she had selected me for Upward Bound, I was so excited. I knew that impressing Mrs. Goodman was not to be taken for granted. Moreover, I knew that when Gwen Goodman summoned you, you came, and where she sent you, you went. As we say in the church, I had been "volun-told!"

In my junior year of high school, my big sister Joyce, who, eleven years my senior, had been something of a second mother to me since infancy, gave me her old Pontiac Sunbird hatchback to get to and from work and my extracurricular activities. Early Saturday mornings, I picked up three of my friends who were also in the program. Hershell, Clinton, Cattrell, and I would put together our quarters and dollars to buy gas, about ninety-nine cents per gallon in the mid-1980s, and head to the campus of Savannah State for our Upward Bound classes.

During the summer, we stayed in dormitories on campus and took college preparatory classes for six weeks. We also took special summer trips that expanded our imagination, providing exposure to arts, beauty, history, and culture in places that children from low-income families might not otherwise have an opportunity to visit. One long bus trip took us all the way up the East Coast from Savannah to New York City. We had such fun, visiting the most famous sights, including the Empire State Building and the Statue of Liberty. We even went to a theater to see the musical *Mama, I Want to*

Sing. Little did I know then that just five years later I would pack my bags, move to New York, and spend a decade there, studying in seminary and serving in one of the city's most influential churches.

We also visited Atlanta, and the four-hour bus trip there was my first visit to the Martin Luther King Jr. Center for Nonviolent Social Change. I had been fascinated and inspired by Dr. King since my first exposure to him during elementary school. I don't recall learning much about him in school, but to show their support for a national effort to make Dr. King's birthday a federal holiday, many parents across the country, including mine, pulled their children out of school on his birthday in those years. In my area, we wound up at the May Street Y (YMCA) for teach-ins about Dr. King's life that sought to make the day away from school meaningful for us kids. As I stood inside the King Center as a teenager, next to exhibits that showcased his Nobel Peace Prize and the suit he wore to meet with President Johnson, I got goose bumps reading Dr. King's words in his own handwriting.

We also traveled to the Upward Bound Olympics, a regional competition amongst high school students on campuses around the state, like Albany State, Georgia Southern College (now University), Paine College, and Fort Valley State College (now University). The Upward Bound campus teams would compete with one another in sports like softball, volleyball, and basketball and in academic competitions like math bowls, chess tournaments, and persuasive and extemporaneous public speaking. For the latter, a student would reach into a basket, pick out a random piece of paper with a topic, and take just a few minutes to prepare and deliver remarks. That, of course, was the competition for me.

It was the summer of 1986, and I drew the topic "Should the United States impose sanctions on the Apartheid government in South Africa? If so, why? Or, why not?" Having followed the issue in the news, I quickly composed an argument against the Reagan administration's policy of so-called constructive engagement, which used various incentives, instead of sanctions, to engage and encourage South Africa's then white-minority government to move away from apartheid. I argued that approach was a wholly unacceptable response that enabled this oppressive regime in its violent subjugation and dehumanization of Black South Africans, who were denied the right to vote in a country where they made up the majority. How, I asked, could the United States, having rejected de jure racial segregation as a contradiction of its human and civil rights ideals some two decades earlier, now turn a blind eye and continue business as usual with a regime even more brutal than what Black citizens had encountered in the Jim Crow era? Just as boycotts and other acts of nonviolent resistance were morally right and politically effective against American apartheid, they would be in South Africa. A new America, having learned the lessons of its own recent past, should and must lead an international coalition of sanctions, I argued. I used the words of Dr. King: "Injustice anywhere is a threat to justice everywhere." I won first place trophies that year and every year in both extemporaneous and persuasive public speaking. I was finding my own voice on issues that I would spend a lifetime addressing in a space that affirmed both my right and my ability to speak and be heard.

Those summers at Savannah State exposed me to new worlds and helped me see myself on a college campus as a real college student. So, when the time came, the question was not *if* I was going to college but *where*. Even that was not much of a question, though. I made up my mind that I was going where Dr. King went. I was going to Morehouse College.

Morehouse, a small historically Black, all-male school in the heart of Atlanta, has long been heralded for producing proud, confident Black men who are leaders in the public square. A 1948 graduate, Dr. King first read Henry David Thoreau's essay "Civil Disobedience" while a student there. In the school newspaper, *The Maroon Tiger*, an eighteen-year-old King, or M. L., as he was affectionately called then, observed that the late Eugene Talmadge, the ardent and hate-filled segregationist governor of Georgia, held a Phi Beta Kappa key. "By all measuring rods, Mr. Talmadge could think critically and intensively; yet he contends that I am an inferior being. Are those the types of men we call educated? We must remember that intelligence is not enough. Intelligence plus character—that is the goal of true education." Benjamin Elijah Mays, then president of Morehouse, a towering Christian intellectual and perhaps the last of the great schoolmasters, would later express a similar concern in his 1969 book, *Disturbed About Man*. "I am disturbed, I am uneasy about man because we have no guarantee that when we train a man's mind, we will train his heart; no guarantee that when we increase a man's knowledge, we will increase his goodness. There is no necessary correlation between knowledge and goodness."

The intentional pedagogical tradition at Morehouse has always insisted on both training the head and tuning the heart. Truly, the Morehouse men I encountered were eloquent speakers and strong leaders, several of them preachers with a polished presence, exuding the so-called Morehouse Mystique. Even brothers in the barbershop who had not gone to college knew of Morehouse's grand tradition of excellence. Having been elected president of my high school senior class and voted "Most Likely to Succeed," I felt I was meant to be a Morehouse man.

The summer after my graduation in 1987, my parents drove me to Atlanta and dropped me off at Morehouse for this new phase of my journey. As we parted, I looked to my parents with expectant eyes and hoped that they would give me some spending money to help until I could learn my way around the city and find a job. But Dad instead typically quoted the King James translation of a scripture (Acts 3:6), expressing what Peter said to the lame beggar who expected some alms as the apostles entered the temple. "Silver and gold have I none, but such as I have give I thee," Dad said. "The grace of the Lord Jesus Christ be with you, son." He and my mom then gave me a great big hug, got in the car, and drove off into the horizon. My parents had no money. I'd have to work hard and trust God.

Morehouse had awarded me a small scholarship, but without federal Pell Grants and low-interest student loans college would not have been affordable for me. That truth informs my work as a U.S. senator today, as student debt has skyrocketed, leaving students and their families laden with big debt. It is a huge burden on ordinary people and hardworking American families. Making college more accessible and affordable for our children and relieving the student debt of millions of Americans is among my highest priorities. It would strengthen our economy, spur entrepreneurialism and growth, and strengthen America's technological and competitive edge in a twenty-first-century world.

At the time, work helped to cover the gaps in my tuition costs and provided my only spending money. Days after arriving in Atlanta, I contacted Ron Jenkins, a Morehouse graduate who worked as a health educator in Georgia's Department of Human Resources. I'd met him and his boss, Dr. Virginia Floyd, a Spelman graduate whom everyone called Ginger, when I worked as a teen peer educator in high school. Ginger, who was director of the Family Health Branch, hired me in a part-time role, helping to strengthen the state's teen pregnancy prevention programs, with Ron as my immediate supervisor. While there I traveled throughout Georgia during the summer months, working with Teen Peer Programs, and wrote a statewide curriculum guide called "Educating Teens for Positive Peer Intervention." The manual was used for many years to train teen peer educators in Georgia. Proud of my work and seeing the relationship between high teen pregnancy rates and high infant mortality rates, Dr. Floyd suggested that Governor Joe Frank Harris appoint me to the Southern Regional Task Force on Infant Mortality. At age nineteen, I became the only teenager on a task force of governor appointees from sixteen southern states.

Morehouse continued to broaden my horizons. Every day I walked in a reality that was different from what the world shows and tells us about Black men. The student body had jumped to 2,343 students in my freshman year, an increase of 850 from the previous decade. Just the sight of so many of us young Black men together, engaged in the process of higher learning, affirmed my own humanity. The indoctrination of what it means to be a Morehouse man began from day one. Freshman Week was filled with speakers sharing the institution's revered history and the world-changing accomplishments of its most outstanding alumni—men like the former Atlanta mayor Maynard Jackson, the former Georgia state senator Julian Bond, the historian, author, and *Ebony* magazine's top editor Lerone Bennett Jr., *Jet* magazine's top editor Robert E. Johnson, the filmmaker Spike Lee, and one of the greatest preachers and theologians of the twentieth century, Howard Thurman, whose final resting place is on the campus grounds. "Over the heads of her students, Morehouse holds a crown that she challenges them to grow tall enough to wear," said Thurman, who graduated as valedictorian in 1923.

Upperclassmen served as proctors during Freshman Week, and before dawn one morning they banged on all doors of all the freshman dormitories. With the older brothers ordering us to get up, we quickly threw on clothes and shoes, stumbled onto the yard, and began a slow jog, chanting through the streets around campus, waking up our schoolmates and rivals at Clark, Morris Brown, and Spelman Colleges. These historically Black institutions, along with Morehouse, the Morehouse School of Medicine, and the Interdenominational Theological Center, at the time formed the Atlanta University Center Consortium. Hundreds of Morehouse freshmen and upperclassmen jogged past their gates and dormitories in the predawn hours chanting,

Rain can't stop the House
Sleet can't stop the House
Snow can't stop the House
Nobody stops the House
Clark can't stop the House
Brown can't stop the House
Spelman may shock the House
But nobody stops the House.

Morehouse really gasses up its students. But for every bit of confidence, we are imbued with a sense of responsibility, the "fierce urgency of now," and the recognition that we must bring our gifts to the enterprise of human progress. I felt it strongly, as if Dr. King, whose life-size bronze image stood resolutely outside the international chapel named in his honor, were pointing a finger directly at me.

From my first days at Morehouse, I found my second home among the budding preachers inside that chapel. I knew when I left Morehouse, I wanted to attend seminary, and I found a dedicated mentor in the legendary Lawrence E. Carter Sr., who became the first dean of the Martin Luther King Jr. International Chapel after its completion in 1979. Since then, he has ushered hundreds of young Black men into ministry, college and university teaching, and some of the most powerful and prominent pulpits in the nation. He also has guided his students into business and the marketplace with a commitment to building "the beloved community," bringing head, heart, and hands to the work of human enterprise.

Dean Carter, who is also a religion professor and the college's archivist and curator, believes God sent him to Morehouse. He was in the tenth grade in his hometown of Columbus, Ohio, when More-house's most famous graduate tried to recruit him to the college. The teenage Carter had accompanied the superintendent of schools in his hometown to a church to hear Dr. King speak and afterward encountered the visiting minister in the pastor's study.

"What's your name?" Dr. King asked him.

When the young man responded, King asked if he was consider-ing college and more specifically Morehouse. The teenager told King that a neighbor had talked him out of going to Morehouse, and Dr. King tried to persuade him otherwise. Dr. King's advocacy for his alma mater didn't win that time, and Carter ended up at the Virginia University of Lynchburg. While there in 1961, he again had a chance to hear Dr. King speak. A math teacher invited Carter to a local high school, where Dr. King delivered a powerful speech titled "The American Dream" (not to be confused with his later "I Have a Dream" speech). Dean Carter has said that King's speech that night was the most riveting oratory he'd ever heard—so much so that he called his mother when he made it back to campus and asked if he could transfer to Morehouse. He wanted to be taught by the teachers who had taught King. His mother refused to allow him to transfer, but he decided then to do the next best thing: at-tend the graduate school where King had received his theological education at Boston University.

Carter was one month from graduating with a master's degree in theology when King was shot to death in Memphis on April 4, 1968. The young seminarian had taken his girlfriend, Marva (who a year later became his wife), on a date to a theater on campus to see a play about the assassination of President Abraham Lincoln when he learned about King's assassination. Devastated, Carter and his date left the theater and walked silently, holding hands, into the night. They came upon a chapel, entered, and sat in the dark. Dean Carter remembers staring up at the stained-glass window and praying aloud, "Lord, help me to do something significant for Martin Luther King Jr. before I close my eyes."

A decade later, when two trusted pastors suggested he apply to become head of the new Martin Luther King Jr. International Chapel being built at Morehouse, Carter put aside his desire to become pastor of a church and applied to Morehouse. The opportunity at Morehouse seemed to him the perfect chance to keep alive the incubator that had produced a Martin Luther King Jr. As a candidate for the job, Carter was invited to deliver a trial sermon at Morehouse in December 1977. The chapel was packed that day as he slowly delivered his message, "The Treasure in Your Trash." When he sat down, he looked up and saw the crowd standing and applauding. Dean Carter said he clearly heard a voice that he believes was the Lord whispering, "You will be the new dean." But his faith was about to be tested because Carter didn't hear another word from Morehouse for nearly a year and a half. He would later learn that as many as five hundred candidates had applied for the job. In 1979, he completed his doctorate from Boston University and finally got the call from Morehouse. The news created quite a buzz, given that the new dean was not a Morehouse man. But he just kept his head down and began molding lives, building a living memorial to his hero.

Soon after I arrived on campus in the fall of 1987, I got to inter-
act with Dean Carter when I competed to become the student
speaker at a joint freshman convocation between Morehouse and
Spelman. The convocation was held early each fall at the historic
Friendship Baptist Church, an influential Black congregation once
led by the father of Maynard Jackson. The church's historical connection to the college runs deep. Morehouse's first location in Atlanta was in the basement of Friendship in 1879, after the institution
relocated from Augusta. Spelman was actually started in the basement of the same church just two years later. Dean Carter and the
Broadway actor Lamar Alford, who was at the time the dramatist
in residence, selected me as the speaker from Morehouse.

On Convocation Day, the Spelman speaker, a freshman named
Keisha McClellan, went first, wowing the crowd with her soft-
spoken yet commanding voice. Her message and manner of delivering it had a way of drawing you in, leaving the crowd riveted. When
she finished, the pastor, the Reverend William Guy, a Morehouse
man and the father of the actress Jasmine Guy, who would rise to
fame in the coming years, stood to introduce me. "Now coming
before us, and I don't envy him, is Raphael Warnock," Reverend
Guy said. I spoke about our responsibility as African American students to get an education and translate it into the kind of social
transformation that would make a difference in the world. As I
brought my remarks to a close, I quoted the last line of a Robert
Frost poem: "And miles to go before I sleep."

Riffing off the refrain, I asserted, "Until racism and bigotry are
ended, we cannot sleep! Until poverty is eliminated, and hunger is
eviscerated, we cannot sleep!" With my voice rising to a climax, I

argued, "Until every child has a chance, we cannot sleep!" My peers and the parishioners of Friendship Church who were unusually staid and reserved for a Black Baptist church were standing and shouting "Amen" as I closed. "Until justice rolls down like waters and righteousness as a mighty stream, we cannot sleep! We must move on!"

That speech helped to establish me as a leader on campus at an exciting time. Many Black students with the academic backgrounds to get into majority-white Ivy League schools were choosing historically Black colleges and universities to connect more strongly to their history and culture. During my freshman year, the Morehouse class of 1979 graduate Spike Lee released his groundbreaking film *School Daze*, with its provocative and entertaining presentation of life on a Black college campus. Millions of Americans were witnessing a step show and other practices and traditions of Black fraternity and sorority life for the first time.

In sharp contrast to television programming prior to that time, my schoolmates and I also saw our lives being played out on the small screen that year as *A Different World*, the popular spin-off of *The Cosby Show*, hit the airwaves and made Reverend Guy's daughter Jasmine a star. We intimately related to Denise Huxtable, the Huxtable daughter who was planning to apply to Princeton, where her older sister went, until a talk with her grandfather persuaded her to go to his and her parents' fictional Black alma mater, Hillman College in Virginia. We saw ourselves in the students Whitley (Jasmine's character, a prissy southern girl with a deep drawl), Dwayne Wayne (her less refined boyfriend), Ron (the awkward, funny friend), and all the others, including a young Jada Pinkett Smith, playing a college freshman named Lena. Some of the cutaway footage was even shot on Spelman's campus. It was a groundbreaking show, depicting for a broad, racially diverse audience the lives of young African Americans, like us, whose struggles centered mostly on the issues of college life, not crime, drugs, or gang culture.

I wasn't as much of a socialite as those characters, though. My conservative, Pentecostal "church boy" upbringing didn't allow me to spend much time in the big Atlanta clubs, where many of my schoolmates hung out. Plus, I've never been much of a dancer, and I didn't have much cash to spare. I had a small group of friends who were all bookish, and we hung out on the yard, most often at Manley College Center, a plaza area at Spelman. We also went out to eat when we had cash. Of course, the "yo' mama" jokes were in no short supply. We did silly stuff and made some bad decisions like every other college student. I remember earning a few speeding tickets on that boring four-hour drive from Atlanta to Savannah and back during the breaks. But I stayed pretty clear of the hard partying that extended the college matriculation of many of my peers to five, six, seven, and even more years. A psychology major and religion minor, I wanted to finish strong in four years and go directly to seminary. I also didn't date much. As outgoing as I was, I was still somewhat awkward when it came to actually asking a girl out. And it didn't help that I was as skinny as a string bean.

My freshman roommate was a guy named Andrew Campbell who was a Biology/premed major from the D.C. suburbs. I thought I had good study habits until I met him. His study habits were far superior to mine, and he was just as disciplined as he was smart. I'd climb into bed for the night, and he'd be hunched over, studying under the lamplight at his small desk. When I turned over late at night, he'd still be at it. Sometimes I got tired just watching Andrew study. But it paid off. Andrew would go on to become a pediatric oncologist, dedicating his life to the work of providing healing and hope to the youngest of cancer patients, sickle-cell patients, and their families. I joined the ministry while he entered medicine, but he, no less than me, is doing the Lord's work.

Being away from my close family for the first time was tough, especially during my freshman year. So I made trips back to Savannah as frequently as I could. For one of my initial trips home, I took a Greyhound bus with Debbie Williams, a Spelman student and a dear friend since we had met in the eighth grade. On other occasions, my big brothers drove to Morehouse to pick me up. At the beginning of Christmas break during my freshman year, the dorms quickly emptied as students headed back home for the holidays. The bustling campus started to look like a ghost town. Finally, my big brother Jeffrey pulled up into the open parking lot in his tractor trailer, driving bobtail. We threw my luggage into the sleeper, and I occasionally tried my hand at talking on the CB radio as we traded jokes and stories on the bumpy four-hour drive back to Savannah. Sometimes, Keith picked me up or drove me back to Atlanta in his sporty Toyota Celica. I felt cool, zipping much too fast down the highway in the car with him. Getting me through college was a family affair.

The trips home became less frequent as I got busier on campus, particularly with the Chapel Assistants, a student-led organization that had been started in 1979 by Dean Carter for students planning to attend seminary. He made sure we spent time with the alumni, thought leaders, and ministers who often stopped by the chapel to share their messages of social activism. In them, I saw modern-day versions of the kind of preacher I wanted to be. In both my sophomore and my junior years, my peers elected me president of the organization—a position more often held by seniors. That year, the Chapel Assistants decided that we would join other school clubs and choose a queen to represent us in the homecoming parade. When I alone got to ride next to her on top of the backseat of a convertible, the brothers nicknamed me the Imperial President.

Serving and learning beside those guys were some of the best years of my life, but I was still insecure about my financial situation. I worked hard during the year and all summer, but most of my money helped to pay my tuition and purchase clothes and other necessities. One semester, after I had worked and saved all summer to pay tuition and buy books, a coat, and clothes, half of my clothes were stolen from both the washer and dryer of the Days Inn motel where Morehouse had housed some of us to deal with its overflow of students. I can still recall the queasy feeling in the pit of my stomach when I opened those machines and discovered that so many of the clothes that I had worked so hard to buy were gone. I'd finally been able to upgrade my wardrobe a bit, and this pushed me almost back to square one. It was a rough winter.

At Morehouse, the Student Government Association president and other school leaders dressed up for big school convocations as if they were headed to Wall Street jobs. My new position was one of school leadership, but I had one suit to my name. I shared my discomfort with Dean Carter. "Dean, I don't have enough suits," I told him, feeling a bit embarrassed. It may sound superficial, and perhaps it was, but Dean Carter, who knew something about poverty himself, shrugged it off. "Oh, don't worry about that," he said, peeking into my future. "Where you're headed, suits will be the least of your worries."

Dean Carter opened many doors to new opportunities. I was a junior in April 1990 when Ralph Abernathy, Dr. King's closest friend and his first lieutenant in the civil rights movement, died. The family anointed Dean Carter to handle every detail of the funeral and burial, and he asked me to be his assistant. I corresponded with speakers, handled logistics, and did whatever the dean asked me to do. The four-hour service at West Hunter Street Baptist Church in southwest Atlanta, where Reverend Abernathy had been pastor, flowed smoothly and in the tradition of such services for the movement's top leaders. Afterward, Abernathy's casket was placed inside a green wooden wagon, which was pulled by two mules. King's body had been transported to his burial ground two decades earlier in the same manner. The funeral procession, including twenty-two limousines, lasted two hours.

At the end of my junior year, I went to the chapel to see Dean Carter and noticed a note on his desk. The note said that *the* Sixth Avenue Baptist Church in Birmingham was looking to hire an intern for that summer of 1990. I needed a job and asked him about it. As it turned out, Dean Carter said he was planning to talk to me about it because he thought it would be a perfect fit. As I sat in his office, he returned a call to the church's pastor, the Reverend John Thomas Porter. When Reverend Porter answered, Dean Carter said, "I have just the young man for you."

Reverend Porter and his Sixth Avenue Baptist Church both played crucial roles in the historic campaign to desegregate Birmingham in April 1963. Years before, when Porter was a student at Alabama State College, he had served as a pulpit assistant to Dr. King, then the new young pastor at Dexter Avenue Baptist Church before the bus boycott launched him into destiny. Afterward, he served as a pulpit assistant to Martin Luther King Sr. at Ebenezer Baptist Church while studying at the Morehouse School of Religion. Then, in December 1962, when Reverend Porter was called to become pastor of Sixth Avenue Baptist Church, Dr. King preached at his installation service. The message that night was "A Knock at Midnight," the same sermon I had listened to repeatedly as a kid. Surely, I thought, this match was divine.

From my first interactions with Reverend Porter and his congregation, I felt an instant connection. On the weekend that I was to be introduced to the congregation and preach my first sermon there, the church paid to fly my mother and me from Savannah to Birmingham. Reverend Porter wanted Mom to feel comfortable, knowing that her son would be in good hands. At twenty years old, being flown somewhere to preach made me feel extra special, but along with that came a strong sense of responsibility.

I was trying to find my own voice as an emerging young preacher with a deep desire to use the scriptures to talk about the real-life stuff of the day. An idea came to me one day, and I just started writing what became my sermon that Sunday, a message called "Listen to the Music." It was taken from Psalm 137, when the Israelites were in captivity in Babylon and yearning for their homeland:

> By the rivers of Babylon, there we sat down, yea, we wept, when we remembered Zion.
> We hanged our harps upon the willows in the midst thereof.
> For there they that carried us away captive required of us a song; and they that wasted us required of us mirth, saying,
> Sing us one of the songs of Zion.
> How shall we sing the Lord's song in a strange land?

I talked about how songs, music, and poetry reflect the tenor of the time. Just as the psalmists of that biblical era wrote of the Israelites' pain, so, too, were the musicians of my day reflecting the times in their songs and the lyrics of hip-hop about drug culture, addiction, violence, and oppression, I said. In closing, I urged young people to hear the beat of a different drummer, to hear the drumbeat of faith and embrace a God who loves them. The congregation responded to the message enthusiastically. I would preach several times that summer.

Sixth Avenue was a vibrant congregation with lots of young people, and I was assigned to them. The church arranged for me to stay in the lovely home of one of the members, a home economics teacher named Annie Crawford. And to ensure that I was able to get around town all summer, I was given the keys to the church's big station wagon. It was functional, but being a single, young man, I thought cruising through town in a brown station wagon emblazoned with the words "Sixth Avenue Baptist Church" was not the coolest ride. But it was a surefire way of keeping me on the straight and narrow.

I was energetic and got along well with the kids. We planned events just for them (Taco Night, Pizza Night, and so on) and then broke into groups by age for real conversations about peer pressure and the challenges of being young Christians. We ended with a mini service led by the kids.

Reverend Porter mentored me and often regaled me with stories about Dr. King. My soul was a sponge. I especially enjoyed hearing about King's preaching in the months prior to the 1955 Montgomery Bus Boycott that launched him into destiny. He would write out a full manuscript of a sermon. But when preaching time came in the service, he would walk over to the lectern, leaving the manuscript on his chair and in eyeshot of those who gathered. Every Sunday, the erudite young preacher, still wrapping up the requirements of a Boston University PhD, memorized the sermon and mesmerized his listeners.

As I prepared to return to Morehouse for my senior year, I sat down to work on my financial aid. I always filled out my own paperwork and figured out how to put the pieces together to cover my costs. This time, though, when I added up my Pell Grant, loan, scholarship, and money earned over the summer, I was still $7,000 short for my tuition. That gap was far beyond my ability to close on my own, and for a bleak moment my finishing college seemed in jeopardy. But I'd made it too far to even consider having to quit. I decided to talk to Reverend Porter to ask if Sixth Avenue could help. When I shared my dilemma, Reverend Porter looked at the numbers and agreed to take care of the balance. I will be forever grateful for the church's investment in me.

By the time I returned to Morehouse for my senior year, Iraq had invaded its neighbor Kuwait. The invasion prompted international condemnation and sanctions on Iraq, but the drumbeat of war was beating. Many students' fathers, uncles, and other family members had served in Vietnam and returned different men, if they returned at all. Some of our friends were in the reserves and the National Guard. We were worried that a new war could be just as catastrophic. So I worked with other students to plan a peace vigil. We invited local, state, and national political leaders, but on the day of our event just one showed up: Congressman John Lewis.

At the time, Representative Lewis was still new in Congress, serving in only his second term. But his long years of civil rights activism made him tower high above the crowd. This was the same John Lewis who in his early twenties had stepped to the front of the civil rights movement as one of the "Big Six," joining Dr. King, James Farmer, A. Philip Randolph, Roy Wilkins, and Whitney Young in strategizing how to confront segregation. The same John Lewis who was beaten and bloodied by Alabama state troopers while trying to cross the Edmund Pettus Bridge on "Bloody Sunday." The same son of sharecroppers who had earned the respect of the nation. It was my first time meeting him, and he was gracious and kind enough to stay around, chatting with the students. His presence among us that day, when he had little to gain personally or politically, spoke more eloquently to me than anything he said.

Later that school year, I began dating seriously for the first time.

Darlene was a Spelman sophomore, majoring in early childhood education. She wanted to be a teacher, like both of her parents. We were friends, and the relationship just blossomed organically. We had been dating a few months when she invited me home during spring break to meet her parents. I rode to Nashville with a classmate and stayed with my girlfriend's family in their guest room. They were a warm family who made me feel at home. She and I dated the rest of my senior year and my first year of seminary. I was not ready for marriage then, and the relationship ended. But our friendship and respect for each other have remained across the years through marriage to other people and, in my case, divorce, the death of parents, and the birth of children.

In May 1991, I graduated from Morehouse with a bachelor's degree in psychology. There's nothing like seeing more than four hundred Black men in caps and gowns, educated and eager to carry their gifts into the world. My parents came over to my dorm room as we prepared to march out onto the campus green, where Morehouse holds its commencement exercises every year. I was already wearing my cap and gown when they arrived, and we took some pictures. Then I removed my gown and placed it on my mother. I placed my cap on my father's head. I was proud of my achievement, the first college graduate in the family. They had given me that which is truly essential, a foundation for success rooted in faith, love, a sense of self-worth, and a healthy sense of humor through life's many challenges. This was our moment, a hallelujah moment for the village that now included not just my parents and family but also the Morehouse community and the folks at Sixth Avenue Church. I returned there as an intern after my senior year and, having connected so strongly with the social gospel vision of the progressive Baptists surrounding the movement, I decided to be baptized in the Baptist tradition and was ordained therein to Christian ministry. Sixth Avenue became a crucial part of my village. The village that has helped me time and time again make a way out of no way.

CHAPTER 4

New York State of Mind

The acceptance letter to Harvard Divinity School came first. I liked the idea of Harvard. Who wouldn't want to say he graduated from such a prestigious institution? More acceptances followed, and suddenly the question of where to attend graduate school became a toss-up. I couldn't really make a bad choice with so many fine options. But when I considered the full experience I wanted—academic rigor, life in a vibrant city, and opportunities to serve and learn in the kind of ministry that I could lead someday—Union Theological Seminary won the matchup.

I arrived in New York in the fall of 1991 with big plans to learn as much as I could from the seminary's first-rate faculty and visit churches with some of the most storied reputations in the country. I wanted to hear great preaching and see ministry up close in an urban, hardscrabble environment at the crossroads of the world. I planned to walk and take the subway around town and sit inside the grand Gothic-inspired sanctuaries at Marble Collegiate Church, one of the oldest Protestant congregations in North America where the Reverend Norman Vincent Peale, the prolific author of *The Power of Positive Thinking*, had served as pastor for half a century; and at Riverside Church, which had been considered the citadel of Protestant liberalism and was the place in April 1967 where Dr. King delivered his powerful speech condemning the Vietnam War. Just two years before I arrived in New York, Dr. James A. Forbes Jr. had become the first African American senior minister of Riverside, which by then was one of the most prominent multicultural and interdenominational congregations in the country. Like me, Dr. Forbes had deep Pentecostal roots. He had graduated from Union and had long taught homiletics, the study of preaching, there, so naturally I was drawn to him. I also planned to take the subway to Bedford-Stuyvesant in Brooklyn to hear the Reverend Dr. William Augustus Jones Jr., a past president of our denomination, the Progressive National Baptist Convention, a powerful preacher, activist, and pastor of Bethany Baptist Church. Preaching in the same neighborhood was the Reverend Dr. Gary V. Simpson, a dynamic, young Union graduate who had recently assumed the pastorate of the Concord Baptist Church of Christ, succeeding the Reverend Dr. Gardner C. Taylor, widely regarded as the dean of Black preaching and once listed by Baylor University as among the dozen most effective preachers in the English-speaking world. I certainly have not heard a finer preacher anywhere than Gardner Taylor. His preaching was Shakespearean and majestic, unmatched in eloquence and possessing a poetic and musical quality that drew deeply from scripture and a wide array of sources. But he was by no means given to the impulse to pander or entertain that ensnares too many preachers, instead preaching always with great substance, theological acumen, and integrity. In 1993, Taylor gave the pre-inauguration sermon at an interfaith service for Bill Clinton, who later awarded him the Presidential Medal of Freedom. He indeed was a national treasure and a spiritual genius. And of course, I'd go to Harlem to visit the legendary Abyssinian Baptist Church, where the Reverend Dr. Calvin O. Butts III, also a Union graduate and a Morehouse man, and a well-known activist preacher, served as pastor.

But first, I needed a job, and I figured working on staff at a church would give me more of the kind of experience I needed for full-time ministry. Two weeks after I arrived in New York, I called Abyssinian, introduced myself, and asked for an appointment with Reverend Butts. I was shocked and slightly taken aback when his assistant told me that the earliest appointment I could get with him was in two months. Being the young, brash Morehouse man that I was, I suppose I thought that he, a fellow Morehouse man, would make the time to see me sooner. I had met Reverend Butts just months before my graduation, when he visited the college and Dean Carter pulled aside a few chapel assistants to meet him. I had to find another way to get to him.

As it turned out, Butts's wife, Patricia, worked in the Human Resources Department at Union Seminary, and she was a Spelman woman who had met Reverend Butts while they were attending the sister-brother schools. Using that connection, I introduced myself to her one day. When she offered to help me if ever there was anything she could do, I told her that I was trying to get a meeting with her husband and had been told he wasn't available for two months.

"We'll see what we can do about that," she said.

Out of the blue one day a short time later, she called. "My husband is in his office, and if you can get to Harlem, he can see you."

I hopped in a cab and headed to Harlem to meet Reverend Butts. We had a good conversation, and he said he remembered meeting me at Morehouse. He then invited me to church the following Sunday. Within the next two weeks, Reverend Butts hired me as an intern minister at Abyssinian. That was the beginning of a new, decade-long period of growth and transformation for me, as I moved between the ivory towers of Union and the ebony trenches of Harlem and ministry at Abyssinian.

At Union, I felt fortunate to be taught by a faculty that was second to none and included five African American scholars. Dr. Cornel West had taught at Union a few years before I arrived. When I got there, the African American faculty included Dr. Delores S. Williams, who had received her doctorate from Union and was one of the early contributors to womanist theology, which points out the contradictions of white feminist and Black theologies, neither of which is sufficiently attentive to Black women living at the intersection of racial and gender discrimination. Womanist theology argues for a multidimensional analysis of oppression to include racial, gender, class, and heterosexist bias, systems of marginalization, and their implications for a faith whose mission is human wholeness and freedom. Dr. Williams was the first woman to be named to the seminary's prestigious Paul Tillich Chair, honoring the German American philosopher who had taught at Union more than two decades and is widely considered one of the most influential theologians of the twentieth century. The historic announcement was a huge moment for Black faculty and students, and we were all filled with such pride. Womanists from all over the country came for the seminary's celebration, which typically draws few people outside the university and the honoree's family. Harlem's faith leaders and dignitaries came out to celebrate Dr. Williams as well.

The other African American faculty members included Dr. Vincent Wimbush, a Morehouse graduate and an accomplished New Testament scholar who was doing groundbreaking work on the Bible and its uses in American culture, and Dr. James Melvin Washington, a brilliant church historian who had the rare gift of being both a first-rate scholar and a penetrating preacher. Moreover, Dr. Washington had the most encyclopedic mind I've ever encountered. He'd list primary sources by heart from history and other disciplines during his lectures, sometimes even quoting chapters and footnotes. The Reverend Dr. Carolyn Ann Knight, a Union graduate who would become one of the most sought-after preachers in the Black church, was also teaching homiletics. And then there was Dr. James H. Cone, the father of Black liberation theology and one of the most important theologians of the twentieth century.

In my first days at Union, the seminary held a chapel service to bring together the new students and faculty. As we were leaving James Memorial Chapel, I bumped into Dr. Cone, and he introduced himself. I responded in kind. "I know who *you* are," I said, explaining that I had first encountered his work as a high school student and budding young minister. Through the years, I took several courses he taught, including Introduction to Theology in my first semester. When I turned in one of my first assignments in his class, he wrote on the top of my paper, "You have the ability to do doctoral work." His note affirmed and acknowledged my potential as a scholar, which was significant to me because he was known as a rigorous taskmaster. Students warned that he put more books on his syllabus than any other professor, but we also knew that he held the same high expectations of us that he did for himself. He was a very disciplined man who jogged five miles a day and read and wrote eight hours every day, except on Sundays.

In my third year at Union, I took Dr. Cone's course on Dr. King and Malcolm X, based on his recently published book *Martin & Malcolm & America: A Dream or a Nightmare*. The book and the course juxtaposed the countervailing approaches of these two clerics—King, the integrationist, and Malcolm X, the nationalist—in the Black freedom struggle. Dr. Cone argued that the leaders moved closer in thought as King came face-to-face with his "shattered dreams" in the years after four innocent little girls died in the bombing of the Sixteenth Street Baptist Church in Birmingham less than a month after his 1963 "I Have a Dream" speech. King realized that he had underestimated the depth of racism and the intractability of white supremacy in this country; meanwhile, as he broke with Elijah Muhammad's Nation of Islam, Malcolm had begun to moderate his sharp nationalist views, developing a more universal perspective on the struggles of marginalized people all over the globe before his assassination in 1965. I didn't agree with everything Dr. Cone said, and we certainly had our share of disagreements over the years. But he strengthened my ability to think more deeply and to interrogate my faith and what that means to the struggle as a Christian in the quest for justice.

Four other faculty members at Union would also meaningfully influence my thinking about scripture, Christian tradition, and the meaning and implications of Christian faith and practice in the world. Professor of Old Testament Dr. Phyllis Trible applied the tools of literary criticism and feminist hermeneutics to scripture in ways that made the ancient stories come alive in the continuing chronicles of people of faith. Dr. Christopher Morse, who had the best sense of humor of all my professors, urged students to ask probing questions that tested the doctrinal claims of the church. What does it mean to truly be faithful? Dr. Morse saw that as the task of Christian theology, loving God with my mind as well as my heart and spirit. Dr. Larry Rasmussen, an extraordinary professor of Christian ethics, would eventually serve with Dr. Cone as an adviser to my master's thesis comparing the activist ministries of Dietrich Bonhoeffer and Martin Luther King Jr. And Dr. Robin Scroggs was a New Testament professor who provided me with an intellectual framework for thinking about the apostle Paul, his impact on the first-century church, and the implications of his thinking for the twenty-first-century church on a whole range of issues, including sexism and human sexuality.

I pushed myself to live up to my professors' high expectations and my own. I loved the challenge, but during my first year at Union, I began struggling with feelings of melancholy and uncertainty. Part of me longed for the familiar—my family, the slow, easy pace of Savannah, the quick southern smiles and warmth. New York and its people, in their haste to keep up, can seem at first distant. Had I made the right decision to attend Union? Did I really have a future at Abyssinian? I ran into Reverend Knight one day at the Pit, a center of student life at Union, whose big Gothic buildings are arranged around a quadrangle. Reverend Knight seemed accessible and approachable, and she had a great reputation as a preacher. I'd heard her preach a revival at Abyssinian and knew she was friends with Reverend Butts. I shared with her my uncertainty, and she encouraged me to stay at Union. It was the right place for me, she said, and there would be many opportunities for me at Abyssinian.

"You're going to do well here," she said confidently.

Time melted the initial New York chill, and I soon settled into my new life. Much of my social life that first year centered on Hastings Hall, where I lived on the sixth floor. Hastings had individual dorm rooms and common living spaces. People often congregated in the kitchen or the hallways, and like at Morehouse some of the best learning took place when we engaged one another in discussion beyond the classroom. My classmates and peers at Union have been among the smartest people I have ever known, and our frustration and criticism of the church came from a place of deep love for the church, its mission and its promise. But we were not always serious.

I didn't have a computer the first year, and a friend from that inner circle, JoAnne Terrell, allowed me to type my papers on her computer in her apartment. She was in the first year of the doctoral program, and we often critiqued each other's work. We also told jokes. One day, she and I were walking down Hastings Hall with another friend, when I broke into a spontaneous rendition of the old Negro spiritual "Swing Low Sweet Chariot."

After the chorus, I took the lead on the solo verse, singing, "I looked over Jordan and what did I see?"

Both ladies piped in, singing on cue: "Coming for to carry me home."

I continued, singing with the same serious face and robust voice: "A little old lady cooking black-eyed peas."

JoAnne fell out laughing. I'd caught her off guard by swapping the line about "a band of angels coming after me" with my own playful lyrics signifying the common culinary delights of Southern soul food as eschatological, that is, "out of this world!"

Sometimes, if I called JoAnne and she didn't answer, I'd leave a sermonette in my sing-preach revivalist voice, whooping about how God is always there. Good humor helped us get through even the toughest days.

Many of my classmates remain my lifelong friends and accountability partners as we've sought over the years to be faithful to our assignments and vocation as ministers, providing leadership in the local parish and pastoral care in chaplaincy at hospitals and other institutional settings; seminarians and university professors, engaging students with head and heart; and Christian activists in the public square. We still encourage one another, laugh a lot, love, and endeavor to keep one another honest about the things that matter. Several of the women have been trailblazers, breaking through ecclesiastical glass ceilings. Among them are the Reverend Dr. Leslie D. Callahan, first female pastor of St. Paul's Baptist Church in Philadelphia, and the Reverend Dr. Kanyere Eaton, first female pastor of Fellowship Covenant Church, Bronx, New York. Nearly every summer for more than a dozen years, I have traveled to Martha's Vineyard to preach at the First Congregational Church of West Tisbury, where my friend the Reverend Cathlin Baker, who was in my circle at Union, is pastor. She was the first female pastor in the church's 335-year history when she assumed the office in 2008. When I made it to the runoff in my campaign for the U.S. Senate, Cathlin drove from Massachusetts with her husband, Bill, two children, a friend, and her dog to help me campaign. And she was among the few friends and family in the room with me when I was declared the winner.

At Union, I also became friends with two other Hastings residents, Jonathan Cutler and Beth Stroud. Jonathan was a brilliant guy who was Jewish, yet not particularly religious, though he was working on a master's degree in religion. Beth was just as smart, a member of the United Methodist Church and openly gay. The three of us were enrolled in Dr. Cone's Introduction to Theology, and sometimes we moved our conversation from the classroom into the Hastings kitchen, or we'd grab dinner just down the street on Broadway, talk, argue, and trade books. I suspect we all were curious at first about one another's backgrounds, and we became quite an interesting trio: me, the southern boy fresh from Morehouse College who was always carefully dressed in neat slacks, sometimes a suit, or crisply starched and pressed jeans with one of a collection of colorful sweaters that were popular at the time (when I could afford it, I vastly improved my wardrobe); the two of them, by contrast, were liberal northeasterners with altogether different fashion sensibilities, reliably casual and comfortable. It was a source of laughter for each of us.

Union was a great place for all kinds of diversity—white, Black, gay, straight, and foreign students from all over the globe, including

South Africans whose homeland was emerging from the grip of apartheid. I'd never had a Jewish friend and, while there were clearly gay students at Morehouse and Spelman, many of them, including some friends of mine, came out *after* college. Coming from a conservative Pentecostal background, I'd accepted the teachings of the church, that homosexuality was a sin. All my life, I'd heard preachers point to the Bible to tell the story of how God had destroyed the cities of Sodom and Gomorrah because of the prevalence of sin, which had long been interpreted as homosexuality. My mind had begun to open as a student at Morehouse, but my evolution on the issue accelerated at Union as I was given the tools to look at the scriptures and the reading of scriptures critically, systematically, and within historical context. Faith is both a divine and human undertaking. That's why white slave owners, for example, had once used the Bible to justify slavery, yet our African American ancestors knew in their bones that God did not intend for them to be slaves. The late great theologian Howard Thurman often told the story of his grandmother, a former slave and devout Christian who had never learned to read but loved hearing him read to her from the Bible, except the writings attributed to Paul the Apostle. Because of her experience, she didn't want to hear anything from Paul. When Thurman finally asked her why, she told him that the master's white preacher, who occasionally held a service for the enslaved, always chose to focus on select biblical writings, particularly verses like the Deutero-Pauline passage that reads, "Slaves, be obedient to them that are your masters . . . as unto Christ." The spirituals and the Black church freedom movement are expressions of the myriad ways in which slaves like Thurman's grandmother clearly turned from that Ephesians text to Exodus where God told Moses to tell Pharaoh to "let my people go." They knew something the slave masters did not know. Their faith was a freedom faith.

M̲y friendship with Beth and later other gay men and women who love God and love the church as much as I do and had a deep desire to serve challenged my earlier thinking. Gay, lesbian, and transgender folk live inside an experience that others do not. I don't know what it's like to have that part of your identity declared anathema. No matter how you live it out. But Union introduced me to a fellowship of thinkers and disciples whose lives challenged me and changed me. It's really the conversion experience that comes from walking with people.

My friend Beth never hid that she was gay, but when she was going through the church ordination process in our third year at Union, she shared with me her worry that at any moment her life could implode. Her denomination prohibited "self-avowed practicing" gay clergy. Beth would go on to serve as an ordained United Methodist pastor in Pennsylvania for six years, but after she shared with her congregation that she lived in a committed relationship with another woman, her superior filed a complaint against her. She faced a church trial in 2004 and was found guilty of "practices declared by the United Methodist Church to be incompatible with Christian teaching." And she was stripped of her clergy credentials. My heart broke for her. We hadn't talked in years at the time, but I called her to offer my prayers and support.

. . .

In January 1995, I got to take my first trip outside the country after signing up for a study immersion trip to Haiti with a group of fellow students from Union. The trip was arranged by Dr. Tom Driver, a theology professor, ethicist, and activist. At the time of our trip, Jean-Bertrand Aristide, who became Haiti's first democratically elected president in 1991 but was overthrown by a military coup the same year, had just returned to office. Aristide had been a Catholic priest, a proponent of liberation theology, with its sharp emphasis on justice for the poor, and a figure of some controversy. As I learned the history of the Haitian people, I was inspired by their strength, by how they had created their own language, Haitian Creole, during the years of slavery from the mix of native tongues spoken by the Africans transported there from different parts of the continent. It was a language that the Africans could understand, and, even though it included French vocabulary, their masters could not. Ultimately, the enslaved revolted and freed themselves from French colonial rule, becoming the first state established by a successful slave revolt.

Our group spent the first few days of a two-week trip living in Port-au-Prince, the capital, in the home of a missionary named Michael who took care of a group of Haitian boys. From the outside, the house looked like a mansion, but inside there was no running water. Michael did not want the boys to grow accustomed to a standard of living that was far above most Haitians. We traveled on the back of a pickup truck or in brightly decorated taxi buses called tap taps, so stuffed with passengers that some chose to ride outside, clinging dangerously to the sides and tops of the vehicles as we rocked and bumped up and down rocky, hilly terrain with few paved roads. The backdrop of lush, beautiful mountains, jutting toward the sky, belied the extreme poverty in the poorest neighborhoods of one of the poorest countries in the world. It wasn't just the clusters of tiny huts dotting the landscape but the clinic I visited, which in some cases did not even have mattresses for the beds, let alone adequate medical equipment, or the sight of hungry children and murky streams that were their only sources of water that spoke to the severe lack of resources. But at one point we had to steer around an overturned bus that had apparently been in the same spot for a long while, and it occurred to me that we Americans take so much for granted, like the easy availability of vaccines to prevent disease, medicines to heal sick bodies, and heavy machinery that could have moved that wrecked vehicle out of the way in no time.

I was struck by the sight of Martin Luther King Avenue in Port-au-Prince, and I stood where it intersected with Boulevard Toussaint Louverture, named in honor of the Haitian general who led most of the slave rebellion from 1791 to 1803. I saw, too, another world, the light-skinned elite, driving their luxury vehicles up the hills to gated communities beyond the mostly dark-skinned masses at the foot of those hills. This, too, was the awful legacy of slavery and colonialism.

One afternoon, we students were assigned to families, who graciously allowed us to spend a few hours inhabiting their worlds. I went to the market with my family to shop for the main part of the evening meal and watched uncomfortably as they picked out a live goat, which was then slaughtered, skinned, and chopped for the family's transport home. When we made it back to their little hut, the mother and other family members disappeared to a separate area to cook that goat. Her husband, the children, and I sat around, mostly looking at one another, straining to communicate, despite the Haitian Creole-to-English dictionary I'd brought along for the trip. Later, I made it through dinner and fought back the queasiness without offending the generous family who seemed so proud to share their bounty with this stranger from America.

After two weeks, I returned to New York. I had been darkened a shade or two by all those days under the blazing sun, and I'd been transformed by the story of a people who overthrew their colonizers, survived neocolonial dictators, struggled to build a democratic republic, and endured so much—both natural and man-made disasters. And I wondered why America, the wealthiest and most powerful nation in the world, couldn't do more for the people of Haiti. I thought about that family who had welcomed me into their lives, and I realized that the only difference between me and them was a windstorm. Both of our ancestors were stolen and transported from Africa to the New World on slave ships. My ancestors landed in the North; theirs in the South. A windstorm could have made all the difference. We were so close, yet our realities were so far.

While Union expanded my mind, Abyssinian showed me how to put my faith into action in the world around me. The spirit of the church's former pastor the late legendary U.S. congressman Adam

Clayton Powell Jr. was still very much alive, though he'd been gone nearly two decades by then. The church's older members could not tell me enough about the man they considered a courageous champion for Harlem and for ordinary people like them throughout the country. He was a strategist and prolific legislator who pushed forth transformative domestic legislation in his twenty-six years in Congress. In 1944, Powell was the first African American elected to Congress from New York, and for a decade he was one of just two African Americans in the entire U.S. House of Representatives.

Powell defiantly pushed a civil rights agenda before there was a mass movement for such, and when he rose to become head of the powerful House Committee on Education and Labor, he artfully guided the passage of nearly fifty pieces of important social legislation. Many were groundbreaking measures, encapsulating President John F. Kennedy's New Frontier and his successor Lyndon B. Johnson's War on Poverty. The legislation increased the minimum wage and provided funding for education for the deaf, nutritious school lunches, and youth vocational training, as well as for elementary schools and public libraries. The committee also would supervise new programs, such as Head Start, which gave many poor children a fighting chance with early preschool education, and Upward Bound.

I'd been a free-lunch kid and a beneficiary of some of those programs, so I know the difference that good public policy can make. Investing in children is so worthwhile because they might grow up and become U.S. senators, or if not, then good plumbers, coders, teachers, productive citizens. Powell, who had replaced his own father and namesake as pastor of Abyssinian, knew this and translated that understanding into effective public policy. But no matter how important his job was in the nation's capital, Harlem's congressman still made his way home on Sundays to preach at Abyssinian. This brand of ministry—where the practical meets the spiritual—resonated with me. It extended beyond the pulpit into the public space to feed the people with knowledge as much as food, crusade for them, fuel movements for social change, and, as a legislator, protect them with good laws.

Powell certainly had his colorful side and shortcomings, but his congregation never forgot the courage he demonstrated when it mattered most. When he died in 1972, the Reverend Dr. Samuel DeWitt Proctor was named pastor of Abyssinian. Proctor, a mentor to the Reverend Jesse Jackson, had been president of North Carolina Agricultural and Technical State University, a historically Black college in Greensboro, when Jackson was the school's student body president and football team quarterback. Even earlier in his career, Proctor had served as president of Virginia Union University, another HBCU whose school of theology now bears his name. A lifelong leader and trailblazer, Proctor had been the only Black student in his first year at Crozer Theological Seminary in Upland, Pennsylvania, where he received a bachelor of divinity degree, and he later returned to lecture at his alma mater. There he met a young student named Martin Luther King Jr. Proctor befriended the young leader, and the two stayed in touch through the years. Dr. King followed Dr. Proctor, who five years prior earned the doctorate in theology from Boston University School of Theology. Prior to coming to Abyssinian, Proctor had headed up the

Peace Corps in Africa and later held the Martin Luther King Jr. chair at Rutgers University, a teaching position he maintained even while serving as Abysinnian's pastor.

At Abyssinian, Proctor brought a steady yet vibrant style of leadership. He had just retired as senior pastor in 1989, two years before my tenure began, and he was much sought after as a speaker, continuing to travel all over the country to address audiences. Fortunately for me, he still visited Abyssinian occasionally, and I got to hear his spellbinding oratory. He drew you in with his engaging storytelling, humor, and keen analysis and kept you captivated without ever even raising his voice. Proctor was a supreme example of a real thinker in the pulpit. In 1997, this preacher who so loved teaching was sitting in a classroom and talking to college students in Iowa, the heart of America, when he slumped over from a fatal heart attack. By then, I'd risen to assistant pastor of Abyssinian and was honored to help plan his funeral.

Calvin Butts, Proctor's replacement, had started at Abyssinian under him in 1972. Then in his early twenties, Butts began as youth pastor and rose to executive pastor. He was Abyssinian's new senior pastor when I started under him, and I got a front-row seat to his rise as Harlem's ardent voice, a fresh firebrand, blazing his own path in a prominent ministry behind pastors who had left mammoth footprints on the trail. The year before I got there, Butts had taken on the alcohol and tobacco industries for their billboard advertisements targeting poor communities. He even climbed on ladders to reach billboards in Harlem and painted over alcohol and tobacco ads to dramatize the issue and make a statement. The protests spread to other cities, too, garnering major attention and ultimately compelled a major billboard advertising company in the city to remove liquor and cigarette advertisements from billboards within five blocks of places of worship, schools, and playgrounds.

In 1993, with the growing popularity of gangsta rap, Butts turned his attention to an industry he believed was peddling a different kind of death with its violent imagery and misogynistic lyrics. Butts argued that the record industry was exploiting young Black rappers by amplifying the most stereotypical images of Black life for commercial purposes and that the messages in the music were consistent with racist and sexist assumptions about Black women. One Saturday in June of that year, Butts drew hundreds of supporters to a rally that began in the church sanctuary and then poured out onto the sidewalk right outside Abyssinian. He gave a speech condemning negative rap. And I also gave a speech challenging the misogynistic themes in gangsta rap, and calling for music that reflects a more balanced and realistic view of life in communities like Harlem. Butts had publicized the protest in the media and asked congregants and supporters to bring recordings of the music on CDs and cassette tapes, which were piled in the middle of the street. Butts also had a steamroller on hand with plans to crush the pile for dramatic effect, but a group of teenagers and young adults showed up at the scene in support of the rappers and stood between the pile in the street and the steamroller. Some of them shouted angrily that our protest was out of touch with what was happening in the street. To defuse the tension, Butts called off plans to use the steamroller. He instead took supporters on a bus to Sony Corporation headquarters in midtown Manhattan and dumped the pile there.

I was twenty-three years old at the time, part of the generation being confronted, and I could see both sides. While I certainly did not condone the violence and disrespect for women in the rap lyrics and videos, I also understood the rappers' argument that they speak a hard truth about what's really going on in their world. Both things can be true at the same time. That was a dynamic conversation that continues today about the responsibility of artists and other influencers on our children; about culture and the commodification of Black lives; about commercialism and the struggle for human dignity; and also about the challenges and pitfalls of respectability politics. What I witnessed then, though, was a minister in real time working outside the box, insisting that the word must become flesh and live among the people.

A big part of that approach was the Abyssinian Development Corporation, a nonprofit founded by Butts, which played a significant role in the revitalization of Harlem by providing affordable housing, spurring commercial development for businesses, and even helping build a public school with a social justice bent. The Thurgood Marshall Academy for Learning and Social Change first opened in 1993, but when the school moved to its permanent home in 2004, it was the first new public school that had been built in Harlem in fifty years. Likewise, when the Abyssinian Development Corporation teamed with the nonprofit Community Association of the East Harlem Triangle and succeeded in bringing Pathmark to the corner of 125th Street and Lexington Avenue in 1999, the area was considered a food desert, without a chain supermarket in the neighborhood for nearly three decades. The community activist Alice Wragg Kornegay had pushed for a supermarket in East Harlem since

1980 and was a founding member of East Harlem Triangle. She died three years before seeing her vision realized. Through these pioneering ventures, I got a chance to see how the church could combine moral capital with financial capital to meet the people's tangible needs.

As influential as his activism was, Reverend Butts wrestled, sometimes publicly, with whether he should run for mayor, or Congress, or some other public office that would enable him to effect change on a larger scale. Clearly, there was still much work to be done in the civil rights/social action arena. When I look back on my time at Abyssinian, as I immersed myself in Powell's legacy and watched Butts up close, I believe that is when the thought first occurred to me: "Maybe I'll run for the U.S. Congress someday."

Over the next decade at Abyssinian, I would be promoted from intern minister to youth pastor to assistant pastor while earning two master's degrees—a master of divinity and a master of philosophy— and beginning doctoral studies in systematic theology, all at Union Seminary. I was proud when my master's thesis earned the highest possible grade, a much-sought-after "Credit with Distinction." The thesis, titled "Churchmen, Church Martyrs: The Activist Ecclesiologies of Dietrich Bonhoeffer and Martin Luther King Jr.," compared the activism and martyrdom of the men. Bonhoeffer was a German Lutheran pastor and theologian who traveled to New York as a young scholar in 1930 to study at Union for a year. He was introduced to Abyssinian, where he ended up teaching Sunday school. Bonhoeffer returned to Germany and was vocal in his resistance to the Nazi government and its persecution of the Jews. He was ultimately hanged by the Nazis for his activism and his alleged plot to assassinate Adolf Hitler. Both Bonhoeffer and King died at thirty-nine years old and have inspired generations with their courage and convictions. Both were also pastors who pushed the boundaries of the church. And both were organic intellectuals who refused to be confined to the academy.

Soon enough, my time would come to step out of the academy on my own.

In the early 1990s New York City was hot with racial tension, still bubbling over from a spate of racially motivated attacks and killings during the 1980s. When I arrived in the city, New Yorkers were still protesting the murder of Yusuf Hawkins, a sixteen-year-old Black teenager who was shot to death in the Bensonhurst neighborhood of Brooklyn on August 23, 1989. Yusuf and three friends had gone there that evening to check out a used car, when they were accosted by a group of about thirty youths, all but one of whom were white and some of whom wielded baseball bats. During the attack, Yusuf was shot twice in the chest. According to media accounts, the attack was instigated by an eighteen-year-old, who was so angry about his ex-girlfriend telling him she was inviting her Black and brown friends to a party that he gathered youths from the neighborhood to attack them; the mob wrongly assumed Yusuf and his crew were the guests. The ex-boyfriend told the police a somewhat different story—that his ex had threatened to send her Black male friends to beat him up and that is why he and his friends assumed Yusuf was there. One thing became clear: Yusuf was not connected to or aware of any of this. The murder of the unsuspecting teenager caused massive outrage, and crowds of mostly Black protesters, led by the Reverend Al Sharpton, marched through the insulated neighborhood to demand justice. Many of its mostly white residents resented the protests, waved hateful signs, and used racial slurs to harass the protesters. But the marchers kept coming back, expressing anguish and demanding justice, as the cases of those arrested and charged wound their way through the courts.

There had been other racially motivated killings: Willie Turks, the thirty-four-year-old Black Metropolitan Transportation Authority worker who was pulled from a car by a white mob and beaten and stomped to death in 1982; Eleanor Bumpurs, a sixty-six-year-old, mentally disturbed Black woman, shot to death by police as they tried to evict her from her home in October 1984; and Michael Griffith, a twenty-three-year-old Black man who, along with his friend, was attacked by a white mob outside a pizza parlor and chased onto a highway, where he was fatally struck by a passing car in an area of Queens called Howard Beach in December 1986. When Spike Lee's movie *Do the Right Thing* hit the big screen in 1989—exploring the racial tension in a Brooklyn neighborhood, Bed-Stuy, between its African American residents and the Italian American owner of a local pizzeria and ending with the killing of an unarmed Black man by the police—this was art imitating life in its rawest form.

Black men seemed in peril. They had been marginalized by society and targeted by police. Mass incarceration had begun to siphon scores of them from their communities, so they were missing from their families. A generation of children was growing up fatherless, or visiting their daddies in jail, perhaps even presuming that life would land them there, too.

And then, in 1999, a police shooting would rock New York City.

On February 4 of that year four New York City police officers in plain clothes shot a Black man, a twenty-three-year-old Guinean immigrant named Amadou Diallo, at about 12:40 a.m. in the vestibule of his own apartment building in the Bronx. The officers later said they mistook him for a serial rape suspect who had last struck about a year prior and thought he was going for a gun when he reached into his pocket. The officers fired forty-one shots, striking Diallo nineteen times. He had no weapon. He was trying to pull out his wallet.

Just a year and a half before that in August 1997, a thirty-year-old Haitian immigrant named Abner Louima had been arrested outside a Brooklyn nightclub and then taken to a police precinct, where he was brutally beaten and sodomized with a broken broomstick or the handle of a toilet plunger. The attack left injuries so severe that Louima needed multiple corrective surgeries. New Yorkers took to the streets, with demonstrators marching to city hall and the precinct where the torture had taken place.

Before the officers even went to trial in the Louima case, Diallo was shot. The shooting was like lighter fluid tossed into a burning flame. Once again, the city exploded. Outraged New Yorkers poured back into the city streets daily and, in recurring waves, made their way to 1 Police Plaza in downtown Manhattan, where they crossed a threshold that assured their arrests. And there were droves of arrests.

As I watched the protests, something inside me clicked this time.

I knew I had to go. It wasn't just that Diallo looked like me. But seeing his merciless killing, after all the other incidents, underscored the vulnerability of navigating the world in Black skin. He could have been me; I could have been him. He was just a hardworking young Black man, saving up money to go to college. I hurt for his heartbroken mother, who had watched her son travel to America with such hope. I hurt for his interrupted dreams and for my people whose skin alone made us such targets of hatred and violence.

Some of my seminary classmates were feeling the same. At least one of them, the Reverend Anthony Lee, now a Maryland-based pastor, was snatched and thrown against a gate by four plain clothes police officers who bolted from a rickety looking car and ran toward him one cold winter night as he was walking back to the seminary. Not knowing whether the men were officers or muggers, he decided that it was best not to run. In a very tense moment, as they were frisking him, one officer yelled "gun" although he was unarmed. Seeing his life flash before him, he said, "I am a student at Union Theological Seminary. My ID is in my right front pocket." After everything checked out, one officer advised, "Don't act so nervous the next time."

Given what was happening around us and sometimes to us, it didn't make much sense for us to be talking about justice in the classroom and singing about it in church if we weren't willing to get in the struggle in the streets. So I gathered up a small group, and we took the subway as close as we could and walked the rest of the way to the precinct. Throngs of others were already there, some with signs, calling for justice. As one group of protesters crossed the line of demarcation, were handcuffed, and were put in the back of a police van, the next group stepped up. My group just flowed with the crowd, moving closer to the line and our eventual arrest. I'd never been arrested before, but I knew without a doubt that I was doing the right thing, that this was my time to get in the fight, to put my body in the game, to participate in the civil disobedience that I had heretofore just read about or witnessed from afar.

Finally, I was handcuffed and led to the back of a police van. Congressman Eliot Engel, who represented part of the Bronx, was in the van, as was the Reverend Michael Eric Dyson, who was teaching at the time at Columbia University. We were all transported to the precinct, processed, and released. There was cautious hope in the community that the protests would push the then mayor, Rudolph Giuliani, past the arrogance he had displayed to citizens' previous complaints about police brutality and racism and the need to address them. The police commissioner, Howard Safir, had not suspended the four officers involved, and in his one-year tenure Safir had shown little interest in addressing police brutality. A Bronx grand jury indicted the officers on charges of second-degree murder, but after an appeals judge ordered a change of venue to Albany, the state capital, because of "public clamor," a jury of four Black and eight white jurors acquitted the officers of all charges on February 25, 2000. And any hope that our outrage and protests might prompt meaningful change was further dashed when an internal New York Police Department investigation found that the officers did not merit any disciplinary action since they had not violated department guidelines.

The outcome was disheartening. But I was forever changed. I'd brought my ministry to the streets, and there was no turning back.

CHAPTER 5

Stepping Out on My Own

In December 1999, one of my mentors, the Reverend John Thomas Porter, announced plans to retire from Sixth Avenue Baptist Church in Birmingham. He had returned to Sixth Avenue, the church where he grew up, as a young preacher in 1962, just as the civil rights movement was heating up in that city. He and the new congregation became a vital part of the movement that effectively dramatized its human rights concerns and successfully pushed the nation to translate them into landmark legislation. Led by Pastor Porter, who was jailed three times during the protests, members of Sixth Avenue had laid their bodies on the line as part of that work of redemption. Reverend Porter's image is immortalized, along with that of the Reverends A. D. King (Dr. King's brother) and Nelson H. Smith, in the statue of three ministers praying at Kelly Ingram Park, where Birmingham police and firemen unleashed dogs and fire hoses strong enough to rip the bark off trees on peaceful protesters, including children. Sixth Avenue also served as a source of comfort and healing for the whole community that painful day when three of the four little girls killed at the neighboring Sixteenth Street Baptist Church were eulogized in its sanctuary by Martin Luther King Jr.

The church remained vibrant and was always teeming with young families and children, and the ministry devoted many resources to keeping them engaged. Attending to the spiritual needs of the youths was key to the church's growth and impact, as I learned during my time interning there. That ministry bore real fruit. Among those who grew up at Sixth Avenue under the mentorship of Reverend Porter was Dr. Freeman A. Hrabowski III, who in 1992 was named president of the University of Maryland, Baltimore County. Hrabowski, a mathematician, was one of just a handful of African Americans leading predominantly white institutions of higher learning in the country at the time. He has since transformed his university into one of the nation's top producers of engineers and scientists of color. To this day, Hrabowski says that one of his most formative examples of effective leadership was Reverend Porter.

I felt a strong calling there. After my summers at Sixth Avenue, Reverend Porter had invited me back to preach twice a year, at Christmastime and in the summer. I loved returning to Sixth Avenue and thought of it as a second home. So, when I preached during the Christmas holidays in 1999, I met with Reverend Porter after worship to discuss my interest in applying to become the new pastor. Baptist pastors are recommended by a search committee of the church's members and elected by a vote of the full congregation, unlike denominations where a presiding bishop appoints the head of the church. I told him that I recognized Baptist churches tended to prefer married family men in the church's top leadership role, and I asked if he thought it would matter that I was still single. While I had been dating and wanted to get married someday, I had no immediate prospects. I'd seen guys rush into marriage for the sake of getting a church, but I took both marriage and the church too seriously to trivialize one to secure the other. Reverend Porter told me that it shouldn't matter and that he didn't think it would.

The church convened a committee of members, independent of Reverend Porter, to conduct a national pastoral search, and I entered the application process by submitting a letter of interest. The timing seemed perfect. I had begun to feel growing pains after eight years at Abyssinian, where I had risen from intern to assistant pastor. I was still working on my doctorate, but I was ready to lead my own church. Nothing would have pleased me more than to return to Birmingham to serve at Sixth Avenue.

As the search for Reverend Porter's successor continued, plans were simultaneously under way to celebrate the church's longtime leader, who was more than just a beloved pastor but also one of the most respected religious figures in Alabama. So I was honored to join the congregation and other sons, daughters, and friends of the ministry at a local hotel ballroom for the grand occasion and to give a brief tribute about how much Reverend Porter's mentorship had meant to me.

• • •

I had hoped to hear from the search committee, but months passed without even a word. Then, one day, I returned home to my apartment in New York and pulled a letter from my mailbox. It was from the search committee at Sixth Avenue. I read eagerly and quickly, and my eyes fell on the words "We reviewed your application, and you do not meet our qualifications." I was stunned. I read the letter again, noticing that while my name and address were correct at the top of the letter, the salutation contained the name of another candidate. I stood there in shock, holding the letter. Not only had I not made it past the first round in the process, but I'd been sent a basic form letter that had been cut and pasted together without even enough care to get my name right. This hurt deeply.

I'd never assumed I was a shoo-in for a position as significant as this one. But I thought that after a relationship of nearly a decade, Dr. Porter's mentorship of me, the church's financial investment in me, my having been baptized and ordained there, and my frequent return visits to preach, I would have at least been seriously considered. I'd felt confident that I would certainly get an interview and a chance to make the case for why I was ready to serve in this capacity. I'd been raised up at Sixth Avenue. And oh, how I loved to preach from that grand pulpit. Birmingham, too, had a special pull for me with its storied civil rights movement history.

I'd long been drawn to this history and its transformative possibilities within the larger American story. It was the work I wanted to do, and I imagined myself—a person who had been mentored by the person who was mentored by Dr. King—serving in that noble tradition and standing in that beautiful edifice as the pastor, ready to take Sixth Avenue to the next level. But it was not to be. And sitting with the weight of that knowledge in my chest made for a long, restless night.

I sought God in prayer.

Mornings are a big part of my prayer life. The psalmist says, "Early will I seek thee." There's something to me very holy about dawn. The sky is dark. The air is thin and crisp. And the world is quiet. No matter where I am, whether I'm in my house or on vacation at the beach, this is when I most often go to God and lay my life out bare. I can sense God's presence. And from this place emerges a peace and calm reassurance that a larger purpose is being worked out in my life. My job is to be quiet and still, even as I work. To listen, learn, and follow.

My early morning devotional is rooted in my upbringing, from hearing my mother's whispered prayers on the other side of the door of the bathroom in the wee hours of the morning.

The great theologian Howard Thurman also has been an inspiration and model for my spirituality. He talked in his sermons about "the inward sea" and about "the centering moment" where you refocus your thoughts, anxieties, and prayers in the presence of God. For me, that centering may be meditating on a psalm, or one verse of a psalm, like "The steps of a good person are ordered by the Lord" (Psalm 37:23). Or when I feel challenged or troubled in some way, it may be "The Lord is my light and my salvation; whom shall I fear? The Lord is the strength of my life; of whom shall I be afraid?" (Psalm 27:1). Or "God is our refuge and strength, a very present help in trouble" (Psalm 46:1). Or verses from Psalm 139, my favorite: "O Lord, you have searched me and known me. You know when I sit down and when I rise up; you discern my thoughts from far away . . . Search me, O God, and know my heart; test me and know my thoughts. See if there is any wicked way in me, and lead me in the way everlasting."

I just focus on the verses or one single verse or even a line. I won't so much talk to God right then as focus and try to listen for what Thurman called "the sound of the genuine." While in that meditative moment, the things that trouble me will sometimes disrupt that space. I feel them quietly, push them to the margins, and place again at the center my mantra for the day, *The steps of a righteous person are ordered by the Lord.*

My prayer emerges from that place of calm assurance. Prayer for me is more about listening than talking. Too often, people's version of prayer is doing all the talking. My most common prayer to God is one I've said in my own words since I was a kid: "Give me wisdom, knowledge, and understanding. Guide my feet. Order my steps. Direct my path."

So while I was disappointed by that letter, I remained guided by the sense that nothing can ultimately thwart the purposes of God. And my job is to be faithful to the process with its turns, disappointments, and setbacks. Ultimately, there is meaning to be gathered, lessons to be learned, and opportunities to grow. We often learn more from the disappointments than from the victories. Looking back all these years later, I recognize that had I gone to Sixth Avenue, my life might look very different right now.

At the time, though, all I knew for sure was that I had been called to be a pastor somewhere. I had started feeling restless in 1997, around the time that my brother Keith was arrested back home and I became his lead advocate, pushing for a more just sentence. I had been given great opportunities at Abyssinian, and Dr. Butts supported my desire to step out on my own. Abyssinian had always been the kind of place that trained and launched young ministers into powerful pulpits across the country. After being turned down at Sixth Avenue, I applied at New York churches—in White Plains and in New Rochelle. I was waiting to hear back from one of the churches in the spring of 2000 when Reverend Butts got an invitation to speak for "Men's Day" at St. James' Episcopal Church in Baltimore. He wasn't available, so as he sometimes did, he recommended me.

"You will not be disappointed," he assured the Men's Day Committee, buttressing his endorsement.

I traveled to Baltimore to preach with every intention of living up to my boss's expectation. I preached a sermon, titled "In the Meantime." It was about how to live faithfully and joyfully through life's transitional spaces, when you are between where you are and where you are headed. How do you live faithfully when you sense deep in your heart that there is more in store for your life but you're between the burdens of the past and the hopes and promises of the future? I used as a reference the biblical story of David, the shepherd boy who was anointed by the high priest and judge Samuel to be the next king to succeed Saul. The Lord sent Samuel to the house of

Jesse, David's father, to anoint one of Jesse's sons for the role. Jesse paraded each of his seven older sons before the high priest with confidence that one of them, with their good looks, superior size, and strength, was the chosen king. But they were not. When Samuel asked if there was another son, Jesse finally brought David, the youngest and the smallest, from the fields. David was the one. Samuel followed God's instructions and anointed the boy, but here's the key: After he was anointed, David didn't go immediately to the palace. He went back to the pasture, minding sheep, stepping in sheep manure, doing the lowly work of a shepherd boy, doing whatever was required of him until God's appointed time. Therein lies the example of how we should live when there is evidence of glory and possibility but we're in that space of preparation, a space when all we really have is God's promise, "I will be with you."

"Faith is not always saying to this mountain, 'Be removed.' Sometimes faith," I argued that morning, "is leaning with your back against the looming shadow of the mountain, secure in the knowledge that God is with you. Faith is trusting God through life's interludes and liminal spaces. Faith is being a good shepherd boy on your way to being a great soldier and a great soldier on your way to being a mighty king. Faith is living with grace and courage in the meantime." As the congregation heard the preacher that morning, I'm not so sure how much they knew that the preacher was preaching also to himself! Sometimes, the preacher has to do just that: preach to himself.

I met some wonderful people that Sunday at St. James', including the Reverend Michael B. Curry, who served as the church's rector. He had recently been named bishop of the North Carolina diocese, and this was one of his few remaining Sundays at St. James'. He was later named presiding bishop and primate of the Episcopal Church, the first African American to head the denomination, and he became more widely known in 2018, when he delivered the sermon at the wedding of Prince Harry and Meghan Markle. Also sitting in the congregation that day were some visitors from the nearby Douglas Memorial Community Church, a prominent Baltimore congregation with a rich history dating back to the early twentieth century. The church was looking for a pastor, and different members of the search committee, independent of one another, reached out to me and asked me to apply. Some of the members had heard me preach at St. James', and others had seen me in a 1999 article in *Ebony* magazine about young leaders.

I would learn later that Douglas Memorial was born in rebellion in 1925, when a group of dissident members split from Bethel AME Church, then the denomination's most prestigious congregation in Baltimore, because they wanted to keep their pastor. African Methodist Episcopal pastors are itinerants, sometimes serving only a few short years in one place before being reassigned by the presiding bishop. Bethel's pastor, the Reverend Frederick Douglas, was being reassigned. But he became the head of the new breakaway church, Cosmopolitan AME. When Cosmopolitan later refused to pledge its allegiance to the AME denomination, the church changed its affiliation and became part of the growing Community Church movement of independent nondenominational congregations. The name of the church was changed in 1938 to honor its founding pastor, Douglas, a renegade who supported the ordination of women as pastors—a radical stance in the early and mid-twentieth century.

Douglas was followed by Marion C. Bascom, a poetic preacher and firebrand who later marched with Dr. King in Alabama, led marches and protests in Baltimore, and served Douglas Memorial for forty-six years. The church had grown to about seven hundred members, including some well-known African American families, like that of Kurt Schmoke, the first African American to be elected mayor of Baltimore in 1987. Bascom's successor, the Reverend Dr. Brad Braxton, a young Rhodes scholar, had left the church after a five-year tenure for a teaching job at Wake Forest University. The search committee was looking to replace him.

I entered the application process at Douglas by sending my résumé and CDs of my preaching, and I was invited to Baltimore to interview with the search committee. I took the train down from New York, met with the search committee, and was scheduled to preach at a confidential location to an assigned group of them on that Sunday night. The Reverend Dr. Harold A. Carter Jr., who had been a roommate of Reverend Porter's at Alabama State University, had opened his sanctuary at the New Shiloh Baptist Church in Baltimore for that part of the process. But the Saturday morning before I was set to preach, I woke up and discovered that my voice was gone—something that rarely happens to me, even if I get a cold. I was worried that I might be unable to speak the next day, let alone preach. I nursed my throat with every remedy I could remember—lemon juice, hot tea, and over-the-counter medications—and by Sunday my voice had just partially returned. Nevertheless, I preached the best I could with my voice going in and out and with little ability to project much beyond a whisper. I had to trust totally in God. Later, I would interpret that experience as a reminder that my future was in God's hands. As the Lord says in Zechariah 4:6, "not by might nor by power, but by my Spirit."

Whatever my gifts and preparation, if I were to land the job at Douglas, it would be by the grace of God.

I later got the call that I was the finalist, and I took the train from New York once again for a "candidate's weekend," which included dinner in the social hall of the church with the Board of Stewards and lay leaders. I got to stand before them, give remarks, and respond to their questions. I preached that Sunday morning, and later that afternoon the church elected me as the new pastor of Douglas Memorial Community Church. I knew that this was the right place at the right time. And I was thrilled.

I started as senior pastor at Douglas in January 2001 at thirty-one years old. This was my appointed time to lead, and I was ready to serve and give my congregation my best. The members welcomed me warmly, and we set my official investiture ceremony and weekend celebration for September. I spent the intervening months getting to know my new community, church, and members.

Just before the Easter holidays, I was invited by a local state senator to be a chaplain for the day and offer a prayer at the opening of the legislative session. This was an exciting opportunity because it would give me a chance to meet my state legislators just as I was learning my way around. I prepared a standard prayer and arrived ready to deliver it. But when I made it there that morning, I learned that legislators had been looking at the disparities in the application of the death penalty and would be debating that day whether to impose a moratorium until the issue could be thoroughly reviewed.

There we were in the Lenten season, remembering that solemn march that leads to Calvary, focusing on the one who was put to death there, and legislators were about to debate this important issue. I knew that I couldn't be a preacher in the prophetic tradition to which I had been called and stand in that state legislative chamber and pray a standard prayer. Prophets disturb us, shake us out of our complacency, declare God's dream for our lives. So I tucked my prepared prayer in my pocket and prayed the kind of prayer where preachers talk to God and others who are listening at the same time. I asked God to "remind us that every Sunday we preach and sing in the name of a death row inmate, a man born in a barrio called Bethlehem, raised in a ghetto called Nazareth, a man who was brought before the state on trumped-up charges, convicted by the state without due process, and executed one dark Friday." I told them that God "declares solidarity with the most marginalized, those on the underside of justice." And I pleaded with God to "help us hear so we might know what is right."

As it turned out, a reporter from a local television station was there, and my opening prayer made the news. A couple weeks later, I brought a few members of the church to the statehouse with an old rugged cross, and we held a prayer vigil on the steps of the state capitol. Eventually, the moratorium was approved, and several years later the state would abolish the death penalty.

The protest at the capital that day in 2001 helped to jump-start the kind of ministry I wanted to build at Douglas, a ministry that was engaged in the issues facing the community, a ministry that stood not in judgment of people but beside them, fighting with them and for them. As I thought about the major issues confronting Baltimore at the time, the growing rate of HIV/AIDS in the city rose to the top of the list. I quickly realized the church sat in a zip code where pockets of the community had an HIV/AIDS infection rate nearly as high as that of some sub-Saharan African nations, but the subject was still taboo in most churches. Antiretroviral drugs to combat the disease were still prohibitively expensive, and African Americans were dying disproportionately, many as modern-day lepers. The rejection of these afflicted members of our society and the church's reticence and hostility toward them were largely driven by homophobia. Raised in conservative church circles, I had seen this dynamic up close. Gay men and women have always served in the church, yet their humanity and identity are not fully embraced.

As a single, straight man in Baltimore and a new pastor in a new town, I knew that addressing the HIV/AIDS issue early and directly would cause some to question my own sexuality. But what kind of pastor would I be if I allowed myself to be silenced by that kind of stigma? I would, in fact, be contributing to the twisted logic of homophobia. Besides, people were getting sick and dying. Gay people. Straight people. God's people. Perhaps I had been called to this place at this time so that I might stretch toward living into the power and promise of my own name. Raphael. The Lord heals.

For my installation ceremony, I decided to build the activities around HIV/AIDS awareness to signal to my church and community the kind of ministry we would build together. The members got behind the idea, and we planned a wonderful weekend, with a daylong symposium that brought together theologians and biblical scholars to help the religious community think through the issue and find the courage to confront our fears with honesty and power. The event also offered sessions with clinicians and public health experts. In media interviews, I quoted the Old Testament prophet Hosea saying, "My people are destroyed for lack of knowledge." And I urged the clergy to lead the way in getting tested to stress the importance of all knowing their status to help create an environment free from stigma. Later the same evening, the members, our guests, and I marched through the community behind a banner that read, THE CHURCH RESPONDS TO AIDS.

That weekend, I was particularly moved by a section of the AIDS Memorial Quilt—individual three-by-six-foot cloth panels, each dedicated to an individual lost to AIDS—which our planning committee had arranged to hang stoically, powerfully inside the sanctuary behind the pulpit for the weekend. The full quilt by then had attracted thousands of panels from all over the country, but even the section loaned to us as part of a traveling exhibit was a quiet reminder that too many sons, daughters, and loved ones had already died in silence and shame. The quilt remained there as a memorial for months.

I kept pushing to modernize our programming. At the investiture weekend, I joined other church folks, Baltimore dignitaries, and guests, all dressed in our finest, at the Renaissance Baltimore Harborplace Hotel for a dinner showcase of the arts. The banquet featured church musicians, as well as a local jazz band that played a beautiful rendition of Duke Ellington's "Come Sunday." My goal was to break down the rigid rules between sacred and secular music forms. Jazz, gospel, and rhythm and blues all come from the same place, the anguished ruminations of a subjugated people speaking to God and each other in their own voice. An acquaintance from Abyssinian, the veteran actor Ossie Davis, beloved as much for his dedication to Dr. King and the civil rights movement as for his film work, was our guest speaker.

The Sunday services were especially poignant for me with Reverend Porter delivering the morning sermon, followed later that evening by Reverend Butts. Both pastors had believed in me when I was just a young man with a dream and they had been there for me throughout the journey. My mom and dad, my first teachers and spiritual examples, as well as two of my sisters, Joyce and Valencia, were there, too, and they were full of joy and excitement for me. The Abyssinian choirs traveled from New York and joined the choirs at Douglas in forming a mass choir for the event that filled the church's large balcony and made extraordinary music.

The occasion was everything that I hoped it would be—a grateful nod to my past, serious acknowledgment that God had called me to this ministry for such a time as this, and an atmosphere of excitement and hope for the future. I was excited for what we could do together. I thought of Douglas as a bridge, a place full of well-educated professionals with stable lives, big jobs, and hearts even bigger than their bank accounts. They were a progressive congregation that wanted to be part of lifting the community, and I looked forward to many years of working together beyond the walls of our building.

In my closing remarks that Sunday evening, I harked back to my suggestion that members of the clergy lead by example with HIV/AIDS testing. I suggested that we have a service with all clergy,

dressed in their sacred vestments, parading together to a testing fa-
cility. I knew that act would preach louder than any sermon about
the need to get tested. It also would destigmatize the disease and
begin to change the narrative that HIV/AIDS is a sickness, not a sin.

So the following January in observance of Dr. King's birthday,
I gave fellow members of the clergy a chance to do just that. As
part of our Martin Luther King Day service, my church summoned
a mobile health unit to conduct on-site HIV/AIDS testing in our
parking lot. Many of the ministers of various churches in the area
had told me they would participate but did not show up. Nevertheless, I preached a message about the "unholy trinity of silence,
shame, and stigma" and encouraged the audience to stand in solidarity with those who were sick and those who were afraid to let
them know that we were in this together. And then I led the way
out of the church to the parking lot to take an HIV/AIDS test. I felt
strongly that compassion and the bearing of one another's burdens
was what it means for the word of God to become flesh.

I had long been connected with the fight against HIV/AIDS.
While living in New York, I had been active in a group called the
National Black Leadership Commission on AIDS, which Debra
Fraser-Howze had founded in 1987. The group's mission was to
mobilize Black leadership, including ministers, to lead the fight in
their communities in part by advocating for policy changes that
addressed the disparities in health and resources. I wanted to continue that work in Baltimore; so a year after I became senior pastor
at Douglas, I helped organize a local chapter of the group to keep
the issue at the forefront of discussions about how to confront
major challenges facing the city, and I served as vice-chairman.

"We're overrepresented by the virus and underrepresented by funds," I told the media about our city when we announced the Baltimore chapter.

According to the Centers for Disease Control and Prevention, in 2002, AIDS was the second-leading cause of death among Baltimore residents aged twenty-five to forty-four, behind only homicide. Nationwide, new infections and AIDS cases had started to decline, but Baltimore still had one of the highest per capita caseloads in the country. A total of twelve thousand city residents were HIV positive in 2000, and by 2002 an overwhelming majority of them—85 percent—were African American. The church and the community could no longer look away. We had to do something.

The commission began lobbying city officials, and in December 2002, Baltimore's mayor, Martin O'Malley, declared a state of emergency in the city's HIV/AIDS crisis. At a press conference announcing the declaration, he called for public and private entities to work together for prevention, education, and treatment initiatives.

I came to love Baltimore. While I was performing my pastoral duties, I was also working on my doctoral dissertation. Just thirty minutes north of the nation's capital by train, Baltimore still had a southern feel, not folksy like the Deep South, but still warm and southern. I got to enjoy real crab cakes and learned quickly about the east side–west side and big high school rivalries. Baltimore is a beautiful port city that, despite its glass and metal skyscrapers, huge sports arenas, and beautifully developed downtown, maintains a small-town aura. Its historic row houses look different from one neighborhood to the next—from the picturesque, expansive brick homes that house the city's wealthiest residents to the crumbling wood frame houses in the poorer sections.

I lived downtown near the Inner Harbor. My rowhouse, built at the turn of the twentieth century, had a rooftop deck, where I could see the skyline and harbor. On summer nights and fall days, I loved sitting out there, enjoying the atmosphere. It provided the perfect place for respite and reflection.

Like many urban areas across the nation, Baltimore is a city with two faces: its old-moneyed communities with wealth dating back generations, top-ranked academic and medical institutions, and Inner Harbor tourist district gleaming with fine restaurants, shopping, and entertainment venues on one side; and on the other, desperation, poverty, and broken neighborhoods besieged by drugs and crime. The critically acclaimed HBO series *The Wire* premiered in 2002, showcasing for the world Baltimore's seediest side.

Douglas is housed in an old Greek Revival–style building that dates to 1857, when it was constructed for Madison Avenue Methodist Episcopal Church. With four fluted white columns sitting on cast-iron bases across the front, granite stairs, and wrought-iron railings and gate, the building maintains much of its original character and has been listed on the National Register of Historic Places since 1992. The congregation skewed older, too, so one of the first personnel changes I made was to hire a youth pastor. Taking a cue from Reverend Porter, I recognized that to have sustained growth, we needed to raise a generation of youths who would bring their own children back and keep the momentum going.

School picture,
age eight.

Posing with my sister Valencia
(standing in blue) and two of our
childhood friends in the neighborhood
near the Kayton Homes public
housing development, where we grew
up. Valencia and I were the babies of
the bunch in our large, blended
family of twelve children.

My big brother Keith and our
parents, celebrating his high school
graduation. Though he was five
years older, Keith was the brother
closest to me in age.

Standing on the streets of New York City as a teenager during my first visit there. I got to sightsee and attend a Broadway show during the trip, made possible by the federal Upward Bound program, which opened my eyes to the wide world beyond Savannah.

My parents, Jonathan and Verlene Warnock, were my first teachers and role models. They raised my siblings and me in a large, loving family full of laughter. My father was pastor of a small Pentecostal church while I was growing up, but in his later years he supported my mother as she became his pastor.

Dad as a young man. He was a World War II veteran and an entrepreneur who saw worth in old junk cars, which he salvaged during the week. On Sundays, he worked as a pastor, helping to salvage broken lives.

Standing with my proud parents as I became the first in our large family to graduate from a four-year college. Getting me through Morehouse College was a family affair.

I gathered a group of fellow seminary students to join the explosive protests in New York City after the police shooting of Amadou Diallo. His merciless killing showed the vulnerability of navigating the world in Black skin. It was a transformative moment that led to my first arrest.

Standing in front of a picture of the Reverend Adam Clayton Powell Jr. during my early days at Union.

With Ossie Davis and my Abyssinian comrades at my initiation
banquet at Douglas Memorial Community Church in Baltimore.

Getting my Union PhD.

With Magic Johnson for an HIV/AIDS event I hosted at my Baltimore church.

Standing with my proud father after preaching. As a kid, I wanted to be a preacher just like my dad. It was Father's Day when I called to tell him that I had been selected as the new pastor of the historic Ebenezer Baptist Church.

Posing with my parents and most of my siblings. It's tough to get all twelve of us in the same room at the same time. But eight of us are pictured here with our parents. *Left to right:* Leon, Valencia, me, Mom, Joyce (slightly behind Mom), Dad, Wandetta, Jeffrey, Terry, and Frank.

Dad enjoying time with his youngest child, Valencia, and her children. Soon after I became a pastor in Baltimore, Valencia and her children joined me there and ultimately made Baltimore their home. Pictured here *(left to right)* are Mark, Dad, Valencia (slightly behind Dad), Markeyah, and Diamond.

Singing "We Shall Overcome" with Senator Obama on
MLK Sunday 2008, Ebenezer Baptist Church.

Sharing the Ebenezer pulpit in 2008
with then senator Barack Obama.
When I invited Senator Obama
to Ebenezer before the Democratic
primary, he was locked in a battle
with then senator Hillary Clinton
to win the party's nomination in the
race for president of the United States.

Protesting the planned execution of death row inmate Troy Davis. His case drew international attention because of significant data that raised questions about his guilt. Standing, facing the camera *(left to right)* are: Amnesty International USA executive director Larry Cox, then NAACP president Ben Jealous, me, and (looking back) Davis's nephew, De'Juan Davis-Correia, who has since graduated from Morehouse College.

The evening of Troy Davis's execution.

Cutting the ribbon for the new Martin Luther King, Sr. Community Resources Complex.
I was proud to complete this $8 million building as a living memorial to Daddy King, who
served as senior pastor of Ebenezer for forty-four years. Pictured *(left to right)* are his only
daughter, Christine King Farris; me; my mother, Verlene Warnock; Esther Jean Roberts,
wife of my predecessor, the Reverend Joseph L. Roberts; and Naomi King, widow of
A. D. King, the younger brother of Dr. Martin Luther King Jr.

At the pulpit of Ebenezer.

Protesting the state of Georgia's refusal to expand Medicaid to the working poor
who can't afford private health insurance. During this sit-in outside the governor's office,
we were confronted by a state police officer before being arrested. Seated beside me
(left to right) are the Reverend Shanan Jones, executive pastor at Ebenezer,
and the Reverend Francys Johnson, then state president of the NAACP.

Standing behind Congressman John Lewis in the Ebenezer pulpit. Before
I decided to run for the U.S. Senate, I sought Congressman Lewis's mentorship.
I was his pastor, but I was clear that he was the elder statesman.

Showing presidential candidate Pete Buttigieg around the old Ebenezer Baptist Church. People travel from all over the world to stand in the sanctuary where the Reverend Dr. Martin Luther King Jr. once stood as pastor. The historic church, now called Heritage Sanctuary, is across the street from my current church.

On the campaign trail with Jon Ossoff.

Giving fist bumps (not handshakes) in a local barbershop during the campaign. My campaign workers and I wore masks and kept the proper social distance when we dropped in on a local barbershop during my campaign for the U.S. Senate, but soon the COVID-19 pandemic would shut down the world and change the nature of campaigning.

Campaigning in the age of COVID-19.

Campaigning in Warner Robins, Georgia. We held these kinds of outdoor rallies across the state of Georgia to keep people safe during the pandemic as I campaigned for the Senate. Supporters were eager to get outside in the fresh air.

Holding Alvin the Dog. Alvin became a star during the campaign when he was featured in my commercials during the runoff. Those commercials were among the most popular of the entire campaign.

Sharing the stage with then vice president elect Kamala Harris and my fellow candidate Jon Ossoff during the runoff campaign. Our Georgia Senate campaigns were so significant to Democrats regaining power in the Senate that the party's national leaders campaigned with us.

Walking in the White House after watching President Joe Biden sign legislation making Juneteenth a national holiday. The measure received overwhelmingly bipartisan support in the House and passed unanimously in the Senate.

Spending precious time on vacation with my children, Chloé and Caleb. The hardest part of my job is being away from them during the week. But when I miss them, I remind myself that I'm working to build a better world for them and for all children.

By the time I arrived in Baltimore, my younger sister, Valencia, had become a single mother, raising three children on her own. She needed a fresh start and decided to relocate to Baltimore with me. We had always been close, and it was good to have her in the same city and, for the first time since our childhood, in the same house. Valencia had become the second in our family to graduate from college, and with a bachelor's degree in social work, she quickly found a job. After about three months, she moved into her own apartment.

It had been difficult for Valencia to leave her children at home in Savannah with our mother, but she didn't want to pull them out of school in the middle of the year. She needed time to get settled. Besides, she knew they were in great hands. When it was time for her to go pick up the children in Savannah, I was unsure when they all would return. But one Sunday I looked out from the pulpit, and there was Valencia, sitting in the sanctuary with my two nieces, then fourteen and eight, and my eleven-year-old nephew beside her. I was delighted to have them as members of my church, and the kids were active in the youth ministry. With no children of my own at the time, I enjoyed spending time with them, showing them around Baltimore, and I even got to play Uncle Dad on the occasions that Valencia had to travel for work.

Valencia's youngest daughter, Diamond, looks like me and sometimes was mistaken as my daughter when we were out. According to her mother, Diamond's personality is a bit like mine, too, seeming at times older than her years. When she was first introduced to her Sunday school class, the teacher told the students that she was Reverend Warnock's niece, to which they responded with oohs and aahs. One of the kids asked excitedly, "What does it feel like to be Reverend Warnock's niece?"

I was told that Diamond responded, "It don't feel like nothing." I was just Uncle Ray.

By 2004, my roots were just starting to set at Douglas Memorial when I returned home to a phone message from Dr. Bernee Dunson, a dentist I'd known briefly while he attended Abyssinian. Now he was living in Atlanta and worshipping at the iconic Ebenezer Baptist Church. Bernee's message said his pastor was retiring and that he and his wife, Hillary, had been talking.

"Wouldn't it be nice if Raphael came down to be our pastor," he told her.

I'd just begun working on a long-term master plan, and there was so much more I wanted to accomplish at Douglas. But Ebenezer had been Dr. King's church. And I was intrigued.

CHAPTER 6

Spirit of the Kings

Soon after I returned the call about the pastoral search at Ebenezer, I sent a brief email message to Reverend Butts.

"Ebenezer needs a pastor," I said. "And I'm wondering if I should apply."

He responded quickly and unequivocally: "Please apply. We need our best and our brightest in pulpits as important as Ebenezer."

Reverend Butts's confidence in me filled me with gratitude, and I began to reflect on his words "pulpits as important as Ebenezer." Even the thought of asking to step into that historic pulpit as pastor humbled me. This was Dr. King's church; at least that's how I'd always thought of Ebenezer. It was the place where the man I'd admired and tried to model for most of my life had served as co-pastor in the 1960s until his death in 1968. It was the mother church of the civil rights movement, the place where Dr. King not only preached his message of love, freedom, and justice to the world but also got to preach Sunday morning sermons, marry couples, comfort bereaved families, and just be M. L., as the old-timers called him, a son and servant of the ministry. It was Dr. King's home church, the place where the movement's most visible soldier brought his weary soul to find sweet rest and the inspiration to fight another day.

Among public figures in American life, King has always been for me one of the clearest examples of faith in action, a depth of spiritual commitment and moral courage that lends itself to a life project much larger than one's lifetime. From childhood, his voice captivated me and his vision of "the beloved community" inspired me to fight for change. Although I was born more than a year after his death, Martin Luther King Jr., more than anybody or anything else, recruited me to Morehouse College. As a college intern minister at Sixth Avenue Baptist Church, I had been mentored by Reverend Porter, who had been King's pulpit assistant as a college intern at Dexter Avenue Baptist Church in Montgomery. In New York, I had witnessed close up the activist ministry of Reverend Butts as he responded to the challenges of affordable housing and police brutality in New York in the 1990s. Could it be that the kid from the projects who wanted so badly all those years ago to attend Martin Luther King's alma mater might become the pastor of his church? No matter the final outcome of Ebenezer's pastoral search process, the opportunity to preach there just once would be a great honor. To actually serve there would be a dream. The thought of it all gave me goose bumps.

I was moved, too, by the history of this congregation and the King family's deep roots there. By late 2004, just four people had served as senior pastors since the church's founding in 1886. And two of those previous pastors were Dr. King's maternal grandfather and father. His grandfather the Reverend Adam Daniel Williams assumed the pastorate at Ebenezer with just seventeen members in 1894. The son of slaves, Reverend Williams had little formal education, but he became a preacher, like his own father and the community ministers who tutored him. After becoming pastor of Ebenezer, Reverend Williams earned a certificate from a ministry training program at Atlanta Baptist College, which later became Morehouse. The church grew to four hundred members in just under a decade and moved to various locations as the congregation continued to grow. People were drawn to Reverend Williams, who was one of the pioneers of what was known as the Black social gospel. In that work, he preached about more than just personal salvation and often used the pulpit to advocate for the development of Black businesses, home ownership, and human rights. He helped organize the first Atlanta chapter of the National Association for the Advancement of Colored People (NAACP) in 1917, became its branch president, and spearheaded efforts to register Black voters. Williams's courage was astounding during this time of brutal racism in the Atlanta area and the entire South. Just two years earlier, a group of white supremacists had burned a cross on Stone Mountain, just outside Atlanta, reinvigorating the Ku Klux Klan and its intimidation and terror tactics against Black residents. Just eleven years before Williams helped create the NAACP chapter, dozens of Black men and women were murdered at random by white mobs and Black-owned businesses looted during the Atlanta race riot of 1906.

All of my ministry training, preparation, and leadership had happened at churches that, like Ebenezer, had served as social gospel stations led by social gospel ministers. John Porter's Sixth Avenue, a place of resistance and refuge for the mourners of precious little girls killed at the Sixteenth Street Church during the civil rights movement. Abyssinian, where Adam Clayton Powell Jr. had served and where before that, his father, Adam Clayton Powell Sr., built a ministry of refuge for the people of Harlem during the years of the Great Depression. Douglas Memorial was also a movement church, leading the fight for integration in the 1960s, under the leadership of Marion Bascom. As I entered Ebenezer's pastoral search process, I was seeking not to put on their shoes but to stand on their shoulders so that I, too, might see and pursue a vision of the beloved community and play my part in the continuing march toward the promised land.

Under Reverend Williams's leadership, Ebenezer grew into one of Atlanta's most prominent congregations. The church sat in a thriving Black community, known as Sweet Auburn, and the stately redbrick edifice that would become known to the world would be completed in 1922. By then, Reverend Williams's only surviving child, Alberta Christine Williams, was being courted by a young preacher named Michael King, whose older sister had been a boarder in the family's home. The two would remain a couple for several years, while she earned a two-year teaching certificate from Hampton Normal and Agricultural Institute in Virginia (now

Hampton University). With the encouragement of the Williams family, King, too, continued his education, completing high school at Bryant Preparatory Institute and enrolling in Morehouse's three-year minister's degree program in 1926. The couple had announced their engagement at a Sunday service at Ebenezer two years earlier and would marry there on Thanksgiving Day in 1926. The newlyweds moved into an upstairs bedroom in the Williams family home and soon began raising their own family. Three children came quickly—Willie Christine in 1927, Michael junior in 1929, and Alfred Daniel in 1930.

The elder King held preaching jobs at two other churches in town, but when his father-in-law died in 1931, he ascended to become pastor of Ebenezer. King would ultimately lead Ebenezer for forty-four years. His wife, Alberta, a gifted musician, formed the church choir, played the organ faithfully on Sundays for many of those years, and served dutifully beside him. And all the Kings were raised to appreciate the depth of their family's roots in Ebenezer. Indeed, the story of the Kings is intermingled with that of Ebenezer. King family members celebrated their greatest joys there—baby blessings, baptisms, weddings. The church's story is in part their story.

Two years after stepping into the Ebenezer pulpit, King officially changed his name to Martin Luther King Sr. While his mother had insisted that she'd named him Michael after the archangel, King's father argued that he'd given his son the first names of each of his brothers, Martin and Luther. But King didn't have a birth certificate, and he grew up being called Mike. When King's father died in 1933, though, King filed the appropriate papers to change his name and fulfill his father's dying wish. He also changed the name of his namesake.

Like his father-in-law, King would become a respected civic and civil rights leader, ultimately serving on executive committees of Atlanta's NAACP and the Atlanta Civic and Political League. In 1939, King senior pushed for a march on city hall as part of a massive voter registration drive, which more conservative clergy opposed. From the pulpit of Ebenezer, he told the crowd of more than a thousand people who had rallied there, "I ain't gonna plow no more mules. I'll never step off the road again to let white folks pass. I am going to move forward toward freedom, and I'm hoping everybody here today is going right along with me!"

King senior would go on to protest policies that paid white teachers more than Black teachers with the same credentials; these efforts led to a gradual adjustment until there wasn't such racial disparity. He also urged other progressive Baptist preachers at the National Baptist Convention, which his father-in-law had been part of organizing decades earlier, to pressure President Franklin D. Roosevelt into ending racially discriminatory practices on trains. Young Martin Luther King Jr. saw this bold activism modeled in his father's personal life and preached from the pulpit of Ebenezer. The younger King would witness his father furiously leaving a shoe shop with him after a clerk insisted that father and son enter through the back door. "You take it like everybody else, and stop being so high and mighty," King senior recalled the store clerk telling him. With his son watching, the father had a decision to make.

"I could see he was confused by what was going on. After all, he only wanted a pair of shoes to wear," King senior recalled. "When I told him we were leaving, he seemed ready to cry . . . As we drove back toward Auburn Avenue, I was able to speak quietly about the whole episode in the store, but the questions, the confusions, remained in his eyes."

Over time, the congregation at Ebenezer started to refer to King senior with parental deference as Daddy King. He relished his role as head of one of the city's most influential congregations and was known for his bold, blunt personality, which he used at will with considerable political influence. In the fall of 1960, his pronouncement of support for a certain political candidate would help change American history.

On October 19, 1960, King junior had been arrested after joining student protesters in a campaign to desegregate snack bars and restaurants in Atlanta's department stores. The younger King was quickly rising as a powerful, influential voice in the civil rights movement that had begun spreading throughout the nation after the successful, yearlong Montgomery bus boycott that began in December 1955. At the time, King junior served as pastor of Dexter Avenue Baptist Church in Montgomery and helped to organize the boycott, but his father had called him home to Atlanta to serve as co-pastor of Ebenezer.

After King was arrested with the students, a judge from neighboring DeKalb County asserted that King junior's arrest violated the terms of a suspended sentence issued in an earlier misdemeanor traffic citation. He had been stopped by police and ticketed for driving on his Alabama license three months after having moved back home to Georgia. The judge had sentenced him at the time to a one-year suspended jail sentence and a $25 fine, which King junior paid. The same judge revoked the suspended sentence and ordered King junior to serve four months of hard labor on a state road gang. The movement's lawyers called every political operative they knew, including sympathizers inside the presidential campaign of then senator John F. Kennedy. Citizens also flooded the governor's office with calls. A few of Kennedy's aides urged him to make a statement in support of King's release, but they were hearing that Governor Ernest Vandiver of Georgia had promised to get King out of jail if Kennedy made no public statement on the case. Instead, an aide persuaded Kennedy to place a private call to King junior's wife, Coretta, who was pregnant at the time, to express concern and support. It was a well-timed, fateful move.

The next day the judge ordered the release of King junior who by then had spent eight nights in three different jails. During a spontaneous mass meeting at Ebenezer a jubilant Daddy King announced that he would be voting for Kennedy. The Republican presidential candidate, Richard Nixon, had declined comment on King junior's arrest.

"It took courage to call my daughter-in-law at a time like this," King senior said of Kennedy. "He has the moral courage to stand up for what he knows is right . . . I've got all my votes and I've got a suitcase, and I'm going to take them up there and dump them in his lap."

The crowd offered thunderous applause, and King junior's friend and aide the Reverend Ralph Abernathy urged them to "take off your Nixon buttons." Two weeks later, Kennedy eked out a narrow victory over Nixon, due in large part to the support of Black voters. In the previous presidential election, as per exit polls, Black voters nationwide had voted for a Democrat over Dwight Eisenhower, the Republican candidate, by a margin of 60 percent to 40 percent. But in 1960, they voted for Kennedy by about 70 percent to 30 percent. This sacred right of Black voters to participate in our democracy had helped to tip the scales in favor of their chosen candidate.

Ebenezer at once gave King junior a firm anchor to serve in the ministry he loved and the freedom to go on a moment's notice where the movement called him. And no matter where he was called, he remained committed to the life of the congregation. Part of the younger King's legacy at Ebenezer is a lasting tradition called the Birth Month Clubs. As the church grew, King junior wanted to find a way to keep members connected, and so he came up with an idea for congregants to join clubs, based on their birthday months. Each club would find ways for the members to socialize and celebrate together outside church and, when needed, console one another.

Unfortunately, life would bring the King family more than their share of tragedy and suffering, and they laid that, too, on the altar of Ebenezer. The younger King's tenure as co-pastor would last a short eight years and end in heartbreak for his family and the nation when he was assassinated on a Memphis balcony in April 1968. A private funeral service for family, close friends, politicians, and dignitaries was held at Ebenezer, followed by a public one at Morehouse.

Five months later, Daddy King installed his youngest child,

Alfred Daniel, called A. D., as co-pastor. With a voice reminiscent of his brother's, A. D. King had not achieved similar prominence, but he had been active in the civil rights movement while also serving as pastor of Baptist churches in Birmingham, Louisville, and elsewhere. The brothers sometimes traveled together, and A. D. was staying at the Lorraine Motel in a room just below his brother's during that tragic trip to Memphis. Then, on the morning of July 21, 1969, less than a year after he became co-pastor, A. D., a married father of five, was found dead in the bottom of the family's backyard swimming pool. His death was ruled an accidental drowning.

And so Ebenezer and the Kings bore another family funeral. Then, just five years later, the King family was struck by grief again.

It was a regular Sunday morning service on June 30, 1974, when members noticed a stranger, a young Black man, seated alone in the main audience section of Ebenezer and invited him to attend the men's adult Sunday school class. The visitor complied and even introduced himself, saying he was from Ohio. When services started, he moved to the front of the church near its new organ. The organ sat on the floor level, and Mrs. King sat before it, playing "The Lord's Prayer." Members closed their eyes in preparation for the usual prayer, but instead they heard a commotion in the front. A voice yelled something about "taking over." And there was the stranger who had been welcomed to Sunday school, standing in front of the sanctuary with guns in his hands. He was close enough to Mrs. King to touch her when he fired at her and then at the church deacon, Edward Boykin, who was standing nearby. A sixty-five-year-old woman who was identified as Mrs. Jimmie Mitchell also was shot. The gunman kept firing randomly, emptying his gun into the crowd. Pandemonium ensued as most of the worshippers fled the sanctuary or dived beneath pews. A few men rushed from the choir and wrestled the gunman to the church floor and took his guns. The victims were whisked away in ambulances to the hospital, where Mrs. King and Deacon Boykin were pronounced dead. The third victim survived.

Marcus Wayne Chenault Jr., a twenty-three-year-old from Dayton, Ohio, told authorities that he had traveled to Atlanta to kill Reverend King but shot Mrs. King because she was closer to him. He professed a disdain for Christianity and Black ministers. Chenault was charged with two counts of murder and aggravated assault, and despite claims of insanity he was convicted and sentenced to the death penalty. His sentence was upheld on appeal, but he was eventually resentenced to life in prison, in part because of the King family's opposition to the death penalty. Chenault would die in prison of a fatal stroke two decades later.

The shooting left Ebenezer adrift. A huge part of its anchor was gone. A member immediately placed a call to the Reverend Dr. Joseph Roberts, a thirty-nine-year-old Presbyterian minister who was working as director of corporate and social mission at the Presbyterian church's national office in Atlanta. Ebenezer's leaders had offered him the opportunity to work as Reverend King's co-pastor, but Roberts wasn't a fan of the two-chiefs structure and had declined. But he had preached there on and off as a guest minister. In fact, Roberts was supposed to deliver the sermon at Ebenezer on the morning of the shooting, but he'd had to cancel for scheduling reasons. Just hours after the shooting, a member called and insisted that it was time for Roberts to reconsider coming to Ebenezer.

Roberts recalled years later that Daddy King had him meet with a group of people at the church and then one night in November 1974 asked his congregation to come to a meeting. About four hundred members showed up, and as Roberts recalled, Daddy King stood and made an announcement: "Now I'm tired. I've been through enough. I've lost two sons . . . I got to give this thing up."

The congregation was shocked. Was Daddy King retiring? He continued, "Now it'll be a dog's breakfast if I just try to get somebody in here and elect them . . . I'm gonna tell you who you need to get as your new preacher so we won't have a whole lot of confusion and this thing will go right . . . You know that Presbyterian boy who I've had over here every now and then . . . y'all ought to call him as the pastor."

The chairman of the Deacon Board jumped up and said, "He's not even a Baptist."

Daddy King shot back: "That doesn't matter, I can make him a Baptist overnight."

And with that, the congregation voted unanimously for Roberts to become the next pastor of Ebenezer. The following day, Daddy King called him with the news. Roberts said he had to tie up some loose ends in his current position and couldn't begin for another nine months. Then, in August 1975, Daddy King retired after forty-four extraordinary years at the helm of Ebenezer Baptist Church. Roberts became the church's fourth pastor and the first one in eighty-one years who wasn't a member of the King family.

Daddy King became pastor emeritus, but he still showed up at his church office nearly every day. And he still carried considerable political influence—so much so that when the former Georgia governor Jimmy Carter considered seeking higher office, he paid Daddy King a visit to ask for his support. In King's recounting of that meeting in his memoir, Carter told King he'd decided to run.

"Run for what?" King asked.

"Why, for the presidency," Carter responded.

"The presidency?" King asked, surprised. "Of what?"

"The United States," Carter added.

Carter knew that Black people across the country would be hesitant about voting for a white southerner, and he needed Daddy King's support. King senior mulled over the request. He liked Carter and had gotten along well with him during his tenure as governor. One thing gave King senior pause, though: the thought that his old friend Nelson Rockefeller a Republican, also might seek the office.

"Governor," King responded, "I'll tell you what. I'm pleased that you've come to me, but I have to be honest with you and say that only if a certain Republican does not run could I consider lending my support to your candidacy. Otherwise, I'd have no problem at all."

Rockefeller chose not to run, and Daddy King would go on to support Carter and stand by him, even when Carter's own words got him into trouble a couple of times with Black voters. Carter won the presidency by a narrow margin in 1976 with the overwhelming support of Black voters (83 percent). Daddy King liked the access that his support gave him to the White House. One day in his office the retired pastor asked his assistant to call the President. She dialed the number to the White House, and put the pastor on the line. He announced to the operator in his characteristically gruff voice, "This is Martin Luther King Sr. Is the president busy?"

The operator must have said yes.

"I understand. Tell him to call me back in fifteen minutes!"

Many years later, I would have an opportunity to introduce President Carter at the New Baptist Covenant Summit, an event he had planned at the Hilton Atlanta on September 15, 2016, as part of his work to unite all Baptists. I shared that story, and Carter smiled that big, famous smile and confirmed that he indeed returned that call to Daddy King.

Roberts was welcomed warmly inside Ebenezer (the Baptists outside the congregation were another story). He was an accomplished administrator, scholarly minister, and certainly no stranger to Ebenezer. He was soothing and familiar to a congregation still struggling with so much loss. Daddy King would die of a heart attack in 1984. His four-hour funeral at Ebenezer would draw former and future U.S. presidents, national and state legislators, big- and small-city mayors, civil rights leaders, millionaires, and ordinary working folks.

Roberts would serve the ministry with distinction for the next thirty years. He created extensive outreach programs to the community. As a student at Morehouse in the early 1990s, I visited Ebenezer one Sunday morning while Reverend Roberts was pastor. As I sat in the balcony, I was filled with nostalgia, imagining Dr. King in that pulpit. I never could have imagined then that I would ever even have a shot of returning to this church as pastor. A few years later, Roberts would spearhead the construction of a thirty-two-thousand-square-foot sanctuary across the street from the historic building on Auburn Avenue. The beautiful new church, built to seat about twenty-four hundred people, opened in 1999, starting a new era for the church as the twentieth century wound to a close.

After much thought and prayer, I submitted my application on the day of the deadline. A short time later, I was selected to be one of the ten to interview in Atlanta with the search committee for the position. The committee was headed by the longtime Ebenezer members Deacon Phillip Finch and the Board of Trustees chairman, Leroy R. Johnson. Finch had grown up in Ebenezer, had been baptized by Daddy King, and was on post as an usher, serving while on break from college, on the day that a gunman murdered Mrs. King and Deacon Boykin. Johnson, who had served in the Georgia Senate from 1963 to 1975, had been the first Black state senator elected in Georgia since Reconstruction. A 1970 *New York Times Magazine* story called him "the single most powerful black politician in Dixie." Johnson was so politically connected that he was able to secure the legal paperwork and political support for Muhammad Ali's first boxing match in three years, in October 1970, after he'd been banned from boxing for his refusal to respond to the Vietnam draft.

Ebenezer's congregation was full of political heavyweights, community servants, and civil rights movement icons, including Congressman John Lewis, Christine King Farris (Dr. King's older sister), and Coretta Scott King (Dr. King's widow). Because the selection process for the finalists was private, my interview with the committee was held at Johnson's home. I felt comfortable in that space and told the committee that I was deeply honored even to be considered. I expressed what Dr. King had meant to me and how he had shown us all how to make the gospel's love ethic come alive in the church and the public square. I spoke about how Ebenezer represented what the Christian gospel should be for all churches: love come alive in personal interactions and systems. And I shared what I'd done at Abyssinian and Douglas to model that.

Near the end of the interview, Sarah Reed, an elderly member of the search committee and retired secretary of the church, leaned back to speak. The story of Mrs. Reed and her husband, Lewis, has become part of Ebenezer lore. The couple was married at Ebenezer by Daddy King, but they ended up getting a divorce and eventually marrying other people. Those marriages, too, ended in divorce, but the former couple bumped into each other one day, rekindled their romance, and married each other a second time. Daddy King officiated, and at the end he admonished, "Y'all stay together this time, all right?"

So Mrs. Reed, who was in her midseventies by the time of my interview, told me she appreciated my commitment. "But please tell me about your family," she added.

There it was. I'd figured my status as a single man might be an issue, but I pretended not to know what she was really asking. I proceeded to tell her about my wonderful parents and siblings.

She persisted: "Do you have a wife?"

I told her that I wasn't yet married and that, although I didn't think it should matter, I wanted to get married someday.

A few weeks later, I received a letter from the search committee. The committee thanked me for participating in the interview process for the position but said the members had decided to move in a different direction. I was eliminated from further consideration. I was disappointed, of course, but not devastated. From the beginning, I'd reminded myself that I wouldn't lose, no matter the outcome. I had a great church in Baltimore, I was enjoying the ministry there, and I was focused on completing my doctorate. So I turned that corner and got back to my business at Douglas.

About a month later, I traveled to Birmingham because the new pastor at Sixth Avenue had invited me and other sons and daughters of the ministry back to celebrate the church's anniversary. I preached that Sunday at three services and thanked the members for embracing the eager young student I had been fifteen years earlier and for supporting me through the years. It was great seeing so many old faces and meeting new ones. I got on a plane to fly back to Baltimore, and during a layover in Atlanta my cell phone buzzed. It was Deacon Phil Finch from Ebenezer. We exchanged pleasantries, and he expressed that the committee had been very impressed with me and that there had been some new developments with the pastoral search. He seemed purposely vague.

"I know we sent that letter," he said. "But we remain interested in inviting you for a candidate's weekend."

I was shocked. I had moved on. Something had obviously gone awry during the selection process, and the committee was circling back to me. I wondered if there was already a favored candidate and if I was being invited just to check a box, showing an extensive search had been conducted. I told Deacon Finch I needed to think about it. When I called him back, I was straightforward about my concerns.

"If I come, I need to know that I'm being seriously considered," I told him. I asked if he could imagine a scenario where a thirty-five-year-old single man could become pastor of the iconic Ebenezer. He assured me that the committee was seriously considering me. I told myself that if nothing else came of it, I would get to preach at least one sermon at the place that had helped to make Kings. So that is how I approached the weekend, as if it were another important preaching engagement. This would be a process of discernment for the congregation and for me about the direction God was moving us. And I would be fine with the outcome. Unlike the great disappointment I'd experienced when I didn't get the job at Sixth Avenue, I felt this time a great sense of peace.

I agreed to visit Ebenezer on Memorial Day weekend because I knew that many of my own congregation members in Baltimore would be traveling and my absence would be less disruptive. My parents and several of my siblings joined me in Atlanta and sat in the audience while I preached at the 9:00 a.m. and 11:00 a.m. services. Also there to support me and hear me preach was Carolyn Ann Knight, the former Union professor who had encouraged me years earlier when in a low moment I second-guessed my decision to move to New York. Reverend Knight was by then a professor of preaching at the Interdenominational Theological Center in Atlanta, an ecumenical consortium of historically Black seminaries. She was well known to the Ebenezer congregation because she sometimes preached revivals there.

My message that day was "The Power on the Mountain and the Pain in the Valley," which focused on two passages of scripture that follow each other in Matthew 17. The first passage is the story of the Mount of Transfiguration. Jesus takes Peter, James, and John with him on a mountain, and the three disciples experience a high spiritual encounter. Jesus is transfigured before them; Moses and Elijah, long gone, appear to them; and the disciples hear a voice identify Jesus as my beloved son. Peter is so enthralled that he wants to stay on the mountain. But then, in the next passage, on the group's return to the valley, they encounter a man who brings his son to Jesus for healing. The man explains that the child possesses some kind of spirit because he foams at the mouth and throws himself on the ground and at times even into the fire. We might describe the child's ailment today as epilepsy. But something had clearly robbed him of his agency and power in the world. The father tells Jesus that he had brought the boy to the disciples (the remaining nine who did not accompany Jesus on the mountain), but they were unable to help. Jesus rebukes the disciples for their lack of faith and casts out the demon.

Ministers often preach about these passages separately. But I likened them to the high spiritual encounters we have in church and the work we are called to do in the world. What is the relationship between worship and witness, the mountain high and the valley low? Sometimes, we get so caught up in what happens inside our houses of worship that we turn them into monuments. We want to stay right there, rather than realizing that the whole point of the mountaintop experience is to give us the power to go down to the valley, where the pain is, where the suffering is, where there is trouble, to carry out the true mission of the church, love come alive in the world.

The sermon went very well, and the members responded enthusiastically to the message. Days later, the committee informed me that I would be recommended to the full church to become Ebenezer's next pastor. The members, about 2,200 at the time, would get to vote me up or down, and I would need at least 75 percent of the vote to be elected.

The election was held on Father's Day weekend, and the church brought in actual voting machines for members to cast their votes. Later that Sunday afternoon, I got a call from Senator Leroy Johnson.

"Reverend Warnock," he said. "You have been overwhelmingly confirmed and elected by the congregation to be the fifth pastor of Ebenezer Baptist Church."

I had received nearly 90 percent of the vote, he said. I thanked him and then sat with the news in silence for a moment, feeling the weight of history, immense gratitude, and honor. At thirty-five years old, I would be the youngest minister to take on this role there as senior pastor. I had been called to this monumental assignment, and I felt ready.

I picked up the telephone and called my dad, who had been to me the greatest earthly example of a devoted father and pastor. I wished him a happy Father's Day and shared my news. My sister later told me that he was so moved he wept.

If you know anything about the Black church, then you know that the "street committee" is real. The street network is swifter than the internet and had already ignited a buzz inside Douglas Memorial that I was leaving. So I addressed it head-on the next Sunday. I told my congregation that the members of Ebenezer had elected me to be their next pastor and that there were strong reasons why I should accept their offer. I explained what Ebenezer and Dr. King had meant to me and how this opportunity would enable me to return home to Georgia and to live closer to my aging parents. And I reassured them how much I loved them and enjoyed our ministry work together. The news was upsetting for some of the members because I had been there just about four and a half years, and we had expected to have more time together. Yet everyone said they were excited for me and that they could not imagine how I could turn down such an opportunity. After church I stood in the vestibule to greet the members as they departed, and one of my seasoned members, a former beauty queen who was then in her nineties, grabbed my hands and pulled me closer to her.

"Son, I know you're the pastor. But this is Big Mama talking," she said. "I love you. We will hate to lose you. But listen to Big

Mama, you go to that church; chase your dream. The Lord will be with you and with us." And she walked away.

A short time later, I received a letter from a thirteen-year-old congregant named Gillian, the granddaughter of the longtime pastor of Douglas, the Reverend Marion Bascom. She had been eight years old when I started at the church, and I'd watched her grow into a smart, energetic, precocious teenager. "They had been saying you were going to leave, and I didn't believe it," she wrote. "I didn't want to believe it. Honestly, you're the first pastor I ever really listened to."

She went on to describe the impact my sermons had on her in making her own decision to follow Christ. Her letter deeply moved me and let me know how much more difficult than I had imagined it would be to say goodbye. This was the first congregation where I was the spiritual leader, and I felt a great sense of responsibility for my members. When you've walked with a people—counseled them, buried their dead, blessed their children, and stood at their hospital beds—you are connected to their lives. I got into their hearts, and they got into mine. We all understood, though, that I had been summoned to this place in this moment. My soul said yes.

I was heading to a place that I would come to call America's Freedom Church. A church steeped in history. A church that draws people from all over the world who want to stand where the Kings once stood. My charge now was to ensure that Ebenezer remained a real church, a resilient church, not a monument. A church that would be, as it had been for generations, about the mission in the valley. The word "Ebenezer" means "stone of help." It references the scripture in which God empowers the people of Israel in their victory against an attack by the Philistines. "Then Samuel took a stone and set it up between Mizpah and Jeshanah, and named it Ebenezer; for he said, 'Thus far the Lord has helped us'" (1 Samuel 7:12). In a fast-paced, technological world with problems—old and new—I wanted to ensure that Ebenezer would always indeed be a "stone of help," a commemoration of God's salvific acts in the past as inspiration for continuing work into the future. The stone must never become a mere monument; instead, it must be a creative place of refuge, restoration, and resistance, carving out a new world that embraces all of God's children. With such a distinguished history, generations of Ebenezer congregants could truly say, "Thus far the Lord has helped us." I could not wait to see what the Lord and the Lord's people might do next.

CHAPTER 7

Putting On My Own Shoes

Just two months after I was elected senior pastor of Ebenezer, the nation watched with shock and sadness in late August 2005 as Hurricane Katrina battered New Orleans and the surrounding Gulf Coast region. The historic storm overwhelmed the city's protective levee system, and raging floodwaters swept through, leaving 80 percent of the city submerged, at least fifteen hundred people dead in New Orleans alone, and billions of dollars in property damage. Countless numbers of residents were stranded in attics, on rooftops, or in the Superdome for days without electricity or adequate food, water, and supplies in the stifling heat. The world saw the heartbreaking images that emerged in the media over ensuing days and weeks.

Ebenezer's congregation, like the rest of the country, began collecting money to assist the hurricane victims, an estimated 100,000 of whom had evacuated to Atlanta. My tenure at Ebenezer began in October 2005, and we sent a youth ministry team to join a nationwide group of churches participating in the cleanup in New Orleans. The following spring, I became more intimately involved in what was happening in that city through an issue that would come to define my political mission: voting rights.

I invited the Reverend Jesse Jackson to Ebenezer as the guest speaker for the church's 120th anniversary celebration on the third Sunday in March 2006. The next day, I accompanied him to a Concerned Black Clergy meeting, where he explained that an important mayoral election was scheduled to take place in New Orleans in April. The election, which initially was to be held February 4, had been hastily postponed for a couple of months because tens of thousands of voters were unable to return to the devastated city. Before the storm, Black residents made up about 70 percent of the population in New Orleans. By April, nearly half of the city's residents were still scattered throughout the country. After losing so much already, these displaced citizens faced the real threat of losing the right to help choose the leader who would guide their city through its most significant rebuilding effort. Reverend Jackson announced that he was organizing a rally at the Ernest N. Morial Convention Center, which had become an impromptu last-resort shelter during the storm for thousands of wet, hungry, and desperate flood victims as they waited days for help to arrive. He planned to follow that with a march across the Crescent City Connection bridge over the Mississippi River on April 1 to protest the scheduled date of the election. The bridge had its own significance. Three days after the storm, when throngs of people who had been trapped in New Orleans tried to cross the bridge, which seemed at the time their only way out, they were blocked by a line of police officers brandishing guns from a small, predominantly white suburban city, Gretna, located on the west bank of the river. Most of the police officers were white; most of those trying to escape were Black. The officers made the would-be evacuees turn back into the disaster that was New Orleans. The message in the logistics of the rally and march was intentional: don't forget what happened here.

So on April 1, Shanan Jones, a young activist pastor I'd recently hired at Ebenezer, and I joined the Reverends Jesse Jackson and Al Sharpton, other ministers, activists, lawmakers, and entertainers, including John Legend, in New Orleans for the demonstration. An estimated two thousand people attended the rally at the convention center. During the rally, speakers demanded satellite polling places in cities, including those beyond Louisiana, with large numbers of evacuees. A few months earlier, our government had been boasting about liberating Iraq and bringing democracy there. Our national leaders fully supported the enfranchisement of Iraqi citizens who were living in our country and allowed them to register and cast absentee ballots remotely in seven U.S. cities during that country's December 2005 parliamentary elections. I couldn't help thinking, "If democracy is good for Iraq, we ought to try it in Louisiana."

During the rally, I thought about the New Orleans election being just a couple of weeks away on April 22. It was most likely going to happen. The question was, what were we going to do about it? I was standing onstage, next to Bishop Paul Morton, whose home and whose Greater St. Stephen Full Gospel Baptist Church, one of the largest ministries in the city at the time, had been devastated by Hurricane Katrina. Bishop Morton had recently opened a vibrant new location in Atlanta. I leaned over and posed the question to him, and we agreed to meet in Atlanta to strategize.

A few days later, we came up with a plan to transport New Orleans residents from Atlanta on buses at no cost to participate in the election. The only requirement was that they had to sign up beforehand so that we could plan adequately, which included providing enough coach buses for the trip, as well as transportation to get voters to their individual polling places throughout the city. We got the word out to our congregations and went on television and radio, urging New Orleanians to return home to participate in the election. Bishop Morton and his staff would host us on the New Orleans end, providing a place to land, a hot meal for those returning home, and a staging area. Meanwhile, my staff, including the church administrator, Glenda Boone, Reverend Jones, and a host of volunteers, set up a "war room" in the former Christian Education Building connected to the old church to field calls from New Orleanians wanting to sign up for the trip home to vote.

Our war room was as much symbolic as it was practical. There is beautiful, historic video footage of Dr. King on January 15, 1968, celebrating what turned out to be his final birthday in that room. He had been working hard, preparing to kick off his national Poor People's Campaign. Confronted by the backlash against the movement that began in the last couple years of his life, and excoriated even by allies within the movement for his stand against the Vietnam War, King was, by all accounts, quite despondent in those days. His staff had not seen him laugh in a long while, so one of them instructed his friend and staff member Xernona Clayton, to plan something that would make him smile. The video shows Dr. King heading toward the door when the voice of a youthful Andrew Young, who would go on to serve as Atlanta mayor, U.S. congressman, and U.S. ambassador to the UN, pipes in, "Now, some folks celebrate Abraham Lincoln, but we're going to celebrate Martin Luther King Day today. Don't let him out of here." Young then leads the room in an impromptu rendition of "Happy Birthday." A wide smile spreads across Dr. King's face. Clayton then presents him with a shoebox filled with gag gifts, including a cup that says, "We are cooperating with Lyndon Johnson's War on Poverty. Drop coins and bills in the cup." Dr. King burst into laughter.

Ebenezer and Greater St. Stephen raised offerings to help with the costs and to hire a family-owned bus company that had been based in New Orleans and was led by a 1990 Morehouse graduate named Shaun Lain. Lain and his family had evacuated to Atlanta due to Hurricane Katrina, and he connected with our church planners and offered the services of the charter bus company his father had started in 1998. That company, Loews Express, one of the largest Black-owned transportation companies in the southeastern United States at the time, provided the charter buses for the trip from Atlanta to New Orleans. I arranged for teams of election lawyers and health-care workers to accompany voters on the eight-hour road trip.

On the Friday night before the election, we gathered in the sanctuary for a worship rally. I had been searching for music that would encapsulate the moment and was disappointed to find the gospel music of our times lacking in justice and antipoverty themes. While I am moved personally by the old movement songs, I knew this was a new movement. But sadly, I was hard-pressed to find contemporary music in the church that addressed justice, a central theme of scripture. So I turned to an old 1985 Isley Jasper Isley hit, "Caravan of Love," which not only fit the moment but again gave me a chance to break down the wall between secular and sacred music. The choir learned the song and sang it the night of our departure. I preached about our journey, which we were calling our Freedom Caravan. Our caravan of love. We prayed and then set off for New Orleans with four busloads of voters.

One of my closest friends, the Reverend Dr. D. Darrell Griffin, flew in from Chicago to take the trip with me. We had served and grown up together as young ministers at Abyssinian. Our caravan landed at Greater St. Stephen in New Orleans early the next morning, and our gracious New Orleans partners provided us with a hearty meal. We then put the voters on school buses that transported them to the polls. Even eight months later, the smell of decay was still in the air. Gutted buildings were everywhere, as were others in various stages of disrepair. Many businesses remained closed, and one building after another bore the telltale X spray-painted by emergency workers to keep track of the places they had searched for survivors and bodies. The numbers painted between the legs of each X told a silent story of the people who survived and died within those walls. I soaked it all in with such sadness as we rolled past these unintended memorials.

When all the voters had cast their ballots later that afternoon, we climbed on the buses and headed back to Atlanta. I felt proud that Ebenezer was living in its legacy, not on it. I thought of how my dad used to wake me up at 6:00 every morning, and he'd say the same thing, "Put your shoes on, son! Get ready. There's something for you to do." It didn't matter that I'd just arrived in Atlanta when this issue arose or that the Kings who trod before me had left giant footprints. I had to put on my own shoes and do the work that God called *me* to do. And with the help of so many faithful soldiers, I'd stepped up and onto a new path that led first to New Orleans. When the votes were counted, the Democrat who was mayor at the time, Ray Nagin, landed in a runoff with another prominent Democrat, Mitch Landrieu. So a month later Ebenezer and Greater St. Stephen put together another Freedom Caravan and traveled back to New Orleans to ensure its citizens still living in Atlanta were able to exercise their right to vote.

Earlier the same month, I delivered the commencement address at Antioch College in Yellow Springs, Ohio, as a tribute to one of its most famous graduates, Mrs. Coretta Scott King. I'd had the privilege of paying Mrs. King a pastoral visit on January 15 that year, her husband's birthday. Until 2004, Mrs. King had lived in the same modest, redbrick home that she and Dr. King bought together in the 1960s in a working-class community called Vine City. At age seventy-eight, she lived in a beautiful, high-rise apartment that had been purchased for her by Oprah Winfrey in an upscale area of Atlanta called Buckhead. I saw amazing photos of the Kings' lives together that even I, a longtime student of King, had never seen. As her pastor, I told Mrs. King how honored I was to meet her, how much I admired her strength and civil rights advocacy, and how her husband had inspired me to become a minister. She had suffered a stroke and did not speak during our meeting. What I would later learn was that she was also suffering with cancer. Yet she looked as elegant and regal as ever, wearing lipstick and her classic hairstyle without even a strand out of place. I held her hand, prayed and sat with her, and a short while later said goodbye. Fifteen days later, I was saddened with the rest of the nation to hear of her death.

There were multiple services and tributes honoring Mrs. King. But on the evening of February 6, 2006, the civil rights community and those who had been close to Mrs. King and her family gathered at her home church for a memorial service that featured tributes from many of her friends and fellow civil rights warriors, including Andrew Young, Xernona Clayton, the Reverend Jesse Jackson, Congressman John Lewis, and the Reverend Al Sharpton.

As I delivered the 2006 commencement address at Mrs. King's alma mater, I stood knowing that I was not the students' first choice as speaker. Under the school's governance structure, the students get to select a speaker, and they had chosen the comedian Dave Chappelle, who lived in Yellow Springs and whose late father had taught music at the university. But when he was unable to accept the invitation, President Steven Lawry extended it to me. I had met him when I invited him to speak at the civil rights community tribute to Mrs. King at Ebenezer the night before her funeral. I read in the school newspaper that there was some controversy among the students about my selection. How was a Baptist preacher from the South an adequate replacement? Some of the gay students wondered aloud if I were homophobic and whether I would come there and judge them. Antioch is a liberal, avant-garde place. The students did not wear traditional caps and gowns to the graduation ceremony. There was an abundance of blue, green, and pink hair. And the procession of graduates was relaxed and informal, more like a parade I could have witnessed in Greenwich Village. I wondered what the college was like in the late 1940s, when a young Coretta Scott, who had grown up in a rural Alabama town, had made her way there. A talented singer, she double majored in music and elementary education and sang in the church choir in Springfield, Ohio. Coretta experienced racism off campus when it came time for her to work as a student teacher. While the college itself was making an effort to diversify by recruiting nonwhite students, Coretta experienced racial discrimination during her time there when, as part of her education major, she was required to do two years of practice teaching at a school. Yellow Springs public schools were integrated, but all teachers were white, and the town board rejected Coretta's application. She asked the college president to intervene, and he suggested instead that she travel to a nearby town to teach in a school with only a handful of Black students. Disappointed, Coretta chose to fulfill the degree requirement by teaching for both years at an integrated laboratory school on campus. She graduated in 1951 and earned a scholarship to the New England Conservatory of Music in Boston, where she met her husband, who was working on his doctorate at Boston University.

My speech for the 2006 commencement was titled "The Freedom Caravan." I laid out what Ebenezer had just done in New Orleans and likened America to a grand and noble freedom caravan that has had to make many stops throughout history. I talked about how we picked up a new set of passengers at each stop, people who broadened our understanding of what it meant to be a freedom caravan. White people landed on these shores, and Patrick Henry said, "Give me liberty or give me death." And if the slave could speak, he would have said, "Me, too." We had to pick up women, who initially were denied the suffrage. Through the women's suffrage movement, women got the right to vote in 1920. African Americans were not initially seen as part of that caravan. The "three-fifths compromise" designated us as three-fifths of a human being. Our ancestors were born in bondage and then considered second-class citizens during the years of Jim Crow segregation. We had to get on the freedom caravan. People who are differently able, or disabled, had to get on the caravan during the American disabilities movement. And yes, our beautiful gay and lesbian brothers and sisters also have a seat on the caravan. That is the story of America, I said. I invited the students to join us on the caravan, to find their voice, their place, their seat. I told them to heed the words of Horace Mann, the college's first president, who said, "Be ashamed to die until you've won some victory for humanity." Many of these students were suspicious of religion and faith, but I shared with them the role both had played in African Americans' fight for justice. And I was heartened that the students, who had been so skeptical of me, sat in rapt attention for the entire speech. When I finished, the whole place exploded in applause. I think Mrs. King, a proud Antioch alumnus, and Dr. King, who delivered the school's commencement address in 1965, would have been proud.

Those months were busy ones for me as I successfully defended my dissertation in May to earn my doctorate degree from Union Theological Seminary. Then, in June, I was formally installed as pastor of Ebenezer. As I had done in Baltimore, I used the event to signal the kind of ministry I hoped to build with the congregation. The weekend event kicked off on Friday with a symposium on poverty, centered on lessons learned from Hurricane Katrina. When so many poor people were stranded in New Orleans, unable to evacuate before the storm, their desperation in the days afterward illuminated the depth of our country's unfinished business with poverty. Dr. King's final crusade was to be the Poor People's Campaign, but he never made it past Memphis. Others picked up the mantle in the decades afterward, but Katrina showed there was clearly much more work to do. The Reverend Dr. Michael Eric Dyson kicked off the conversation, addressing the topic, "Poverty and the Faith Community: After Katrina." A banquet followed on Saturday evening at a downtown hotel with Andrew Young as the guest speaker and a jazz band, rendering Duke Ellington's "Come Sunday." The highlight of the evening was a special benediction delivered by a beloved preacher in an unexpected way. At the suggestion of Dr. Angela Farris Watkins, the granddaughter of Daddy King, a recording of him, closing out the 1976 Democratic National Convention after he'd helped Jimmy Carter win the nomination, was played to close out my investiture banquet as well. Daddy King's rousing prayer was a perfect way to connect Ebenezer's past to its present and future.

The festivities concluded the next day. It was a proud moment when I looked out into the audience on Sunday morning and saw my maternal grandmother Lucinda Brooks, my parents, and many of my siblings, all there to support me at the installation service. Other members of my village were there to show their support as well—congregants from all three of the churches where I had served as a minister (Sixth Avenue, Abyssinian, and Douglas), classmates from Morehouse and Union. My former Union professor the Reverend Dr. Carolyn Ann Knight delivered the sermon for the morning service, and Dr. Butts preached that evening. The president of Union, Dr. Joseph Hough, gave remarks as the pulpit of Ebenezer was passing from one Union grad to the next. Newly minted as a PhD, I wore my doctoral robe and regalia.

Dean Lawrence Carter, my mentor from Morehouse, presided over the entire event, as he had for my Douglas investiture. It has become somewhat of a tradition among the former chapel assistants to have the man who guided our early steps in ministry guide our installation ceremonies. As a special surprise for me, Dean Carter arranged to send "the Presidential Chair," an oversize wooden chair with African carvings, where the president of Morehouse sits during commencement ceremonies, to the Ebenezer sanctuary for the event. Elders of the congregation performed a ceremony, wrapping me in West African kente cloth in a nod to our African roots, before presenting me with my ordination robe. I then sat in "the Presidential Chair." The moment signified the strong bond between Morehouse and Ebenezer. Three of Ebenezer's five senior pastors and all three of the co-pastors who served under Daddy King had been Morehouse men. The moment also represented the intrinsic connection between education and faith. Morehouse is named after a preacher and steeped in the tradition of the church. "Education and faith are the Tigris and the Euphrates of our freedom journey: twin rivers at the source of our redemption," Dr. Butts says. Both are connected to the struggle for human liberation.

The past is still present at Ebenezer in wonderful ways. The congregation is as vibrant as ever. I love that the membership is so broad based, made up of all kinds of people who include history makers and trailblazers, professionals across every field, as well as working-class brothers and sisters who walk to their community church. We all work side by side in ministry and community outreach.

But in 2007, my activism in a case that involved a former high school athlete named Genarlow Wilson landed me on the opposite side of the issue from a member of my church's Board of Trustees. Genarlow was a seventeen-year-old honors student in 2003, when he and five other young men attended a New Year's Eve party in a hotel room in Douglasville, Georgia, with free-flowing alcohol and marijuana. He received oral sex from a fifteen-year-old girl at the party, and the encounter was videotaped. In February 2005, he was convicted of aggravated child molestation, which was a felony intended to punish adult child predators, and he was sentenced to the minimum ten-year prison term without parole mandated by the law.

While I don't know anyone who would condone the behavior of the teenagers inside that motel room, Wilson's case should never have entered the criminal justice system in the first place. State legislators modified the law in March 2006 to make consensual oral sex between teenagers four or fewer years apart in age a misdemeanor—a change that had been advocated by Wilson's attorney since sexual intercourse between teenagers was already considered a misdemeanor. But the lawmakers did not make the law retroactive, so young Genarlow remained a felon, serving a harsh ten-year sentence in prison.

I got involved in the case in June 2007, when one of my fraternity brothers from Sigma Pi Phi, the oldest Black Greek-letter society for postcollegiate men, called and asked me to attend a press conference announcing the fraternity's support of efforts to free Wilson. Wilson's mother was there, and I got to know her and some of the activists who had been involved in trying to help this young man. I researched the case and was appalled by his treatment, more criminal than just. I could not remain silent or neutral. I jumped in, helping to organize protests and prayers throughout Atlanta. One rally on the courthouse steps in Douglas County drew activists and political figures from across the political spectrum, all of whom believed Wilson had been wrongly convicted and deserved a chance to get his life back.

In June 2007, a superior court judge in Monroe County voided the remainder of Wilson's prison sentence and ordered him released, but before all of us supporters could even celebrate, Georgia's attorney general, Thurbert Baker, appealed the decision to the state supreme court. Baker not only was the highest-ranking African

American elected official in Georgia but also is a member of my congregation and served at the time on the Board of Trustees. All of us at the church had been so proud when Baker, first appointed to the position in 1997, went on to win elections to the position three times. In 2006, he earned more votes than any other Democrat running for statewide office. This case seemed to me the perfect opportunity for him to use his discretion to swing the pendulum back toward justice. I even met with Baker and tried to urge him to withdraw his appeal, but he explained to me that as he saw it, his job was to protect the laws of Georgia, even the bad ones. I didn't understand that reasoning but saw it as my job to be the state's conscience. State lawmakers had acknowledged that the law was bad, and they changed it. Baker would go on to run for governor in 2010 but was defeated in the Democratic primary. We never discussed the case again after I met with him, and Baker remains a respected member of my congregation. Ebenezer is the kind of place where people embrace each other in love and good faith even if they disagree. But I never wavered in my commitment to stand with the young man. I even held a press conference just outside the church with a few supportive deacons and others standing behind me to call for Wilson's release. In October 2007, Wilson and his supporters won a huge victory when the Georgia Supreme Court voted 4–3 to overturn his sentence and ordered him released from prison.

Just days after walking out of prison, Wilson and his mother visited a service at Ebenezer to thank the congregation and me for our support. "No words really can explain how thankful me and my family are," he said to us. "The Bible says there's a time and season for everything. I guess that time finally came."

After Wilson's release, those of us who had supported him stayed the course to help put him on the road to recover from his mistakes and live a life of purpose. I called the president of Morehouse and lobbied for Wilson to be admitted as a student. The radio host Tom Joyner used his radio pulpit to do the same. Wilson was accepted and attended Morehouse on a full-tuition and room-and-board scholarship from the Tom Joyner Foundation. He graduated in 2013 from Morehouse with a degree in sociology, has a job, and is a productive working citizen.

My advocacy on the Wilson case drew me further into the criminal justice arena. During the summer of 2008, I received a letter from a coalition working on behalf of a death row inmate named Troy Davis. Davis had been sentenced to death for the 1989 killing of an off-duty Savannah police officer. But his case was drawing national and international attention because seven of the nine witnesses whose trial testimonies had played a key role in his conviction had recanted or materially changed their stories. I was immediately drawn to the case because Troy hailed from Savannah, and he was about my age. As I read about the case, I recognized the area of town where the crime occurred, and my heart filled with sadness for Mark Allen MacPhail, the twenty-seven-year-old officer who was off duty and working as a security guard when he responded to a disturbance in the Burger King parking lot and was shot to death. I thought of his family and the tragedy of losing a loved one. I'd seen that pain up close, counseling the parents, spouses, children, and siblings of many who had been murdered through the years. But the tragedy could cut both ways. It struck me that Davis had maintained his innocence and that several of those who had testified that he was the shooter recanted their testimonies; some of them said that they had been pressured by the police into lying. One of the two remaining witnesses was a man who some of the witnesses claimed had admitted to being the actual shooter. There seemed to me too much doubt around this case for the state to put Davis to death. But he was a young Black man convicted of killing a white police officer in the South, and I knew that halting this death train might be impossible, no matter how much doubt.

Before long, I began speaking out in the media about the case and rallying to stop the State of Georgia from killing Davis. I joined a long list of people who agreed that there were too many valid questions raised in this case to implement capital punishment. They included even some former high-ranking prosecutors, judges, and lawmakers who had been generally supportive of the death penalty, such as the former FBI director William Sessions, the former Georgia Supreme Court chief justice Norman Fletcher, the former U.S. deputy attorney general Larry Thompson, and the former U.S. attorney for the northern district of Georgia and former congressman Bob Barr. Support to halt Davis's execution came from as high as Pope Benedict XVI, the former president Jimmy Carter, and Archbishop Desmond Tutu. Ben Jealous, head of the NAACP, and Amnesty International also were among those fighting against Davis's execution.

One evening, I drove to Georgia Diagnostic and Classification State Prison in Jackson, Georgia, to visit Troy Davis for the first time. We talked about our upbringing in Savannah, and I was struck by the similarities in our stories. He was raised in a devout

Christian household not far from my own neighborhood. His faith seemed to bring him a measure of peace in this moment. "My life is in God's hands," he told me repeatedly.

I got to know Davis's mother, Virginia Davis, and older sister, Martina Davis-Correia, through our advocacy, and I was impressed by their belief in his innocence and dedication to saving his life. The state had initially planned to execute Davis on July 17, 2007, but the trial court granted a stay to review the case further. Two more execution dates would be set in 2008, and our hopes would be raised when the planned killing was halted. But the case kept winding back to the same place until Davis was out of options.

On March 28, 2011, the U.S. Supreme Court denied an appeal to review the case. Less than a month later, Troy's mother took a nap while sitting up in her chair, and she never woke up. I delivered her eulogy at the family's request. Virginia Davis was sixty-five years old, and her cause of death was listed as natural causes. But I believe she died of a broken heart. She had been a good mother who loved her son, but she knew by then he was going to die. And perhaps, it was just too much. Those of us who believed in Davis knew the best way we could honor her was to keep fighting for him, and we did.

A fourth execution date was set for September 21, 2011. Two days before then, I visited Davis again. He seemed remarkably calm, resolute, at peace with whatever was to come. I sat with him. Prayed with him. He told me that he wanted his life to mean something.

I reminded him of all the citizens and celebrities who had rallied against the inhumanity of his execution, raising important questions about our criminal justice system, and I assured him that in that sense he was already victorious. His life did have meaning and an impact on our system of justice. We said our goodbyes.

As the hours ticked down, I was among those who testified before the Board of Pardons and Parole in a last-ditch effort to have Davis's death sentence commuted. We were not even asking the board to let him out of prison, but just to let him live. I talked about my visits with Davis and his strong faith. I also mentioned the questions surrounding the evidence in the case and held that up as solid justification to keep him alive. Several of Davis's relatives also testified, including a nephew, who said he'd grown up visiting his uncle on death row, but that Davis had been a good influence, encouraging him to stay on the right path. The board heard three hours of testimonies from supporters of Davis, including one of the jurors who had voted during his initial trial to convict him but had come to believe there were enough questions in the case to spare his life. Nevertheless, the board rejected our pleas, and there was nothing else we could do.

On the evening of the scheduled execution, I huddled with Davis's family members outside the prison as our government strapped him to a gurney, stretched out his arms and legs in a contraption that eerily resembled a crucifix, and killed him with an injection of poisons. All in our name. I would later read in the papers that, given a chance for final words, Davis lifted his head, turned to the family of the police officer who had been killed in 1989, and said, "I know all of you still are convinced that I'm the person that killed your father, your son, and your brother, but I am innocent . . . But I am so sorry for your loss. I really am sincerely. . . . For those about to take my life, may God have mercy on all of your souls. God bless you all."

My heart carried the weight of so many dashed hopes as I traveled home to Savannah to eulogize him. A short time later, I made the trip home again to help bury Troy's sister, Martina Davis-Correia, who had fought for him even as her own body grew weak with cancer. She died of breast cancer on December 1, 2011, at forty-four years old. It was as if she willed herself to live until he was executed, and then let go.

It amazes me how a nation that so prides itself on its morals and values continues to justify state-sanctioned murder. The United States remains one of the last places in the Western world that still carries out the death penalty. This brutal practice remains only in other places with human rights records that we as a nation abhor. Twenty-three U.S. states have already abolished the death penalty, and I believe there is a move in this country more in that direction.

The Troy Davis case embodies the larger problems that we see played out across the landscape in death penalty cases. The application of who gets the death penalty is too arbitrary, with deep racial bias. And deep class bias, also. More often than not, capital punishment is for those with no capital. And most of all, the punishment is final. There is no way to bring a person back if the state realizes it made a mistake. This is in part a moral conversation that I believe the faith community can and should lead. Dr. King said it best: "The old law of an eye for an eye leaves everybody blind."

The more time I spent on these cases, talking to families impacted by the criminal justice system, the more I came to understand the even bigger problem of mass incarceration. The United States of America, the land of the free, is by far the incarceration capital of the world. Think about that. The land of the free, the shining city on the hill, shackles more people than any land in the world. Nobody comes even close. And the people incarcerated within those prison walls are disproportionately people of color. In the United States, Georgia has one of the highest incarceration rates. Almost daily, I meet men and women who have come into contact with the criminal justice system, maybe through an arrest that was never prosecuted, but their lives and livelihoods are forever damaged. They have trouble finding a job and decent housing when a background check reveals the arrest record, even if they were never charged or found guilty of a crime. For those who serve time in jail for a crime and go through the heavy work of turning their lives around so that they may return to society, the hurdles to success are even higher. They are no longer in prison, but they remain handcuffed nonetheless. Desperate and angry, many return to crime, perpetuating prison's revolving door.

I agree with the author Michelle Alexander, who calls the mass incarceration of tens of thousands of Black men for nonviolent drug-related offenses and the lifelong consequences they face "the new Jim Crow." They are denied the right to vote in many states, the right to participate in our democracy, and access to upward mobility. I've seen the devastation up close in the case of my brother Keith and my family's twenty-two-year battle to free him. What I learned advocating for him, talking to families across Georgia, and fighting for them has led me and my congregation to get involved in a new kind of Poor People's Campaign, ending mass incarceration.

Ebenezer as a faith community has decided that we cannot be silent on this issue, that we must go beyond just the pastoral care of members who are struggling and address mass incarceration in a more systemic way. I am particularly proud of the work we have done on expungements, a legal process that helps people seal certain types of nonviolent misdemeanor and felony arrests from public view. Through our Record Restriction Summit, we teamed with the Temple, the oldest Jewish congregation in Atlanta, and created a one-stop shop for getting an expungement. The program has brought together representatives of law enforcement, the District Attorney's Office, and the courts—all the parties needed to sign off on the process—at Ebenezer on a Saturday and condensed the usual 120-day process for Fulton County residents into a single day. Hundreds of men and women walked away from our church on those designated Saturdays with the legal paperwork to have their records sealed and brighter outlooks for their futures. This is making grace real and changing people's lives.

In recent years, we've also teamed with other faith communities and national artists for a three-day ending mass incarceration summit in June 2019, which we called "Let My People Go." The title was taken from the book of Exodus, chapter 8, which is so central to African American faith, when the Lord commands Moses to go to Pharaoh and tell him, "Let my people go, so that they may worship me." The summit was the beginning of a much-needed conversation in the faith community about mass incarceration and practical ways we can bring about change. Michelle Alexander was an opening plenary speaker, and she shared some of her thoughts and research from her book. Our special guests included Yusef Salaam and Raymond Santana Jr., two of the five young men wrongly convicted as teenagers of raping a white woman jogging in New York City's Central Park in 1989. They were exonerated by DNA evidence, and their story was told to a new generation in the Netflix miniseries *When They See Us*. About four hundred guests from various religious denominations, including many who were formerly incarcerated, attended the conference, participated in three days of workshops, and walked away with a tool kit to guide them in engaging their faith communities.

The conference led to our ongoing Multifaith Initiative to End Mass Incarceration. We've laid out a three-pronged plan to engage our congregations, change the narrative by sharing the important personal stories of those who are impacted by mass incarceration, and educate our public policy leaders on ways they can partner with us in bringing needed change. As I've said often, we who believe in freedom cannot rest until we dismantle mass incarceration.

And so our work continues.

In January 2008, a political candidate campaigning to become the next president of the United States was filling Americans across the nation with hope. Senator Barack Obama was that candidate, and he was inspiring a growing multiracial coalition that included many young people who had never participated before in the political process. That momentum catapulted him to a first-place finish in the Iowa Democratic caucuses on January 3 that year—a win that shocked the political establishment. At the time, Senator Hillary Clinton, who finished third in Iowa, was considered the frontrunner for the Democratic Party's nomination. She had garnered the support of much of the party's leadership, including many older African American politicians. As I thought about the historic nature of Senator Obama's campaign and what he had just accomplished in Iowa, I decided to invite him to Ebenezer.

The occasion was "King Sunday," the church's annual celebration of Dr. King on the third Sunday in January. Senator Obama accepted my invitation, and the congregation was excited to hear from this young Black man who had the audacity to run for president. But on the morning of January 20, 2008, temperatures dipped into the teens, and weather forecasts of possible snow had shut down churches across Atlanta. My staff and I watched the weather reports closely but decided to move forward with our celebration. By the time the doors of the church opened, people were waiting outside in the cold in a line that snaked down the sidewalk nearly a block. Senator Obama and I shared a few moments of small talk in my study before the service and then walked into the pulpit together. The packed church roared with applause. The pride of the crowd was palpable.

I preached an abbreviated sermon, entitled "Unfinished Business," addressing the final days of Dr. King's ministry, when he talked about the triple evils of racism, poverty, and war. The work of eradicating those evils is left to us, I told the congregation. Then, jokingly, as they say in the Senate, I yielded "the remainder of my time to the distinguished gentleman from Illinois."

It was moving to see Senator Obama standing in the pulpit

known around the world because of Dr. King, who had shared his dream of a country where people would be judged by the content of their character, not the color of their skin. Senator Obama was a hopeful sign that Dr. King's dream could become real. In his speech, Senator Obama urged the crowd to look past the issues that divide us. He said that his message of hope had been derided by critics, yet hope was what the country needed. "It's true. I talk about hope," he said. "I talk about it a lot because the odds of me standing here today are so small, so remote that I couldn't have gotten here without some hope."

He ended with a rousing appeal for people to join him in his quest to bring the nation together. "In the struggle to heal this nation and repair the world, we cannot walk alone," he said. "So, I ask you to walk with me and march with me and join your voices with mine, and together we will sing the song that tears down the walls that divide us and lift up an America that is truly indivisible with liberty and justice for all."

On the same Sunday that Senator Obama visited Ebenezer, his opponent, Senator Clinton, was standing with my pastor, Reverend Butts, at Abyssinian. Obama would go on to win the Democratic nomination, and his election-night victory was among America's most emotional moments. Who could forget Reverend Jesse Jackson's tears? I later attended the inauguration, and as I stood there among the Washington, D.C., crowd, I pulled out my telephone and called my father back in Savannah. I remember the pride and joy in his voice and thought about the ways in which he had seen the arc of history. On that day, he got to see it bend more toward justice.

About a year and a half after that historic moment, the congregation at Ebenezer and I celebrated a proud expansion of our ministry with the groundbreaking of the Martin Luther King, Sr. Community Resources Complex. The project had been on the agenda when I arrived at Ebenezer, and I made it a priority to help bring the church's vision to life. I loved the idea of extending our ministry beyond the sanctuary with a complex that would be a one-stop shop for community services, provided by various nonprofit agencies. These nonprofits would partner with the church in a collaborative venture to meet the needs of our community. This was the perfect way to honor Daddy King, who had been an activist and dedicated community servant while serving as pastor of Ebenezer for forty-four years. Despite a national recession that toppled the housing market and construction industry and stalled the national economy between 2007 and 2009, we at Ebenezer maintained our faith in the vision for the complex. I pressed forward with planning and generating the needed funds, mainly through private and corporate donations and grants. Our vision moved closer to reality with the ceremonial groundbreaking after our morning worship services on Easter Sunday, April 4, 2010. It was the anniversary of Dr. Martin Luther King Jr.'s death, and I couldn't help thinking that he would have been so proud to see his father memorialized in this way.

While construction of the complex was underway, my staff and I worked on building the team of nonprofits that would join us as collaborative partners. Our anchor tenant was Operation HOPE, a financial literacy empowerment program founded by entrepreneur John Hope Bryant in Los Angeles in 1992 in response to the devastation caused by the riots. Bryant was looking to move his organization to Atlanta, and the two of us were introduced by Andrew Young's daughter, Andrea. The timing was fortuitous. Operation HOPE was consistent with the collaborative's mission, and Bryant made plans to open the Hope Financial Literacy Center inside the new complex. Operation HOPE would offer an array of financial services with a three-pronged goal of raising credit scores among residents, moving them from renting to home ownership, and helping entrepreneurs develop their small businesses. A number of other agencies joined the partnership, including Casey Family Programs, which focuses on children in foster care; the Center for Working Families, Inc.; Atlanta Workforce Development Agency; and the Georgia Department of Human Services. The organization 100 Black Men of Atlanta would later bring its youth services operation to the complex.

Like a tree sprouting from fruitful seeds, our beautiful, three-story, orange-brick complex rose from the ground at 101 Jackson Street NE, adjacent to the Horizon Sanctuary and within the Sweet Auburn community known as the King Historic District. The $8 million complex spreads over 32,000 square feet, comprising offices and classrooms, a fellowship hall with a commercial grade kitchen for large church and community gatherings, and a cybercafe. The complex also displays photos of King Sr. and Mrs. King and artifacts from their lives, including his ministerial robe, suits he wore on momentous occasions, and his sermon notes.

The community celebrated the opening of the Martin Luther

King, Sr. Community Resources Complex on November 4, 2012, with Andrew Young as the keynote speaker. A ribbon cutting afterwards drew a host of dignitaries, including Christine King Farris (the daughter of King Sr.) and Naomi King (the daughter-in-law of King Sr. and wife of the late A. D. King), and local elected officials. Knowing how much this occasion meant to me, my mother also traveled from Savannah to join me for the celebration.

The completion of that complex and its enduring presence and impact in the community have been among my most fulfilling accomplishments as pastor of this great church. Our list of partners is ever evolving as the needs of the community and the organizations themselves change. But what gives me great satisfaction is knowing that we at Ebenezer erected more than just a building. We created a vehicle to help our community move beyond charity to real change and self-sufficiency.

Even as the Community Resources Complex was still under construction, I began to think more deeply about how to effect change on a broader scale and whether I could have greater impact by running for public office. I'd seen my pastor, Reverend Butts, wrestle frequently with the same question, though he had not yet taken that step. I decided to schedule a luncheon meeting with a man who seemed a model of what I could become, Congressman John Lewis.

By then, I had been Representative Lewis's pastor for several years, but he was the elder statesman. While I had met him once during college, this was my big chance as a mature adult to thank him for his leadership through the years. There I was having an extended conversation with John Lewis, my parishioner and my hero, over lunch. I told him how much I admired his example. Then, finally, I got to the point.

"I'm thinking about running for office," I told him, followed by an assurance that I would never even consider running against him. He didn't need my assurance, of course, but I wanted him to know all the same. Then I asked if he would mentor me.

Congressman Lewis was as kind and gracious as when I'd first met him and he'd hung around when he had little to gain personally from mingling with a bunch of college students. But I was surprised by his response.

"Oh, you don't need it," he said simply.

His words didn't feel dismissive; that was not his way. He just seemed to be saying there was no magic complicated formula that needed studying. That in his line of work you learn by doing, by showing up, by putting your body in the game.

In the years ahead, a new voting rights initiative would give me a chance to sit beside Congressman Lewis, walk next to him, and crisscross Georgia doing just that.

CHAPTER 8

Making History

For years, the thought of perhaps running for the U.S. House of Representatives sat idly in the back of my mind. From my days at Abyssinian, the model I had seen work well for a young minister, aspiring to national public office, was in the House. Congressman Adam Clayton Powell had left an indelible mark, not just with the antipoverty federal legislation he was able to push through Congress, but in the hearts and minds of the congregation he served with equal passion. I'd heard Dr. Butts's deliberations with himself about whether to run for the House seat to have broader impact. And I'd seen other ministers serve dual roles in the pulpit and the House. Among them were the dynamic Reverend Floyd Flake, who served as pastor of Allen Temple A.M.E. Church in Queens, New York, during my Abyssinian years, and the Reverend William H. Gray III, who was pastor of Bright Hope Baptist Church in Philadelphia when he was elected to the House in 1978. Gray was an impressive figure to me in the late 1980s and early 1990s as he rose to become the first African American chairman of the House Budget Committee and the first to serve as the majority whip. No such model existed in the U.S. Senate. When Carol Moseley Braun became the first African American woman elected to the Senate in 1993, just one other African American had walked that path in the twentieth century, Senator Edward Brooke of Massachusetts. The election of Barack Obama to the Senate from Illinois in 2004 made him just the fifth African American to serve, and the third to be popularly elected. Thus, I never seriously considered the U.S. Senate or thought it was any immediate possibility in Georgia until a member of my church planted that seed one day in 2013.

Lawrence Bell, a young professional who worked in local and state politics, had been attending Ebenezer for a couple years, but we were introduced one-on-one for the first time that year while participating in a church outreach at an all-boys school in Atlanta. Our Men's Ministry had adopted B.E.S.T. Academy, a middle and high school located in one of the poorest, most troubled neighborhoods in west Atlanta. Many of the school's students didn't have even the basic necessities at home, and so the school did what it could to fill in the gaps. To make sure the students at least had clean uniforms, for example, school administrators installed washers and dryers. To provide successful father figures for the boys, the school formed partnerships with community groups and churches, like Ebenezer. While Atlanta is known around the world as the capital of Black excellence and the cradle of the civil rights movement, it is, too, a city of contradictions, a place with deep pockets of poverty, where opportunities and upward mobility are still too limited for the poorest people who live there. So on designated Saturdays the men from Ebenezer would bring care packages of toothbrushes, toothpaste, deodorant, and lotion and spend time with the boys.

On one of those visits, Lawrence, a graduate of Clark Atlanta University, a friendly rival to Morehouse, and I struck up a conversation. He had been drawn to Ebenezer by my activism and preaching of the social gospel. Though he was younger than I, Lawrence, too, had been shaped in that tradition of civil rights engagement and protest. The schools that make up the Atlanta University Center Consortium now—Clark, Morehouse, and Spelman—have long been fertile ground for youthful idealism and activism. In the 1960s, students from those schools, like Julian Bond, Otis Moss Jr., and Marian Wright (later Marian Wright Edelman), were central to the sit-ins, protests, and pickets that led to the desegregation of department stores, restaurants, and other private and public facilities. I heard firsthand stories from the mouths of former student participants whom I had the honor of pastoring at Ebenezer, including Dr. Gwendolyn Middlebrooks; the Reverend Albert Brinson; and the late Lonnie King, a Morehouse man and one of the movement's founders. A boulevard near the campus is named for those students and the Atlanta student movement. And long before he was an award-winning actor, Samuel Jackson was expelled from Morehouse after he and other students locked themselves and the college board of trustees in an administration building for a day and a half as part of a protest over the school's curriculum and governance structure. The Reverend Martin Luther King Sr., who was one of the trustees, was allowed to leave after six hours due to health reasons.

Lawrence and I became friends and continued our conversations. One day, he threw out a suggestion. "You should run for the U.S. Senate." The idea seemed so far-fetched and out of the blue that I laughed.

"Run for the Senate?" I asked. "I think you've consumed too much Communion wine!"

There was no path for an African American Democrat to win a statewide election in the red state of Georgia in 2013, to my mind. I had been in college when Andrew Young, who had walked beside Dr. King, served in the U.S. Congress, run the city of Atlanta as mayor, and negotiated with leaders around the world as a United Nations ambassador, lost in the Democratic primary when he ran for governor in 1990 against Zell Miller, who represented a conservative strain in the party. If someone as beloved as Andrew Young could not win statewide, what chance would I have? Plus, of the nearly two thousand U.S. senators in the country's history to that point, just ten of them had been Black. But Lawrence shot back, "I think you'd be surprised how much the state has changed."

Later, he presented me with data showing an influx of African Americans, more progressive white citizens, and women to Georgia, particularly in the suburbs around Atlanta, over the past several years. The Atlanta metropolitan area had become a fulcrum of a kind of reverse migration of Black folks. My father had been part of that original Great Migration of an estimated six million African Americans who fled the rural South with its racist Jim Crow laws in the early to mid-twentieth century for better job opportunities in northern, midwestern, and western cities. But my father returned soon afterward when his first marriage failed. Since 1975, large southern cities, like Atlanta, have seen increases in the numbers of African Americans, particularly the young and educated, while many northern cities have continued to see their numbers decline.

By 2013, President Obama had entered his second term, and Lawrence believed that I could inspire the same kind of multiracial, multigenerational coalition that had ushered Obama into office. I was intrigued. But the timing had to feel right. In the meantime, I would keep busy with my ministry, building our financial literacy program and workforce development office on the church campus and feeding the hungry while also asking why the hungry have no food. And, whenever possible, I would keep getting into what Congressman Lewis called "good trouble."

I did consider running after Senator Saxby Chambliss, a Republican, announced that he did not plan to seek reelection the next year. The conversation with Lawrence about the changing demographics in Georgia was still fresh in my mind, and I wondered if this would be a good time for me to run for the office. I engaged in that discussion with a few people I trusted and even mentioned my interest in running for the seat to President Obama when he came to speak for Morehouse's commencement ceremony in May. I was on the program to deliver the opening prayer for what is usually a moving, outdoor ceremony. But of all years, Atlantans woke up that day to torrential rain. Morehouse's backup plan for rain on graduation day is to move the ceremony indoors, which then limits the number of guests each graduate can invite. Because Obama's visit had been so highly anticipated, an estimated ten thousand guests were expected to attend. The rain was spotty throughout the day, so the administration took its chances and moved forward with the outdoor graduation. Even the occasional rain didn't dampen the excitement of the graduates and their supporters, who got to hear an inspiring message from the country's first Black president while he was still in office. I had met him before, and as we waited for the processional, we chatted a bit. I mentioned that I was thinking of running for the U.S. Senate seat. He looked at me, raised an eyebrow, and gave me that familiar Obama grin. "Are you sure you want to do that?" he joked, adding that I had a pretty good gig over at Ebenezer.

By that time, the Democratic Party's energy had begun to coalesce around another candidate, Michelle Nunn, the daughter of the legendary former senator Sam Nunn, who had served for twenty-five years. In the small, gossipy world of politics, the word had gotten out that the pastor of Ebenezer was thinking of running for the seat, and the buzz was so loud that I got a visit from Michelle. She told me that while she understood she couldn't tell me what to do, she hoped not to have to run against me. And if I chose not to run, she said, she would be honored to have my support. By then, I had already decided that this was not the right time, and I threw my support behind her. I traveled with her on a few occasions across Georgia, including to my hometown of Savannah, and introduced her to my network of friends and family. State Senator Jason Carter, the grandson of Jimmy Carter and a member of my church, also was running for governor that year, and so I supported both campaigns. Nunn and Carter became the standard-bearers for the Democratic Party that year, but to our disappointment neither of them was successful.

• • •

In January 2014, the Reverend Bernice King, the youngest child of Dr. and Mrs. King, asked me to be the keynote speaker for the King Center's annual celebration, honoring Dr. King on his national holiday. The event is held each year at Ebenezer, but the family and the King Center select the speaker and direct the program. At the time, Georgia was among the southern states refusing to expand Medicaid, as called for in President Obama's Affordable Care Act, to close the coverage gap for those people who earned too much to qualify for Medicaid but did not earn enough to buy private insurance. It was lunacy to me that our public officials, including some who were sitting in the sanctuary for the service, would turn down federal funds to expand the program, thereby punishing the working poor in our state, just to avoid supporting legislation tied to President Obama. So I talked in my speech about how Dr. King had championed the working poor, and I called on our public officials to do the right thing and increase the minimum wage, extend the long-term unemployment benefits program that had been expanded during the 2008 recession and had recently expired, and expand Medicaid.

"Increased productivity and profits have not translated into increased prosperity for those who make the prosperity possible," I said.

Just weeks later, a group of activists and I decided that we needed to dramatize the issue. The group included the Reverend Francys Johnson, an attorney, pastor, and state president of the

NAACP, and the Reverend Timothy McDonald of First Iconium Baptist Church, who was former president of Concerned Black Clergy of Atlanta. At the time, the Moral Mondays movement, under the leadership of the Reverend William Barber, head of the NAACP in North Carolina, was delivering scores of protesters to the state capitol in Raleigh, North Carolina, to challenge the legislature's anti-poor and anti-worker public policies through acts of civil disobedience. We would take a similar tact.

We planned our campaign for mid-March during the legislative session at the state capitol. Protesters flowed into the capitol in waves. I gave a speech, and a group of us sang spirituals in the building's marble rotunda. Some protesters were arrested in the senate gallery as they unfurled a large banner that read, EXPAND MEDICAID, and shouted the same message. Later that afternoon, I led a group of about a dozen protesters to the governor's office, where we held a 1960s-style sit-in, blocking the entrance. When the police arrived and asked us to move, we refused. The police handcuffed us and transported us to Fulton County Jail, and the next wave of protesters took our place. We accomplished our goal of drawing the spotlight to the Medicaid issue, garnering attention from the local media and even *The New York Times*. But I remained frustrated that Republican lawmakers, who made up the overwhelming majority, just dug in their heels, refusing to budge. And Georgia remained among the states that rejected an opportunity to extend health insurance protection through Medicaid to men and women who get up and go to work every day in low-paying industries that serve us yet are unable to afford to take care of themselves when they get sick.

• • •

Soon, though, I got involved in another effort that sought to change the system from the inside out. One day, the state representative Stacey Abrams asked to come and visit with me at my church. I said, "Sure." Abrams, a Spelman graduate, and I had mutual friends. She'd come to Spelman right after I left Morehouse, and she, too, had been brought up in the schools' traditions of activism and leadership. During her term as minority leader of the state house, beginning in 2011, I was a frequent visitor, often as part of a multiracial clergy coalition to advocate for issues, like the expansion of Medicaid, and to protest others, including those terrible gun laws that made such weapons permissible virtually everywhere, including in bars, schools, and religious institutions, on college campuses, and in houses of worship. We found in Stacey a powerful advocate. Around the same time, Stacey and I served on a panel where we talked about leadership to a group of prospective movers and shakers participating in a group called Leadership Buckhead. Stacey also visited Ebenezer on various occasions. The child of two United Methodist ministers, she on one occasion served as the guest speaker for Ebenezer's annual Women's Day program. But on the day of her requested visit with me, Stacey laid out her plans for a new organization she'd started, the New Georgia Project, through which she planned an aggressive outreach to register "low-propensity voters," folks who had been written off as unlikely to vote. These were citizens who felt disconnected; they felt their vote didn't matter; and it became a self-fulfilling prophecy.

Abrams explained that the demographics of Georgia were changing and that research showed there were 800,000 to 1 million eligible but unregistered voters of color in Georgia. She had already raised the funds to hire and train canvassers to go into the neighborhoods, find these potential voters, and register them to vote. We could build a multiracial coalition that could change Georgia by electing principled leadership that represented all the people. She said she needed my help as spokesman for the project.

I didn't have to study long on this proposition. The New Georgia Project was a brilliant idea. Stacey was trying to help realize the dormant political power that Lawrence Bell had described to me a year or so earlier: Black voters, Latino voters, Asian voters, progressive whites, students, and women. I thought to myself that this is the kind of work that could reverse the old southern strategy of appealing to racial resentments and fear as a way of blocking what should be a natural political coalition between people of color, poor and working-class white people, young people, and women for the sake of a progressive political future.

Stacey's voter education, registration, and mobilization strategy reminded me of a sermon the Reverend Jesse Jackson gave in a Philadelphia church in January 1984 during his historic presidential campaign. He likened the potential of voters to the story of David and Goliath. When confronted with Goliath, David had to figure out how to slay the giant. He looked around, and all he saw were some rocks lying around. But he took five smooth stones, put them in his bag, and with perfect aim brought the giant to the ground. In that speech, Jackson had called out the tens of thousands of unregistered voters who had sat out elections that conservative candidates had won by thin margins. The unregistered voters were, he said, "rocks just laying around." We were losing winnable races "by the margin of despair," he said. Then he urged the crowd, "Pick up your slingshot, pick up your rock, declare our time has come."

Ebenezer had already been engaged in its own voter registration drives, setting up in the vestibule after church on some Sundays to capture unregistered potential voters. But the New Georgia Project would enable me to participate in this important endeavor on a much grander scale. I was all in. Before I knew it, I was doing dozens of interviews in the local and national media, explaining what the New Georgia Project was doing. We were registering tens of thousands of voters at a clip that the secretary of state's office was unaccustomed to handling. But instead of pushing to get these voters on the rolls, these public officials seemed to be doing all they could to slow us down. Our canvassers had worked diligently, getting potential voters registered, and we delivered the forms to the appropriate Board of Elections in various counties to be entered electronically into the system. Whether the reason was incompetence or some type of malfeasance, the result was the same: people were being denied the right to the legal franchise. At one point, Stacey, Francys Johnson, and I delivered to the secretary of state's office stacks of boxes filled with slips of paper representing forty thousand voters who had been registered by the New Georgia Project but still were not showing up on the rolls.

Those on the other side, including the then secretary of state, Brian Kemp, a Republican who had well-known ambitions to run for governor, denied that his office had interfered with the process and instead accused us of widespread voter fraud. And with big fanfare, he announced an investigation. Kemp's "investigation" ultimately found there was no wrongdoing by the New Georgia Project. But his intention was to distract us and cast a cloud over the organization. Nevertheless, we stayed focused and by 2017 we would register more than 200,000 new voters.

When Stacey announced her run against Kemp in a trailblazing campaign for governor in the 2018 elections, I assumed the role of board chairman of the New Georgia Project. Though she would fall short by a narrow fifty-five-thousand-vote margin, by September 2019 the New Georgia Project would register a total of half a million new voters—voters who would help us make history in the state in the years ahead. Stacey is clearly a star in the national Democratic Party, and I am glad that she decided to run for governor again. Beyond that, she is just a special human being whose brilliance and foresight enabled her to see the big picture of a new Georgia before it was visible to others. Her leadership has been indispensable in the cultivation of Georgia's new multiracial electoral majority. When we all participate in the political process, we set the terms for a future that embraces all of us and our children.

All the while, speculation continued about whether I would enter electoral politics, especially in the year before 2016 when U.S. senator Johnny Isakson was coming up for reelection. Isakson, a Republican, was one of Georgia's most beloved politicians, and he was respected on both sides of the aisle. He and I were friends, too. In fact, the first time I sat in the well of the House of Representatives for a State of the Union address, I came as a guest of Isakson's in 2011 to see President Obama address a joint session of Congress. That speech came on the heels of the tragedy near Tucson, Arizona, where U.S. representative Gabby Giffords was shot in the head during a meeting with her constituents in a supermarket parking lot. Six people were killed in the shooting, and thirteen others, including Giffords, were injured. In a show of unity, Democrats and Republicans, who usually sat on different sides of the aisle during the annual address, decided that each of them would sit with a legislator or guest from another party that year. I wasn't a legislator, but I was Senator Isakson's "date" for President Obama's speech that evening. Three years later, Senator Isakson invited me to open the U.S. Senate in prayer as a guest chaplain. He also blessed me with tickets to President Obama's first inauguration.

Despite our public policy differences, Johnny Isakson and I had a genuine respect for each other. But policy matters. The people of Georgia needed the health care that he and others were fighting. They also needed voting-rights protections that are best secured at the federal level, and other meaningful legislation aimed at lifting society's most vulnerable. Activists and concerned citizens across the state were urging me to run against Isakson, and I wrestled with the question throughout the summer of 2015. I held a church meeting to find out how the members would feel if I sought the office, and I walked away believing that, while there was some hesitation and resistance, overall I would have my congregation's blessing if I pursued the seat.

There was someone else I consulted about the decision, the

woman I had started dating, Oulèye Ndoye. A friend of hers had introduced us at a New Year's Eve service at Ebenezer. I found her to be very smart and beautiful. She had graduated from Spelman with a bachelor's degree in international studies and received a master's in migration studies from the University of Oxford. In the year or so after we first met, she spent much of her time abroad. But we became friends and saw each other occasionally on her visits back to Atlanta. Oulèye loved politics, and she was very helpful as I talked through whether I should run. I finally decided that this was still not the right time. I needed to attend to the flock, accomplish some other administrative and programmatic objectives at the church. I was not sure that I would ever run for public office at all and that too would be perfectly fine. My passion was not politics but service, and my goal was change. That could happen in many ways. So I put my head down and got back to work in my pastoral ministry.

As the time passed, my relationship with Oulèye grew more serious, and we got engaged at the end of a New Year's Eve service at Ebenezer in 2015. We got married first in a private ceremony in January and then in a larger one at the church on Valentine's Day. Our daughter, Chloé, was born later that year, and our son, Caleb, was born during the Christmas holidays in 2018. Unfortunately, the marriage would not survive, but I am eternally grateful that we produced two amazing, beautiful children, and their mother and I are completely devoted to co-parenting them.

Caleb was still an infant in 2019 when Democrats began lining up to run against Senator David Perdue, who had beaten Michelle Nunn in 2014 and was up for reelection in 2020. Community leaders approached me again with the prospect of running, and again I said no. There was a good field of democratic candidates running in the primary, and I figured one of them would emerge as an able standard-bearer for the party. Besides, I had two young children, including an infant, and I was enjoying every minute I could have with them. But then, one day in August 2019 as I was getting dressed, I picked up my cell phone to read my texts, and a CNN bulletin flashed across the screen. Senator Isakson had announced that because of his failing health, he would not be able to complete his term and planned to retire at the end of the year. The news stunned me, and I knew immediately why my friends were trying to reach me. I took a deep breath and proceeded with my day. This was not an ideal time to think about running for office, but I was determined not to stress about it.

My life has been a series of "not my will, Lord, but Thy will be done" moments. It is my faith that steadies me when life feels chaotic and uncertain. I'm able to rest in the assurance that my life is ultimately in the hands of an almighty God and that if I do everything I can to be faithful, I will somehow end up where I'm supposed to be.

Folks started calling me again, and as I demurred, I figured the party's interest in me as a potential candidate would evaporate, but that didn't happen. I talked to my advisers, close friends, prayed about it, and prayed some more. Finally, I came to realize there may never be a more perfect moment, that life was full of unexpected dips and curves, but that so many people, including me, had put in years of work for this opportunity. After four years of Donald Trump and Trumpism, the country was deeply divided and could use another moral voice. Not another transactional politician—and not even a senator who used to be a pastor but a pastor in the senate—reminding us of the covenant we have with one another as an American people. God was at work. It was time, and I was ready.

I quickly began assembling a campaign team. I had raised no money at all, and Lawrence Bell was my first senior adviser. We interviewed candidates for key positions and chose Jerid Kurtz, who had led several big political campaigns, as our campaign manager. We hired other key personnel, a finance director and consultants, and with less than ten months to introduce me and my message to all of Georgia, we dashed out of the gate.

I officially announced my candidacy on January 30, 2020, with a video tweeted early that morning. The video was aimed simply at introducing me. It captures me walking through an apartment in the Kayton Homes project, where I had grown up, talking about my upbringing in a large, loving family with two devoted parents who had taught us the value of hard work. I talk about graduating from Morehouse, earning a doctorate, and being called to Ebenezer. I end the video sitting in a church pew. "Some might ask why a pastor thinks he should serve in the Senate," I say, staring into the camera. "Well, I've committed my whole life to service and helping people realize their highest potential. I've always thought that my impact doesn't stop at the church door; that's actually where it starts."

The media throughout Georgia trumpeted the news. Stacey tweeted her endorsement right away and tweeted the video: "Reverend Raphael Warnock is a true ally in our fight for justice. That's why I'm proud to endorse him for U.S. Senate here in GA. Take a moment to get to know him & if you can, chip in to support his campaign." Stacey's endorsement and unwavering support meant so much to me.

The same day that I announced my candidacy, the World Health Organization (WHO) declared the outbreak of a new coronavirus "a public health emergency of international concern." We'd been hearing news reports about a mysterious virus that was causing massive sickness in China and was beginning to spread to other parts of the world. But no one fully understood yet how that would play out in the United States. Meanwhile, my team and I fanned out all over Georgia, meeting people, laying out my platform as clearly as possible. I promised to protect our voting rights, fight for access to high-quality, affordable health care, re-create an economy that spurred jobs and upward mobility for all, and push for an end to mass incarceration and for fair treatment for all. The plan for the first few months of the campaign was to build our organization and make sure we had the resources to knock on as many doors as possible, communicate with voters on TV, online, and through other channels, and to make sure we could inspire people with our "Get Out the Vote" events. We attended a few small events and had plans for more. Soon, though, all of it would come to an abrupt halt.

On March 11, 2020, the World Health Organization declared the COVID-19 virus a global pandemic. My church and campaign staffs and I were monitoring the news closely because we had two big events planned the following weekend: the church's 134th anniversary celebration on Sunday, March 15, and a big backyard picnic fundraiser on the same day in Los Angeles, where I was scheduled to fly after the church event. In the early part of the week, I focused on getting hand sanitizer stations set up at strategic locations throughout the church to keep the members safe for one of our biggest events of the year. But news reports regarding the spread of the virus and of the rising death toll worldwide gave me pause.

By Thursday, March 12, the governor of Ohio had announced statewide school closures, President Donald Trump had announced a travel ban from much of Europe, and the National Basketball Association had suspended its season. It was clear to me that having an in-person celebration would put too many people at risk. The staff and I quickly pivoted and began planning a virtual celebration. Just the guest preacher, a small team of singers and musicians, and I would be in the sanctuary. Throughout the week, I was also on the phone at various times with Jerid, Lawrence, and other campaign staff, as well as the Los Angeles host of the planned fundraiser, and we decided to cancel my trip and the campaign event.

The next week, President Trump declared a national emergency, and the country began shutting down to slow the spread of the virus. More schools and businesses closed, and families were instructed to quarantine at home with the members of their households, leaving many loved ones isolated from one another. Health-care facilities and their medical professionals quickly became overwhelmed, providing health and emotional care for those who were sick and dying in sterile hospital rooms without the comfort of loved ones, who were not allowed to visit. The death toll kept rising by the day, and it didn't take long for the numbers to show that the virus was having a disproportionate and deadlier impact on people of color.

Very early in the epidemic, I had the sad duty of eulogizing my first parishioner to succumb to COVID-19. At thirty-six years old, Ron Hill was a beloved high school coach, husband, and father of fifteen-year-old twin daughters who grew up in the Ebenezer Sunday School and the children's ministry. The church and larger community were heartbroken by the news of his sudden death. But there had been news reports of a terrible wave of COVID-related deaths in Albany, Georgia, and many of the people who died had attended one or both of a couple of big funerals in town. We did not want Ron's funeral to produce other funerals, so we had to find a way to conduct the service while everyone sheltered in place. COVID is cruel in this way. It takes those we love, while also making it difficult for us to come together to express our love for one another while in the process of grieving. Everyone, including the bereaved family, stayed sheltered in their homes, while the entire service was conducted on Zoom. As I eulogized Ron from my dining room table, and tried to offer comfort to hundreds of teachers, students, and others who joined the online service, I knew that we had entered strange and bewildering territory.

Church was different. Campaigning was different. For the latter we had to shift our planned approach to reach the masses. There were no more large indoor events, so we worked the phones and videotaped messages to the people of Georgia. We postponed plans to open a campaign headquarters in downtown Atlanta, and my home served that purpose for a long while. I communicated with my staff via the telephone and Zoom. Advisers came only as needed, and we wore masks and stayed distant in the back of my house, away from the areas where I was quarantining with my children. The staff also came and set up a backdrop in my home office for media interviews. We eventually began holding outdoor drive-in rallies to deliver a message of hope and healing in innovative, safe ways.

Americans were already hurting, emotionally exhausted, and scared in May 2020, when a cellphone video captured the brazen murder of George Floyd, a forty-six-year-old African American man, by a white police officer in Minneapolis, Minnesota. And suddenly the Black Lives Matter movement, which had been excoriated by those on the far right, took on even greater urgency, attracting massive crowds of new followers, who risked contracting the virus to join the protests and growing movement for police reform. Like people of goodwill who saw that video across the nation, I was horrified, hurt, and angry that this kind of brutality and inhumanity had happened again.

What could I say as a pastor, as a U.S. Senate candidate, as a fellow human to people who were hurting and likely wondering if there was any hope for racial healing as a nation? I tried to capture our pain the following Sunday as I talked about the George Floyd murder and the pandemic of racism in our land during my sermon, "Renew." We are all mere mortals, made from dust, I said. "For mere dust to try to dominate other dust, to put your dusty knee on the neck of another man, who is already handcuffed and on the ground, for nearly nine minutes with your hand in your pocket is to arrogate to yourself things that belong to God. It is sickness. It is ungodly; it is uncivilized and unjust. George Floyd deserved better than that." Then I called the names of other Black men and women who had been killed by police or in racially motivated incidents across the country. Breonna Taylor. Ahmaud Arbery. Sandra Bland. Atatiana Jefferson. Botham Jean. Tamir Rice. Trayvon Martin. Eric Garner. Emmett Till. They all deserved better than that.

I told the congregation via our virtual broadcast that I, too, had been weeping all week. But I urged them not to give in to cynicism, hate, and despair. "I dropped by your house to tell you don't you dare give up. I know it's dark, but that's when the brightest stars shine. When it's dark, God is up to something . . . I see a new world coming when all God's children can be heard and understood." That Pentecost Sunday, I assured the people that a fresh wind of the Spirit was coming and the old world, where racism and hatred and bitterness prevailed, is passing away. "The old world is breathing its last breath," I said. "It is desperate because it is dying. You can hear its death rattle."

But there would be more suffering.

Rayshard Brooks was sleeping in his car in a Wendy's parking lot in Atlanta the night of June 12, 2020, when he was awakened by the police. The police body and dash cameras show him having what appeared to be a civil and nonconfrontational conversation with the officers, who at some point administered a sobriety test. Following those forty minutes of conversation, Brooks was told that he was under arrest. He was on probation and likely dreaded the thought of returning to prison. He grabbed an officer's taser, took off running, and was pursued. As the police chased him, he turned and fired the taser backward from a considerable distance as he ran. An officer shot his gun thrice at Brooks, who fell to the ground and died at a hospital shortly afterwards. And once again, the nation watched as a much too common ritual of grief took place in another Black church—my church, Ebenezer. After the shooting, I had sat with the family, grieved with them, and listened as Rayshard's widow told me that her twenty-seven-year-old husband had loved to dance, though he just moved from side to side like an old man. I had met the eight-year-old daughter whose birthday he celebrated on what would become his last day. And then I eulogized him.

"We had to come together because there's another virus in the land, and it's killing people," I said at the funeral. "There's COVID-19 and then there's what I call COVID-1619. And they are both deadly. In this land, we've been trying to beat back this virus of racism since 1619, when twenty slaves arrived in Jamestown, Virginia. Mass incarceration is its latest mutation, but it is an old virus that kills people." I reminded them that Rayshard was on probation in a state that, despite reforms, was ground zero for keeping people on probation for extended periods of time and that when Rayshard ran from the police, he was running from that system. "He was trying. He had been digging his way back. And he knew that night that he could lose his liberty," I said. "And afraid of losing his liberty, he lost his life, running from a system that too often makes slaves out of people. This is about a whole system that cries out for renewal and reform." While some would argue that had he not run, he would be alive, the truth is both he and George Floyd are dead. Brooks ran. Floyd did not. Both are dead. Neither is more dead than the other. And therein is the problem. Black parents do not really know what to tell their children in order to keep them alive. And that's not just a Black problem, although it is happening to Black people. That's an American problem.

Later that evening, after I preached at Rayshard Brooks' eulogy, I drove four hours to Savannah to pick up my sister because after twenty-two years the battle to free my brother Keith was coming to a surprising end. He was among the thousands of nonviolent inmates released to serve the rest of their sentences at home under certain conditions as part of a nationwide effort to keep the deadly virus from spreading rapidly in overcrowded prisons. I was ecstatic about finally welcoming my brother home and volunteered to pick him up at the federal prison in Jesup, Georgia. Because we were in the thick of the COVID-19 pandemic, I rented a place via Airbnb, rather than sleep at my elderly mother's home. Though I arrived in the wee hours of the morning, I could barely sleep after lying down. I had visited with my brother on many occasions in many different federal prisons, but this time he would finally be coming home with me. Early the next morning, I picked up my sister Joyce and we drove to Jesup.

When we arrived, my brother was already standing outside on the prison yard with one bag that held all his belongings. Joyce and I ran toward him and embraced him with love, joy, sorrow, and relief. After more than two decades and numerous appeals to no avail, a middle-age man of fifty-five years stood in front of us. So many years had been lost. So much had happened. So much more *could* have happened to him while he was locked up. But he was yet alive. He had navigated prison culture and stayed alive while staying clean. There was really too much to say. So we let the silence speak. He knew. We knew. Those prayers for mercy beneath that oak tree all those years ago and so many other prayers had been answered at last. Children and children's children had been born. Dad had died. But Mom lived to see it. Her son was coming home.

I was back on the road campaigning when the news broke about a month later on July 17, 2020, that the civil rights movement icon Congressman John Lewis had died of pancreatic cancer at eighty years old. I'd known that he had cancer and that the odds were not in his favor. Yet his death still hurt. Another movement general was gone. His bravery and courage during the movement and his fight for voting rights and democracy throughout the rest of his life had made my own Senate race possible. In recent years I'd had the honor of working beside him, busing voters to their polling stations, as part of our church's "Souls to the Polls" initiative. During early voting for a previous election, I invited Congressman Lewis to deliver the Sunday sermon and reminded the congregation of the sacrifices made for their right to vote. He was a testimony to that. Then, after service, Congressman Lewis and I joined many in the congregation, boarding buses that took us to the early voting stations. Ebenezer is the kind of congregation where more folks than not could have driven themselves to the polls and most likely would have done so. But this campaign was more about inspiration than transportation. The buses were wrapped in our SOULS TO THE POLLS signs, so as we rolled through the neighborhoods of Atlanta, we encouraged and reminded citizens of the urgency to vote. This was about bearing witness, and even in his advanced years Congressman Lewis still put his body in the game.

I officiated at Lewis's three-hour funeral at Ebenezer, which drew three former U.S. presidents—George W. Bush, Bill Clinton, and Barack Obama—House Speaker Nancy Pelosi, and several members of Congress. President Obama spoke for us all when he called Congressman Lewis "an American whose faith was tested again and again to produce a man of pure joy and unbreakable perseverance." And the president didn't hold back, warning that Republicans were attacking voting rights "with surgical precision." He described the closing of polling locations, the targeting of minorities and students with restrictive identification laws, and policies that undermined the U.S. Postal Service leading up to a crucial election dependent on mail-in ballots.

"Now, I know this is a celebration of John's life," President Obama said. "There are some who might say we shouldn't dwell on such things. But that's why I'm talking about it. John Lewis devoted his time on this earth fighting the very attacks on democracy . . . that we are seeing circulate right now."

Congressman Lewis had endorsed my Senate campaign, and I'm glad that he got to see me running with a real shot at winning. And I believe he would have been proud of his party's success in November 2020, when Joe Biden won back the White House with Kamala Harris, the first African American, first Asian, and first woman vice president, at his side in the presidential race. And this African American preacher finished on top of a crowded field of twenty-one candidates with 32.9 percent, or 1.6 million votes, in the Georgia special election. Without the required majority, though, I faced a runoff on January 5, 2021, against Kelly Loeffler, the short-term incumbent and multimillionaire businesswoman who had been appointed by Governor Brian Kemp in December 2019 to fill Isakson's seat until the election. Loeffler, co-owner of the Atlanta Dream WNBA team, had entered the Senate as its wealthiest member and quickly aligned herself with President Trump's destructive agenda.

I will be forever grateful to the courageous women of the WNBA, particularly the Atlanta Dream, who publicly supported my campaign. Loeffler seemed to be trying to use her own team as a political pawn by taking a vehement stance against the Black Lives Matter movement with the hope of buttressing her support among those on the extreme right. But that strategy backfired. The issue of police brutality is a real matter of life and death for many of these players and their family members. And they would not be used.

Former Dream star Angel McCoughtry told *The Washington Post* that the players did their homework. "When we wore the Warnock shirts, we didn't just wear them because Kelly denounced the Black Lives Matter," said McCoughtry, who spent ten seasons with the Dream but had moved to the Las Vegas Aces by the political campaign in 2020. "We did our research. We looked at health care. We looked at LGBT rights. We looked at social justice issues."

I met with many of the players over Zoom one night, and we talked about police brutality, voting rights, reproductive rights, health care, and equal rights for the LGBTQ community. They discovered that my views aligned with theirs on issues that were important to them. I also told the players how proud I was of them for dedicating their season to Breonna Taylor, the twenty-six-year-old emergency technician who was shot to death in her home on March 13, 2020, by Louisville, Kentucky, police officers, and for keeping her name alive with the "Say Her Name" campaign. To my great surprise, I learned that players from the Dream and Phoenix Mercury entered the arena for their nationally televised game on August 4, 2020, in black T-shirts that said in white letters, all caps: VOTE WARNOCK. Players from other WNBA teams also started wearing the shirts, and some of the images even went viral on social media.

In the other Senate race, where the Republican senator David Perdue was running for reelection, he failed to capture the majority, with 49.7 percent of the vote. That landed him, too, in a runoff against the Democrat Jon Ossoff, a thirty-three-year-old former executive of a small documentary film company based in England. Suddenly Georgia faced the prospect in the January 5 runoff election of sending not just its first African American and Jewish senators to Washington, D.C., but of sending two Democrats and flipping control of the Senate. The national spotlight turned to Georgia, and the stakes of my election were higher than ever.

As I saw it, the heart and soul of the nation were at risk. With a demagogue occupying the White House and giving his tacit approval, white supremacy was on the rise. The nearly four years of the Donald Trump presidency had seen a resurgence of unabashed, unashamed bigotry on a scale that I had not witnessed before in my lifetime. And I hoped that Georgia—that America—was ready for change. For the rest of the way, I ran with that sense of urgency. Loeffler wasted no time trying to paint me as a scary extremist. It helped that I had been raised in the Warnock household, where thick skin was a must. Supported by people across the nation who recognized the importance of this race, Ossoff and I often campaigned together. We urged Georgians to stay focused and tune out those who were trafficking in fear and division because they had no vision. I didn't know Ossoff before the campaign, but we quickly became friends. We'd both been touched by Congressman Lewis—Ossoff as a former intern in his Washington office and me as Congressman Lewis's pastor and longtime admirer. Ossoff and I began doing more events together, and we would chat and swap notes during the stops. We also posted signs that captured part of our focus: Health, Jobs, Justice. We represented the New Georgia— the Georgia that Lawrence Bell had described and Stacey Abrams had envisioned years earlier.

The national media was scrutinizing this race like few others before in Georgia. A nationally televised debate between Loeffler and me was scheduled for December 6, 2020, and I knew it was crucial for me to perform well. My closest advisers made sure I was keenly aware that the way I responded mattered as much as what I actually said. I was a Black man challenging a white woman, and I couldn't come across as too aggressive. I could get labeled very quickly as "angry," even if I showed moral outrage. It was a delicate dance.

I prepared for the debate, studying all the major issues and carefully considering my opinions. I practiced with Sarah Riggs Amico, a Democrat who played the role of Kelly Loeffler. Amico had run unsuccessfully for lieutenant governor of Georgia when Stacey ran for governor. None of us could have anticipated that Loeffler would so robotically refer to me repeatedly as "radical liberal Raphael Warnock." But by debate time, I was ready. There was no accusation or response I hadn't heard from my team, so I stayed calm and answered the questions, without even acknowledging my opponent's mischaracterization of me.

My team and I felt confident that I did what I needed to do in the debate, and media reports were generally favorable. Many independent polls showed me ahead in the race, so we were cautiously optimistic. We didn't rely too heavily on polling data, though, because history had shown that in racially tinged elections some white voters were not forthright about their candidate choice. So we kept pushing our message across the state. Soon after the Electoral College affirmed Joe Biden's victory, the president-elect campaigned with Jon Ossoff and me in December 2020. Then, on January 3, 2021, two days before the election, Vice President elect Kamala Harris joined us for an outdoor, drive-in rally in my hometown. I followed Jon, whom I was now calling "my brother from another mother." It was such a thrilling moment, walking out onto the stage as Mary J. Blige's "Work That" pumped up the crowd. I paused at the corner of the stage and looked out at the huge parking lot, filled with cars, trucks, and vans and their occupants, honking their horns and hanging out of their vehicles' windows.

"Well, hello, Savannah, Georgia!" I shouted, looking into the crowd of my hometown folks. "Hello, Garden City!"

More honks and waves.

"Wow, it's a beautiful day in Savannah, and you all look like you're ready to win an election," I added. "Listen, I've been traveling all across the state. But I'm always grateful to be home. 'Mid pleasures and palaces, though we may roam, be it ever so humble, there's no place like home.'"

I talked about the importance of the election and stressed that Savannah had a chance to send one of its own to the U.S. Senate for the first time in 150 years. I talked about the new Georgia. And I asked them to urge everyone they knew to get out to vote. I left feeling excited and confident that even amid a deadly pandemic Georgia was changing for the better.

All our hard work and hopes came down to this: election night, January 5, 2021. For much of the evening, I stayed quarantined with an intimate group of family, friends, and campaign staff inside my campaign headquarters about a block from my church. This was Campaign 101 in the age of COVID-19. No normal election night setup in a big hotel ballroom. No long, "who's who" guest list. No party hopping from one campaign celebration to the next. Vaccines were not yet widely available, so those in the room remained masked and appropriately socially distant. The group included my sisters Joyce and Wandetta, my brother Jeffrey, and some of my cousins; friends that I'd grown up with in Savannah; my Union seminary colleague and friend Cathlin Baker and her family; my friend Darrell Griffin from my days at Abyssinian and his son, Miles, a Morehouse student; my close friend Byron Perkins, a Birmingham-based civil rights attorney I befriended during my intern days at Sixth Avenue; and some of my church members. I had insisted that my mother, eighty-two at the time and at high risk for the virus, stay at home under quarantine in Savannah. Despite all the excitement around me, I was calm. I had done all I could to get my message out, and the outcome was in the hands of the people of Georgia now. I believed they were ready for change, but I also knew the old guard wouldn't give in without a fight. I figured the race would be so tight that it would take a day or two to declare a winner, just as the results of the presidential contest had the previous November. I'd even told my family not to bother traveling from Savannah to Atlanta that night to join me. But they ignored me. No way were they going to miss this moment, no matter what it brought. And as it turned out, I was so glad they had not listened to me.

After a full day of working the phones, holding up signs outdoors, ending our campaign in Atlanta, some of our party gathered at a small restaurant right behind the old church, and at one point I joined them there. But around 10:00 p.m., Adam, one of my communications consultants and strategists who was busy crunching the numbers, summoned me back to headquarters, where big television screens were tuned to cable television news stations so that we could follow the election returns. The whole country was watching. When I arrived back at headquarters, Adam pulled me aside to share a surprising update: we could likely get the results that night after all. Given the votes that had been cast already and where the outstanding votes were in the state, things looked promising. I should summon everyone to campaign headquarters, he said, and begin working on a victory speech.

The group at the restaurant scurried back across the street and gathered around the television screens. About 11:40 p.m., a large batch of votes were announced from DeKalb County, a heavily

Democratic area near Atlanta, moving me into the lead with about thirty-five thousand votes over my opponent. The room roared with applause and celebration. We were giddy with excitement. We knew. The remaining votes were in Democratic strongholds.

Around 2:00 a.m., CNN flashed a breaking news banner across the screen, and the host announced, "We can now make a projection in one of the two Georgia Senate runoffs. CNN will now project that Democrat Raphael Warnock is elected to the U.S. Senate, the pastor defeating Republican incumbent Kelly Loeffler. This puts Democrats halfway towards their goal of retaking control of the U.S. Senate."

By now, my friends, family, and staff were in a full celebratory mood, bumping fists, shouting, "We did it!" "Praise God!" "Thank you, Jesus!" Tears flowed all over the room. My sister rushed over and, caught up in the emotion, gave me an impromptu, forbidden hug. She got Mom on the phone.

Moments earlier, even before CNN called the race, I had gone live to thank my supporters. I'd slipped into an office that had been prepared for the speech and had a quiet moment to think about the history we were making. I longed to call my father and share the moment with him, as I had the night President Obama was elected the first time. Georgia voters had made me the first African American from the state to serve in the U.S. Senate and just one of eleven African American senators in the long history of our beloved country.

I looked around the room at my jubilant family and friends, some who had known me since the fifth grade, and I thought about the unlikeliness of it all. Ray, the baby boy of the Warnock clan, who had grown up in the projects and started preaching at eleven years old in a tiny Pentecostal Holiness church, the son of a junkman and a woman who spent her teenage years picking somebody else's cotton, had been picked by the people of Georgia to represent them in the U.S. Senate. And then I looked into the camera, opened my heart, and let the words flow:

Thank you so very much. I come before you as a proud American and as a son of Georgia.

My roots are planted deeply in Georgia soil.

A child who grew up in the Kayton Homes housing projects of Savannah, Georgia. Number 11 out of 12 children. A proud graduate of Morehouse College and the pastor of Ebenezer Baptist Church, the spiritual home of Martin Luther King Jr. and Congressman John Lewis. A son of my late father, who was a pastor, a veteran, and a small-business man, and my mother, who, as a teenager growing up in Waycross, Georgia, used to pick somebody else's cotton. But the other day, because this is America, the eighty-two-year-old hands that used to pick somebody else's cotton went to the polls and picked her youngest son to be a United States senator.

So, I come before you tonight as a man who knows that the improbable journey that led me to this place in this historic moment in America could only happen here. We were told that we couldn't win this election, but tonight we proved that with hope, hard work, and the people by our side anything is possible.

I also cited the words of Dr. King: "We are tied in a single garment of destiny, caught up in an inescapable network of mutuality. Whatever affects one directly affects all indirectly."

I knew that the road ahead would not be easy, but with faith in God and in the strength of the people as our broad and diverse witness, anything, yes anything, is possible. Together, we can build a future that honors the sacrifices of those who came before us and is worthy of the promise that lives in all our children.

CHAPTER 9

Fighting for Our Lives

I slept little the night of the election, but I rose early the next morning, January 6, in a happy, hopeful mood. The people of Georgia had done an amazing thing and elected the state's first African American U.S. senator. All the network and cable news shows were calling, and I did back-to-back interviews from my home office via Zoom all morning. On *The View*, Whoopi Goldberg said she never thought she'd see such change in Georgia, and Sunny Hostin described watching the election returns with her father, who was born and raised in Augusta, Georgia.

"I can tell you from the tears in his eyes that we are so very proud," Hostin said.

As I told the hosts, I hoped to "be a force for good and pulling us all together as we build what Dr. King called the beloved community and respond to the concerns of ordinary people."

In all the interviews, I talked about my pride in the citizens of

Georgia who had rejected cynicism and division and chosen to take a new path forward. I talked about my excitement to work with the incoming president-elect, Biden, and vice president elect, Harris, to deliver legislation to lift the country's most vulnerable citizens and help bring racial and political healing to our country. My election was emblematic of the American dream—that in this land of the free an African American man who grew up in public housing, the eleventh of twelve children, the first in his family to graduate from college, could be elected to the U.S. Senate by a large, multiracial coalition in the South.

"Maybe Americans were finally ready to pull together," I thought, full of optimism. But my exhilaration would be short-lived.

Shortly after 1:00 that afternoon, my cell phone began buzzing with news updates. I picked up my phone, glanced down at the screen, and saw reports concerning the U.S. Capitol. I quickly turned on the television and watched in shock as the most violent attack on the U.S. Capitol since the British burned it down in 1814 unfolded over several hours. Mobs of enraged men and women, waving huge Trump signs and flags, toppled temporary barricades around the perimeter of the Capitol, overtook the U.S. Capitol Police, and beat officers trying to hold back the crowd. The rioters smashed windows of the building, pushed their way inside, and then stormed angrily through the halls in search of democratically elected officials they viewed as enemies. They called for House

Speaker Nancy Pelosi. They even called for their fellow Republican Vice President Mike Pence, who had drawn their ire when he had enough dignity to refuse to interfere with the congressional certification of the presidential election results. Security teams rushed Pelosi and Pence to safe locations just as the rioters were making their way inside the building.

My heart ached for my new colleagues and their staff members, some of whom huddled under desks and behind chairs in the House chamber as they waited to be evacuated. Their faces showed a mixture of shock and fear. What was going on? I could not believe the destruction at one of our country's most hallowed institutions or the disdain for democracy on the contorted faces of the rioters. This wasn't an attack by foreign enemies. These were Americans, driven by the Big Lie, which had been perpetuated by a defeated president, Donald Trump, since the November 3 election: that victory had been stolen from him because of voter fraud. Just before the insurrection, Trump had addressed thousands of his supporters during a rally at the Ellipse outside the White House. During an hourlong speech in which he called out the Georgia Senate elections as having been "rigged," Trump dropped incendiary lies about the election, whipped up rage, and urged protesters to march to the Capitol. Never forget this day, he told them.

As matters deteriorated at the Capitol, Trump supporters gathered at state capitols across the country. Many in the crowds were armed. Georgia's secretary of state, Brad Raffensperger, a Republican, was even evacuated from his office with his staff as a precautionary measure. He had been under constant verbal attack after refusing Trump's urging to alter the state's election results in his favor.

The racist overtones of Trump's claim that the election was stolen are clear. African Americans, many of whom were newly registered, showed up at the polls in unprecedented numbers for both the November 2020 presidential race and the Georgia Senate races. And those votes played a crucial role in unseating an incredulous Trump and sending me and Jon Ossoff to the Senate. The former president's continued claims of widespread voter fraud are just his way of saying that the votes of certain people don't count, can't count, and can't be real because the election outcome was not consistent with the myth of white supremacy.

America's story has always been complicated.

The day of my runoff election and the day afterward both tell us critical things about America today. January 5 represents the hope of an America moving closer to our ideal. But January 6 reveals the dark, ugly underbelly. Both are true. For now, we the people reside somewhere between the two. But we are the latest generation that gets to decide whether we're going to give in to bigotry and fear or push closer to our democratic ideals. I choose hope. I choose inclusivity. I choose equal protection under the law. I choose truth and justice. I choose the beloved community.

This is the conviction and hope that I carried with me to Washington, D.C., on January 20, 2021, for my first official day in office.

The inauguration of President Biden and Vice President Harris was held outside the Capitol on the same steps that had been a site of the violent insurrection just fourteen days earlier. The ceremony was a beautiful, multicultural affair with a theme of unity reverberating through each speech.

"We have learned again that democracy is precious," President Biden said in his address to the nation. "Democracy is fragile. And at this hour, my friends, democracy has prevailed. So now, on this hallowed ground where just days ago violence sought to shake this Capitol's very foundation, we come together as one nation, under God, indivisible, to carry out the peaceful transfer of power as we have for more than two centuries."

Later the same afternoon, Vice President Harris conducted the swearing-in ceremony on the senate floor for me and fellow senators Ossoff and Alex Padilla, who had been appointed by California's governor, Gavin Newsom, to replace Harris. Because of the pandemic, most of my family members were unable to travel to join me. But my sister Valencia drove from her home in Baltimore and watched proudly from the gallery. As part of the ceremonial tradition, a current senator escorted each of us newcomers to the floor to take the oath of office. I chose to be escorted by Senator Tim Kaine, a Democrat and a Catholic, who presented me with a special rosary given to him by Pope Benedict XVI. I chose also to be sworn in using a Bible that had been presented to me by the Ebenezer congregation on the occasion of my installation as the church's fifth senior pastor. My family members, friends, and supporters gathered around televisions and online in their homes to watch the historic ceremony. My children's mother even sent me a video of my two precious little children watching their dad's swearing in with her at home. And I know that my dad was also somewhere smiling in glory, especially because I was sworn in on what would have been his 104th birthday.

Seven days before I began my term in the Senate, the U.S. House of Representatives voted to impeach President Trump on a charge of inciting an insurrection, and his impeachment trial was set early on the Senate agenda. The trial began February 9, and for four days a powerful case was laid out against the former president. It was my first vote from my seat on the senate floor (I had voted on other matters but not from my seat because it takes a few days for the desks to be shuffled and new senators to find where they will be seated in a new Congress). I was among the fifty-seven senators who voted to find the former president guilty. That number included seven Republicans who bravely crossed party lines to hold their party's standard-bearer responsible for his actions. Nevertheless, we were short of the necessary two-thirds vote for a conviction. Forty-three Republican senators voted "not guilty." There was no doubt in my mind that Trump was responsible for what happened at the Capitol that day. He incited those rioters with his baseless claims about a stolen election and voter fraud, despite all the evidence to the contrary as confirmed by judges across the country, including some he had appointed, and despite assurances by senior election officials and the Homeland Security department. Secretary of State Raffensperger, whom Trump tried to pressure to "find" him 11,780 votes, said that the 2020 election cycle was "safe, honest, and secure." Biden's victory was confirmed three times by machine and hand recounts. Yet Trump continues with the lies—lies that have led to subversive attempts at the state level to undermine the very principle on which our nation was built: our democracy.

In the months following the November 2020 election, state legislatures controlled by Republicans introduced at least two hundred fifty voter suppression bills, using voter fraud as a false pretext. In Georgia, legislators approved a draconian new voting law that, among other things, makes it a crime to bring water or food to citizens standing in long lines to vote—lines that seniors and others stand in for as much as six, seven, or even ten hours to exercise their basic constitutional rights. Lines will be made even longer by the actions of those same legislators. The law also limits absentee voting, restricts the hours of use for drop boxes, which undermines part of the whole point of having a drop box, and reduces the period for runoff elections from nine weeks to four and early voting in runoff elections from three weeks to one. The law even provides an easy path for partisan politicians at the state level to overthrow local boards of elections to sway the results, just as Trump had demanded of Raffensperger in a futile attempt to bend the people's will toward his own. These and similar measures passed in other states are a direct attack on the ideal that we as Americans say we hold most dear. This is Jim Crow in new clothes.

I recognize that dangerous, old nemesis. That is why I have made the passage of national voting rights legislation an urgent crusade during my time in office. Federal legislation would offer protection against the disenfranchisement of minority voters, elderly voters, disabled voters, and students. Among other things, the bill would implement same-day voter registration, make Election Day a national holiday so that working people can get to the polls, expand early voting, and ban partisan and racial gerrymandering. There have been times when the voting rights issue seemed dead or when it dropped in priority, even among members of my own party. But I have been relentless, pushing and prodding behind the scenes, as well as at the microphone, fighting to keep this issue alive. As I see it, the right to vote is *the* defining issue of our times, and this moment is a defining time in our history. A time when we must declare that our democracy belongs not to the politicians but to the people.

I believe that democracy is the political enactment of a spiritual idea. It affirms that we are all children of God, that we all have within us a spark of the divine, and therefore a right to help determine the direction of our country and our own destiny within it. My work on voting rights and so many other issues and my decision to venture beyond the relative safety of a sanctuary into this contested terrain of the U.S. Senate aim to give the people, ordinary people, a voice in their own democracy.

There are politicians out there who didn't like that ordinary people in Georgia used their voices to insist on change and send me to the U.S. Senate. Those same politicians are doing all within their power to undermine voting rights and to make it more difficult for *all* Georgia voters to have a say in the next election. So, as I fight for the issues that matter to the people of Georgia, I am fighting to be able to continue in the years ahead doing the work that Georgians sent me to Washington to do.

The voting rights issue is so important to me that I made it the centerpiece of my maiden speech on the floor of the senate on March 17, 2021. I talked about my humble upbringing, my hardworking parents, and my deep roots in Georgia. "In a word, I am Georgia," I said. "A living example and embodiment of its history and its hope, of its pain and promise, the brutality and possibility."

I reminded lawmakers of the history of the staunch segregationists who held the Senate seats from Georgia at the time of my birth, Richard B. Russell and Herman E. Talmadge. After the U.S. Supreme Court outlawed school segregation, Talmadge warned that "blood will run in the streets of Atlanta." His father, Eugene Talmadge, a former Georgia governor, had famously declared that African Americans' place was "at the back door." And he used one word to describe his remedy for keeping African Americans from the polls: "pistols."

"Yet there is something in the American covenant—in its charter documents and its Jeffersonian ideals—that bends toward freedom," I continued. "Led by a preacher and a patriot named King, Americans of all races stood up. History vindicated the movement that sought to bring us closer to our ideals, to lengthen and strengthen the cords of our democracy, and I now hold the seat— the Senate seat—where Herman E. Talmadge sat. And that's why I love America. I love America because we always have a path to make it better, to build a more perfect union."

Then I shifted in my speech to the vicious voter suppression efforts sweeping the country from Georgia to Arizona, from New Hampshire to Florida. "I think that's wrong," I said. "Matter of fact, I think that a vote is a kind of prayer for the kind of world we desire for ourselves and for our children. And our prayers are stronger when we pray together."

Finally, I chided state lawmakers who responded with punitive measures, instead of praise, for voters who had turned out in record numbers during the presidential election and the U.S. Senate races in Georgia. And I urged my colleagues to pass the For the People Act, a voting rights measure introduced earlier that day. "The right to vote is preservative of all other rights," I said. "It is not just another issue alongside other issues. It is foundational. It is the reason why any of us has the privilege of standing here in the first place. It is about the covenant we have with one another as an American people. *E pluribus unum*, out of many, one. It above all else must be protected."

The legislation stalled in the Senate, but the fight is far from over. As long as I have breath, I will keep working to protect the enfranchisement of voters, to preserve our democracy, and to bring this federal legislation to fruition. We as a nation owe a debt of gratitude to Georgians for giving the U.S. Senate the power to deliver legislation that improves the lives of poor and working- and middle-class families and to fight for a more compassionate future for us all. Working for the people of Georgia has been one of the greatest honors of my life, and I have not retreated from the toughest battles. I promised ordinary Americans that I would fight for them; their story is my story. The issues that matter to them matter to me. When I arrived in Washington, D.C., I knew that one of the first orders of business had to be addressing the waves of suffering caused by the pandemic. It was bad enough that families—too many families—were losing loved ones to the deadly virus. By the end of January 2021, a total of 432,189 lives had been lost to COVID-19—a number that had nearly doubled by the end of the year. But hardworking men and women, particularly those in the low-paying service industries, also lost their jobs and the ability to take care of their families. So I got to work quickly, collaborating with my Senate colleagues on the American Rescue Plan, and within my first fifty days in office we were able to deliver one of the country's most substantial economic relief packages, a plan totaling $1.9 trillion, for working- and middle-class families.

It brought me joy to know that this plan was providing a $1,400 economic impact payment per person, expanded earned-income tax credit, and the largest child tax credits in history—measures that experts estimate will cut the child poverty rate in half. The legislation also included extended unemployment insurance, small business support, and more for Americans who were suffering through no fault of their own. Without this support, our people and our country would likely have experienced the kind of widespread devastation unseen since the Great Depression.

The American Rescue Plan also provided help to another group that had been suffering long before the pandemic: Black farmers. Their plight has been on my radar for years as I followed news accounts of the USDA's admission of long-term discrimination against Black farmers in lending and financing practices. I have tremendous respect and appreciation for the essential role that farmers play in our economy and society. My mother picked cotton in rural Georgia in her teen years. One in seven workers in our home state work in agriculture, forestry, or related fields. But Black farmers as a group are nearing extinction, and the role of our government in their dramatically dwindling numbers is difficult to overstate. The pandemic has thrust them into an even more urgent crisis. While campaigning for the Senate seat, I heard from Black farmers, who for decades were unable to get the kind of financing made readily available to white farmers and, as a result, have been saddled with huge debt and the threat of losing their farms. Their dwindling numbers tell the tale: in 1920, Black farmers accounted for 14 percent of all farmers in the United States, but by 2017 their numbers had shrunk to just 1.4 percent. I promised to push for funding to address the inequities, and soon after taking office, I introduced the Emergency Relief for Farmers of Color Act. After consulting with fellow lawmakers, though, we agreed that including the assistance in the pandemic relief bill would be a smoother and faster route to get the farmers the much-needed help, because the pandemic had illuminated and exacerbated their troubles. The American Rescue Plan Act included a total of $5 billion for Black and other minority farmers—$4 billion in debt relief and another $1 billion for technical assistance and training.

I was proud to help our government to finally do right by these farmers and deliver emergency relief to them. My hope was that the funds would help level the playing field a bit so that these men and women could begin the long process of recovering, not just from the struggles caused by the pandemic, but also from decades of unfair government policies and treatment. But before we could get even a dime of the money disbursed to them, conservative groups, one led by the far right adviser to Donald Trump, Stephen Miller, filed lawsuits, claiming reverse discrimination, and a federal judge blocked implementation of the provision. That was deeply disappointing and frustrating. Again, justice has been delayed for these farmers.

I am ever mindful that our nation's farmers have suffered greatly during the pandemic and that these have been desperate times for them. They saw profits evaporate as restaurants were shuttered during the pandemic, and worker shortages made it extremely difficult even to get their produce from their farms to the market. As Americans quarantined at home and drove less, farmers were negatively impacted by the reduced demand for biofuels and the grains used to produce them, particularly corn. In late March 2021, I toured southwest Georgia farms with my colleague Congressman Sanford Bishop and met with farmers and ranchers to discuss these and other issues. I will continue to advocate for all farmers and push for matters that are important to them. For example, I was able to secure at least $100 million in funding to expand broadband coverage across Georgia in the bipartisan infrastructure law. That will be crucial in rural areas to help increase Georgia farmers' competitiveness in the global economy. We can be a government that helps farmers in general while also being attentive and responsive to the particular history of discrimination that has created unique struggles for Black farmers and other farmers of color. We can do both. That is compassionate government. That is good government. Good government and good policies matter. My life is a testament to their power and possibilities. Everything that I have done and will do in this first term stems from this core belief.

The expansion of Medicaid to cover the working poor is good government. These hardworking men and women go to work every day, usually in service industries, earn too much to qualify for Medicaid under the traditional rules, but cannot afford private health insurance because real wages among lower- and middle-wage workers have been stagnant for decades. Under President Obama's Affordable Care Act, the federal government provided a path to close the insurance gap for those Americans by expanding Medicaid to them and covering the bulk of the costs. The federal government covered 100 percent of the costs for the newly insured in the first three years of the expansion, and its share gradually reduced to 90 percent thereafter. That means states could offer Medicaid to those Americans in the gap and after the third year and every year thereafter pay at most just 10 percent of the costs. But it was left to the states to decide whether to expand Medicaid in that way. My home state is among the twelve states that refused the expansion, leaving at least 4 million Americans in those states without coverage. Many of those citizens live in the South, where some state governments have failed to provide basic health-care coverage for their residents. In Georgia, an estimated 646,000 people fall in that insurance coverage gap.

That's why I've been fighting for the expansion of Medicaid in Georgia for years. In 2014, I protested at the statehouse in Georgia and even got arrested trying to push state lawmakers to do the right thing. In 2017, I traveled to Washington, D.C., as part of a multiracial, multireligious coalition who came to protest the GOP's attempt to repeal the Affordable Care Act and to bear witness as Congress prepared to pass the budget—the same budget that included $1.5 trillion in President Trump's tax cuts, much of it for the richest of the rich while making cuts to the Children's Health Insurance Program. I said in my speech that day, "A budget is not just a fiscal document. A national budget is a moral document. It lays bare who we think matters and who doesn't. It is a reflection of our values. Sadly, if this budget were an EKG, it would suggest that America has a heart problem."

We were a nation in need of moral surgery, in need of healing. As ordinary Americans, we could not do the surgery ourselves, but we had come to Washington, D.C., to get the room ready for work that only God could do. After our protest outside the front of the Capitol that day, we moved inside to the Rotunda and began to pray and sing. Capitol Police officers approached us and told us we were not allowed to pray and sing in the Rotunda. When we refused to stop, the officers warned us three times, as is their usual practice, and then arrested us. These days, when I am in Washington, I walk past that Rotunda regularly to get to my office, located just down the hall.

In my workaday life I have moved from agitator to legislator, but in my heart I am still an activist and pastor, fighting for Medicaid expansion, translating my protest into public policy, and standing up for the people I love inside the halls of their own government. So, in July 2021, I introduced, along with fellow senators Ossoff and

Tammy Baldwin of Wisconsin, the Medicaid Saves Lives Act, which would create a federal Medicaid-style program that offers coverage for those eligible Americans living in non-expansion states, like Georgia and Wisconsin. The act also includes a provision that would reduce uncompensated care costs and thus reduce the number of hospital and provider closures in those states. Georgia has seen eight hospitals close over the past decade for lack of paying customers, and all those facilities have been in rural communities. That is a significant issue for all who live in rural areas. Even if you don't need Medicaid and have plenty of money and great insurance, none of it matters in a medical emergency if you live in a rural area and the closest hospital is dozens of miles away. A hospital in your community where you can receive critical care can make all the difference in medical emergencies.

Politicians should not use the people as pawns in cynical political games. Public servants should actually serve. And I can think of no more noble cause than to ensure that the people, especially the working poor living in the wealthiest nation on the planet, have access to quality, affordable health care. It is part of the covenant we have with one another. The refusal of those twelve states to expand Medicaid and to leave so many of their citizens with no coverage and no hope is just bad policy. But policies are not just words on paper. They impact lives for better or worse. And real people are struggling and in some cases even dying unnecessarily because of politics. They are people like Lorie Davis, who lived with her husband, Bob, in Covington, Georgia, and worked as a trauma nurse at Grady Memorial Hospital. But when Lorie was diagnosed with pelvic adhesive disease, a condition that causes chronic pain, her suffering became so great that she had to leave her demanding job as a nurse. To help make ends meet for her family, she found work in the restaurant industry, but she was unable to maintain steady employment.

"She believed in working," I told my colleagues when I shared Lorie's story after introducing the legislation to expand Medicaid. "She understood the dignity of work. But while working, she could not afford health insurance. She made too much to qualify for Medicaid, but not enough to afford other insurance plans."

Lorie waited many years for her Social Security disability claim to be adjudicated, finally qualifying for benefits in 2017. Even then, though, she was unable to qualify for Medicaid because of her and Bob's combined marital income. This left Lorie in the coverage gap—unable to purchase coverage that was financially out of reach. So, like millions of Americans, she tried to survive without health insurance. She relied on her own medical training and on free clinics for treatment of her chronic condition. Imagine that: a trauma nurse who had cared for so many others, unable to receive the care she needed.

"As members of this body, we should be ashamed that in the richest nation in the world, a country with all of our resources, all of our medical technology, that some citizens would choose not to seek treatment—even when they know better—because they fear they cannot afford the price tag of lifesaving care," I said.

Lorie's symptoms worsened in August 2020, yet fearful of the costs she delayed seeking treatment. Her concerns about money left her unable to follow the advice she had undoubtedly given to many of her patients when she worked as a nurse: to seek treatment early. But her own inability to pay kept her away from doctors until she had no other choice. In September 2020, Lorie was admitted to the hospital with pneumonia, and while there she was diagnosed with lung cancer. She died on September 17, 2020.

Lorie is the human face of our public policy. "These are the tragic casualties of the games that politicians play," I told my colleagues. "As a senator who believes in health care as a human right, a sacred obligation, I refuse to stop fighting until Georgians, like Lorie Davis, have access to the care that they need—when they need it."

For every person who loses her life because she cannot afford health insurance, there are tens of thousands of others, surviving in that insurance gap, managing chronic health conditions the best they can. Cynthia English, a forty-six-year-old truck driver who lives in Albany, Georgia, is one of them. She suffers from diabetes and hypertension, but unable to afford health insurance and unable to qualify for Medicaid, she relies on the Samaritan Clinic in her hometown for health care. The name of that clinic certainly resonates with me as a minister, and I'm grateful for the lifesaving work their employees do. But the acts of a few Good Samaritans in a single clinic are not nearly enough to meet a need so great.

The state-level politicians in Georgia and elsewhere who keep refusing to expand Medicaid are taking the people's money and denying them health care, all while the people's taxes are subsidizing health care in other states. One of the many reasons I have supported Stacey Abrams for governor is I know she would insist that the Georgia legislature do the right thing.

• • •

I have had the honor of working on this issue and on others to help our government meet the needs of people, ordinary people, working people, poor people. But I look forward to heading home each weekend to be with my two children and to preach to the flock at Ebenezer. One of the toughest parts of my job in Washington is being away from Chloé and Caleb, whom I love with all my heart. Raising them is a blessing and a gift that I cherish every day. To see things anew, even the smallest of things, through their young eyes of wonderment, curiosity, and joy balances my life and slows me down enough to take it all in. Because I am away from them during the week, I am more intentional when I'm with them. Every moment matters. We spend time at home together playing games, reading, doing ordinary family things. We enjoy riding bikes on the trails— or more often, me pulling them on the trail in a child carrier behind my bike. When it's hot, they fall asleep, and I become the chauffeur. It must be nice to fall asleep anywhere, knowing somebody's got you. On Sundays, we worship together. And on Monday mornings, I get them ready for school and drop them off before heading to the airport and back to Washington to do it all again.

The children and I see one another and talk on FaceTime regularly during the week. But some days, I just want to be home in the same space with them for those sweet, simple moments—a tooth falling out, an extra star at school for good behavior, an extra hug. When I miss them, I remind myself that I am fighting for them and for all children. I am fighting so that they will forever have a home, a sustainable planet where they can breathe freely, and a vibrant and prosperous democracy where they can live freely. A country where they can flourish and grow into their full human potential and pass their gifts on to the next generation.

I was on the plane heading from Washington, D.C., to Atlanta for the Christmas break in 2021, when I noticed a handsome couple sitting in the row ahead of me on the opposite side. They recognized me, and we nodded and waved. When we landed, the couple waited around to chat with me. They introduced themselves, and the husband handed me a blank sheet of paper and asked me to autograph it for their one-year-old son. I'm still not quite accustomed to people asking me for an autograph, but I was honored that they wanted it and wrote a short note, signed it, and handed the paper back to them. The wife then handed me a note that she had written on the back of her airline ticket.

"Thank you! My family and I are big supporters of you," her note began. "We appreciate all that you've done for families. One thing that would be life-changing is student debt relief and forgiveness."

She went on to explain that she and her husband were 2012 and 2016 college graduates, and that she had borrowed $35,000 to complete her education. She said she has paid $20,000 but still owes another $30,000. "It feels endless and defeating," she wrote. "Please fight for all of us. It feels like a government authorized loan trap."

This is the kind of student loan stress that I hear from ordinary people everywhere I go. These are people who have done what they were advised to do as kids—stayed out of trouble, played by the rules, and attended college. But from the day they graduate, they are drowning in a sea of debt. I have heard horror stories about students graduating with six-figure debts with degrees in the humanities that didn't lead to financially commensurate careers. Outstanding college loans have surpassed credit card debt and auto loans to become the second-largest consumer debt after mortgages. Too many of our young people have to mortgage their future in order to have a chance for a future. As the first in my family to go to a four-year college, I was able to rely on Pell Grants and some federal student loans. After four degrees, I ended up with a manageable $30,000 in student loan debt, which I was able to pay off relatively quickly. But no student should have to mortgage their futures to get an education.

Of course, those who are hardest hit by the student loan debt crisis are families with less generational wealth. One proposal that has been heavily discussed in the Biden administration is wiping out the first $50,000 of federal student loan debt per borrower, which I strongly support. I even cosponsored a resolution in February 2021 urging President Biden to use his executive authority to do just that. That measure would be a real boost to our consumer economy, increase home ownership, spur entrepreneurial initiative and innovation from creative young people unburdened by debt, and go a long way toward narrowing the racial wealth gap. In December, I led thirteen of my colleagues in sending a letter to President Biden asking him to continue to waive the interest on student loans for the rest of the pandemic. Those waivers were first granted before I took office, and they are helping to relieve some of the students' financial burdens as they cope with the pandemic. It just makes sense to continue the relief for the duration of this national emergency. And it makes sense to address student debt in substantive, long-lasting ways.

We can help people who are confronting these issues. That is what good government can do, especially in this great country. So much is possible here. My life speaks to those possibilities. I remember the first time I visited the White House as a senator. I was there with leaders of the Congressional Black Caucus from the House side and Senator Cory Booker of New Jersey. I sat there quietly for a moment in awe that, given the start of my journey, I was sitting in the Oval Office with these powerful leaders, discussing how we make progress in this country for ordinary people and engaging President Biden on these issues. Every day that I go to work for the American people, I push to help America live up to its promise for all Americans, including those growing up in communities like the one where I grew up.

We have much work to do yet, even to live up to the promise embedded in our name: the *United* States of America. The postracial America that many hoped would follow the election of Barack Obama, America's first African American president, has not materialized. Instead, we retreated to familiar corners of division, seemingly far from the beloved community that Dr. King described. Suppressive voting rights laws threaten to disenfranchise voters of color. Police brutality continues to be driven largely by a fear of Black bodies. U.S. prisons are filled with a vastly disproportionate share of Black and brown inmates. The real wages of American workers, from Atlanta to Appalachia, have declined for decades, and they find themselves sharing less of the prosperity they create for others. To ignore these realities is to engage in a kind of delusion that keeps us spinning in place, instead of moving toward a more perfect union. This is our unfinished work.

I love our country. I love it enough to hold up a mirror so that we might see ourselves in all our beauty, complexity, and imperfection, and work to be better. The work starts with a basic question: Who do we want to be as a nation? Do we lean toward the hopeful, multiracial majority that showed up in Georgia, ready to move forward on January 5? Or do we fall back to the America that showed up on January 6, bitter, destructive, divisive? Reconciling those two Americas is the daunting challenge ahead. I choose the beloved community. That is the kind of world I want for my beautiful children and for yours. I do not believe that those who seek to divide us will have the last word. But that is left to us. We must put forth a vision of America that embraces all of us, all of our children. While I do this work to build the kind of world I want for my children, I know that they can thrive only to the extent that we build a world where other people's children also have the opportunity to thrive. In that sense, we must build together a more just society and a more humane, inclusive democracy. In a system bedeviled by pernicious schemes of voter suppression, we must insist that our democracy belongs not to the politicians and their sponsors but to the people.

With vision and courage, we *can* live up to the promise and the power of our name. We *can* take all of the broken and beautiful pieces of our complicated American story and weld them together in a new chapter of hope and possibilities. We the people are called to this moment. And as my dad used to say, it's time to get up, get ready, and put our shoes on. Together, we *can* make a way out of no way.

Acknowledgments

Everybody has a story. Scripture tells us that "We live our lives as a tale that is told" (Psalm 90:9 KJV). I am so grateful for those who have assisted me in telling mine as it relates to the larger American story.

First, I want to thank my mother, my siblings, and other family members for their remembrances of key moments in our family history, especially those that predate my birth. Our conversations have enriched both the book and our relationships as we have taken stock anew of the life we have built together.

My campaign and senate staff, including Mark Libell, Lawrence Bell, Jerid Kurtz, Quentin Fulks, Michael Brewer, Meredith Brasher, Meredith Lilly, Joshua Delaney, Annie Wang, Adam Magnus, Lauren Passalacqua, Stuart Guillory, Nicole Marquez, Jamari Torrence, and Brandon Gilkes, have been faithful compatriots with me in my improbable journey to the senate and in my work every day for the people of Georgia. Without them none of this would be possible and for them I am grateful.

Since 2005, I have been honored to serve as senior pastor of Ebenezer Baptist Church. I am grateful for the ministry team that serves alongside me as we bear witness to God's love and justice in the world. They have helped to create many of these stories and have helped to jog my memory so that they now live on the page. Many thanks to the entire staff and especially to my longtime executive assistant, Esther Harris; and to the church's executive pastor, the Reverend John Vaughn. Thanks to Richard DuCree and Andre Jones who have captured many key moments in my ministry in photographs and on video. Thank you, Ebenezer family, for giving me space to think, imagine, pray, push, agitate, and get in the kind of "good trouble" that makes for a more just and peaceful world. Since 1886, you've been making a way out of no way. You are indeed America's Freedom Church.

This project would not be possible without the incredible vision and skill of my book agent, Will Lippincott, and Lisa Frazier Page, world class professionals who have been with me from the beginning of this project. I'm especially thankful for Lisa's expert guidance and her thoughtful encouragement, which pushed me to explore my life story deeply in these pages. I feel like Virginia Smith "got it" from the first time we talked. She is an incredible editor and it has been a joy to work with her and the team at Penguin Random House. I thank the people of Georgia for giving me the honor of my life—serving and representing you in the United States

Senate. Last, but certainly not least, I thank my precious little children who share so much of their dad with others. They are indeed my reason to fight for the highest and the best our democracy has to offer.

All mistakes and omissions are mine.

All glory belongs to God.

Appendix 1

LET MY PEOPLE GO:
THE SCANDAL OF MASS INCARCERATION
IN THE LAND OF THE FREE

William Belden Noble Lecture

Harvard Memorial Church

October 16, 2019

Then the Lord said to Moses, "Go to Pharaoh and say
to him, 'Thus says the Lord: Let my people go, so that
they may worship me.'"

EXODUS 8:1

In the spring of 1968, Martin Luther King Jr. took his last stand
for freedom. In a very real sense, he was summoned to Memphis by
the sacrifice of two sanitation workers, Echol Cole and Robert
Walker, who were literally crushed to death in the back of a trash
truck where they sought shelter from a storm. They were there

because Black sanitation workers were prohibited from riding in the truck with their white counterparts. Viewed as disposable refuse, they could ride only on the back of the truck or in the compactor area. So the Black bodies of Echol Cole and Robert Walker were literally crushed by the vicious machinery of Jim Crow segregation. We should observe that this was four years after the passage of the 1964 Civil Rights Act and three years after the Voting Rights Act of 1965, the key legislative victories of the movement.

Yet, tragically, it was these crushed Black bodies, the latest blow in a long pattern of neglect and abuse, that finally gave fuel to the fledgling Memphis movement, triggering the radical spirit and action of the local Black churches and producing those historic and iconic signs, I AM A MAN. It is a sign of the oppressed that they must organize movements and carry out campaigns to affirm about themselves what ought to be obvious and secure for themselves what ought to be automatic. Said these sanitation workers whose hard yet noble labor secured human dignity for all, "I am a man." Negotiating the interstices of racial and gender oppression in the nineteenth century, Sojourner Truth asked, "Ain't I a woman?" Similarly, activists resisting police brutality and the deadly encounters between law enforcement officers and unarmed citizens as consequences of mass incarceration declare, "Black Lives Matter."

Those who retort, "No, All Lives Matter," manifestly miss the point. It is oppression itself that makes necessary movements to affirm what ought to be obvious; likewise, it is privilege itself that renders one blind to what ought to be obvious. One of the biggest obstacles to genuine human community is a glib, unreflective, and uncritical universalism. Justice demands the recognition that all lives are not imperiled in the same ways.

That is why a weary but committed Martin Luther King Jr. made his way to Memphis. He was there to stand with those who needed a movement, carrying signs bearing an inscription that was at once simple, sublime, and scandalous: I AM A MAN. A little over two months later, he would be slain by an assassin's bullet on the balcony of the Lorraine Motel. His last book, published a year earlier, was titled *Where Do We Go from Here: Chaos or Community?* I ask, "Where indeed?" Specifically, more than half a century after the Poor People's Campaign, where are the places that poor bodies and Black bodies are being crushed by the machinery of the state or the society at large, demanding the attention of the church and the larger faith community?

While recognizing the structural complexity of racism and its inextricable link to and participation in other constituent parts of hegemonic power, including sexism, classism, and militarism, I would argue that today mass incarceration is Jim Crow's most obvious descendant, and like its ancestor its dismantling would represent both massive social and infrastructural transformation and immeasurable transvaluative power in a society still steeped in the ideology of white supremacy. The ideology of white supremacy has created the massive infrastructure of the American carceral state. I argue that this massive and increasingly privatized infrastructure has in turn constructed its own distinct ideology.

And it is this ideology—the distorted, fear-based logic of the carceral state and its construal of blackness as dangerousness and guilt—that imperils Black bodies during routine traffic stops (Sandra Bland, Philando Castile), while running in the rain through one's own gated community (seventeen-year-old Trayvon Martin), while playing in a public park (twelve-year-old Tamir Rice), and while eating ice cream or playing video games with family members in the sanctuary of one's own home (Botham Jean, Atatiana Jefferson). Yet the deadly encounters between police and Black citizens so often in the headlines are as predictable as they are tragic. After all, they are but one manifestation of the massive infrastructure and insatiable appetite of a racialized carceral state. I submit that at root this is a spiritual problem, symptomatic of a sickness in the body politic.

Dr. King understood this. That is why when he, Joseph Lowery, and others formed the Southern Christian Leadership Conference in 1957, the organizational arm of his prophetic witness, their motto was not merely "To end segregation in America" or "To secure voting rights"; their motto was "To redeem the soul of America." That was their motto, focus, and theme. Yet again it is the soul of America that is in trouble.

The United States of America—the land of the free—is, by far, the mass incarceration capital of the world. Think about that. The land of the free, the shining city on the hill, shackles more people than any land in the world. Nobody even comes close in the rates of incarceration or even in the sheer numbers of people incarcerated. It is a scandal and a scar on the soul of America. That we are a nation that comprises 5 percent of the world's population and warehouses nearly 25 percent of the world's prison population is a scandal and a scar on the soul of America. That we lock up people awaiting trial and keep them there for weeks and months and years (remember Kalief Browder) not because they pose a threat to society but because they cannot afford to pay a bail bond is a scandal and a scar on the soul of America. That we criminalize poverty and penalize people for being poor is a scandal and a scar on the soul of America. That we have a greater percentage of our Black population in jails and prisons than did South Africa at the height of apartheid is a scandal and a scar on the soul of America. That in all of our large American cities as many as half of the young Black men are caught up somewhere in the matrix and social control of the criminal justice system and that Black men have been banished from our families, devastating generations of our families, is a scandal and a scar on the soul of America. These men and increasingly women then come out carrying the mark and stigma of "convicted felon" or "ex-felon" and are therefore confronted with all of the legalized barriers against which Martin Luther King Jr. and those who battled the old Jim Crow fought, including discrimination in housing, employment, voting, some professional licenses, public benefits, and student loans. It is a scandal and a scar on the soul of America.

Most of the Black men in America's jails and prisons today are charged with nonviolent drug-related offenses. They are casualties in America's war on drugs. At least, it was a war when the drug was crack and the bodies were Black and brown in places like Detroit, Baltimore, the South Side of Chicago, South Central L.A., certain communities in Atlanta. We had a *war* on drugs. But now that we are talking about opioids and meth and the faces of the human tragedy are white and suburban, suddenly we have a public health emergency, an opioid crisis. Two very different responses to the same problem.

Public health emergencies are addressed through doctors, public health officials, social workers, therapists, and clinics. Wars are prosecuted against enemy combatants who either are killed or become prisoners of war. In places as large as New York, entire communities may well experience daily the trauma of being subjected to "stop and frisk," the tools of a de facto occupation in a democratic republic that makes claims to certain constitutional guarantees like presumed innocence and due process. In places as small as Ferguson, citizen protests are met by military tanks and weapons of war on civilian streets. The truth is that there are a whole lot of people across racial, religious, class, cultural, and generational lines who are self-medicating in the midst of an American crisis— the deep, aching, spiritual void of a culture awash in the broken promises of an individualistic, consumerist impulse of acquisition that even reduces relationships to transactions and short-circuits the difficult but fulfilling work of real intimacy and the joy of genuine community. The data clearly show that Black people and white people use and sell drugs at remarkably similar rates. Yet Black people are 12 percent of the general population and over 50 percent of the prison population.

That is why Michelle Alexander has persuasively argued that the mass incarceration of tens of thousands of Black men for non-violent drug-related offenses and the lifelong consequences that result are constituent parts of "the New Jim Crow." Legally barred from the doors of entry to citizenship, symbolized in the right to vote, and denied access to ladders of opportunity and social upward mobility, those who have served their time in America's prisons or who plead guilty in exchange for little or no actual prison time are not part of a class, Alexander argues, but a permanent caste system. I agree. In theological terms, they are condemned to what I call eternal social damnation. Even in the face of heroic efforts to carve for oneself a path of redemption, ours is an exceedingly punitive system that routinely produces political pariahs and economic lepers, condemned, in a very real sense, to check a box on applications for employment and other applications reminiscent of the ancient biblical stigma "unclean."

There is no clearer example of America's unfinished business with the project of racial justice than the twenty-first-century caste system engendered by its prison-industrial complex. Moreover, I submit that there is no more significant scandal belying the moral credibility and witness of the American churches than their conspicuous silence as this human catastrophe has unfolded now for more than three decades. To be sure, scores of American churches have prison ministries and some even have reclamation ministries for formerly incarcerated individuals. But there is a vast difference between offering pastoral care and spiritual guidance to the incarcerated and formerly incarcerated and challenging, in an organized way, the public policies, laws, and policing practices that lead to the disproportionate incarceration of people of color in the first place. I submit that that is one of the most pressing moral issues of this moment. We need a national, multi-faith, multiracial movement to end the scourge of mass incarceration, the insatiable beast whose massive tentacles place Black children in choke holds and brown babies in cages on both sides of the border.

But how do you build an effective social movement, particularly among church persons, when the primary subjects of its advocacy are those stigmatized by the pejorative label "illegals," in the case of our Latinx sisters and brothers subjected to draconian tactics of immigration enforcement, whether they are citizens or not? How do you win public sympathy and support for "convicted felons"? It is one thing to stand up for Rosa Parks, whom Martin Luther King Jr. called "one of the most respected people in the Negro community." It is quite another to fight for the basic human dignity of persons whose entire humanity has been supplanted by a legal and moral stigma. In many instances, they may well bear real culpability for their condition.

Indeed, this is part of the conundrum posed by racial bias in the criminal justice system. In a world where ordinary Black people must still navigate every day the racial politics of respectability, bearing the burden of being, in the words of that old folk saying, "a credit to the race," those who find themselves caught up in the criminal justice system have not kept their side of the deal. If many outside the African American community view these young Black men who track through the courtrooms of every major American city every single day with fear and contempt, many within their own families and churches harbor feelings of disappointment, anger, and ambivalence. They are the ultimate outsiders, stigmatized for life as both "Black" and "criminal," two words that have long been interchangeable in the Western moral imagination.

Four hundred years after the arrival of more than twenty enslaved Africans in Jamestown, Virginia, the Black body remains the central text in the narrative of a complicated story called

America. For all who would understand who we Americans are and how we arrived, the Black body is essential reading. There is no American wealth without reference to Black people. Yet the Black body is viewed essentially as a problem, sitting at the center of what Gunnar Myrdal characterized in 1944 as the "American dilemma." Four hundred years later, formerly enslaved Black bodies and branded black bodies and lynched black bodies and raped black bodies and segregated Black bodies are now stopped, frisked, groped, searched, handcuffed, incarcerated, paroled, probated, released, but never emancipated Black bodies.

Like many, I have witnessed the human cost of this story and stigma, and I have felt its pain personally, experiencing it in my own family. I am the youngest of seven boys in my family. My brother Keith, who is just above me, is serving time right now in a federal prison. He was sentenced to life, his natural life, in 1997, as a first-time offender in a drug-related offense in which no one was killed and no one was physically hurt. In fact, because the entire crime scenario was created, concocted, and controlled by the federal authorities, no one got high. In this operation, no actual drugs ever hit the streets, and none were removed from the streets. My brother was sentenced to life. He is a veteran of the first Gulf War and has appointed himself as a model prisoner since his incarceration twenty-two years ago. It is the stigma of color and criminality that makes his story not as uncommon as one might think.

But no group is more stigmatized than those persons on death row. After years of steady decline and presumptive death by many criminologists, the death penalty reemerged, as part of a conservative backlash, in the years immediately following the civil rights movement. In a real sense, it is the final fail-safe of white supremacy, for the data clearly show that its use ensures that in the final analysis the lives of white people are to be regarded as more valuable than the lives of Black people. That is why the race of the victim, more than anything else, determines the likelihood that the punishment will be death by execution. And if the victim is white and the presumed perpetrator is African American, the symbolic power of condemning that cardinal trespass is every bit as important as ensuring that the actual African American who committed the offense is executed. That that is still true decades after the era of lynching became exceedingly clear to me a few years ago during my public advocacy for the death row inmate Troy Davis.

By the time I met Troy Davis and became involved with his case, both as pastor to him and his family and as a public advocate for the sparing of his life, he had been on death row for nearly twenty years, convicted in 1991 for the 1989 slaying of the Savannah, Georgia, police officer Mark Allen MacPhail. It was 2008 and we held the first of several rallies for him at Atlanta's historic Ebenezer Baptist Church, where I serve as senior pastor.

Davis's case had already gained national and international attention and brought together unlikely allies in the struggle to save his life. It embodied so clearly all that is wrong with America's deployment of the death penalty that even death penalty proponents, like William Sessions, former head of the FBI, and Bob Barr, a conservative Georgia congressman, stood in agreement with liberals like President Jimmy Carter and Congressman John Lewis against the execution of Troy Davis. The trial provided no physical evidence in support of Davis's conviction. No murder weapon,

DNA evidence, or surveillance tapes were ever produced, and in a trial based largely on eyewitness testimony, seven of the nine witnesses supporting the prosecution's case recanted or materially changed their testimony.

There was so much doubt surrounding this case that on three separate occasions Davis's execution was stayed within minutes of his death. One fall afternoon, I sat, in a pastoral visit, at his cell as he reflected on his life, its meaning, and his hope that somehow his story might be a bridge to a better future and a larger good. We talked. We prayed. We sat silently. We said goodbye.

Two days later, I stood in a prison yard with his family and hundreds of others one fall night, September 21, 2011, as Troy Davis was stretched out and strapped to a gurney, bearing an eerie resemblance to a crucifix, and executed in my name, as a citizen of the state of Georgia, by lethal injection.

In the years that I have continued to fight for Davis and others like him, for the soul of a nation scarred by the scandal of mass incarceration, and for the lives of young Black men like Trayvon Martin, who was tragically endangered and murdered by the stigma of blackness as criminality, I have often reminded myself that I preach each week in memory of a death row inmate convicted on trumped-up charges at the behest of religious authorities and executed by the state without the benefit of due process. The cross, the Roman Empire's method of execution reserved for subversives, is a symbol of stigma and shame. Yet the early followers of Jesus embraced the scandal of the cross, calling it the power of God. To tell that story is to tell the story of stigmatized human beings. To embrace the cross is to bear witness to the truth and power of God subverting human assumptions about truth and power, pointing beyond the tragic limits of a given moment toward the promise of the resurrection. It is to see what an imprisoned exile of a persecuted community saw as he captured in scripture the vision and hope of "a new heaven and a new earth."

That is why Ebenezer Baptist Church, spiritual home of Martin Luther King Jr., has been trying to find a way to faithfully and effectively bear witness to God's justice. This past summer, we organized a national, multiracial, multifaith conference focused on the collective work of dismantling mass incarceration by catalyzing the resources of people of faith and moral courage in a movement that operates at the local, state, and national levels. Our co-conveners were Auburn Theological Seminary in New York and the Temple, the oldest Jewish congregation in Atlanta. We are now at work for the long haul, and we have four objectives:

1. to train and equip pastors, rabbis, imams, and other faith leaders and their teams with practical tools for addressing their ministries to mass incarceration as a social justice issue in their local setting;

2. to identify and coalesce around a strategic legislative agenda at the local, state, and national levels;

3. to organize an interfaith network of partners focused on abolishing mass incarceration; and

4. to lay the groundwork for the development of a new media strategy for reframing the public understanding of the prison-industrial complex and its implications for public safety, quality of life, and so on.

But this national effort taken on in partnership with others builds upon years of advocacy and activism. Seeking to leverage our legacy for good work in the present rather than rest on the historic laurels of a glorious past, we have been busy addressing our ministry, particularly over the last several years, to a criminal justice system that crushes the poor in the incinerator of a biased system whose outcomes are too often more criminal than just. From time to time, we have gotten engaged as public advocates in certain cases; we have raised offerings and have partnered with celebrities like the rapper T.I. and the actor Mark Ruffalo (the Hulk) to bail poor people awaiting trial out of jail; and we raised our voices as part of a coalition of conscience that successfully persuaded the mayor and the council to end cash bail in the city of Atlanta. Moreover, Mayor Keisha Lance Bottoms has committed to closing the city jail and turning it into a youth center that invests in our future.

But much of our work has been focused on expungements (record restrictions). In 2016, we came together with other Fulton County officials to organize and host our very first expungement clinic, a one-stop shop in the church's banquet hall that cleared the arrest records of hundreds of citizens who had been arrested but never convicted. Like millions of Americans who have arrest records, they were either barred or limited in their employment options, rejected in their applications for housing, apartments, and other features of a prosperous and dignified life. These expungement events have been emancipation moments for people looking for a second chance.

I remember the very first one and the joy I felt as I walked into our sanctuary that Saturday morning and realized that almost everyone gathered that day had a record. But then I thought to my-self that in a real sense that's true every Sunday. None of us wants to be forever judged by our worst moment, and each of us has some record that cries out for grace and redemption. Some time after the first event, I was sitting in the chair at the barbershop. My barber was finishing my haircut, and I was rushing to get out of the chair to my next appointment when another patron walked up to me. He said, "Rev, that was a great event y'all had." I said, "What event?" He said, "The expungement event." I politely said, "Thank you," as I was trying to get to my next appointment. He said, "Rev! Wait. You don't understand. You cleared my record. A bad check charge from twenty years ago." I froze. He appeared to be in his late fifties, well dressed, and he looked so "respectable." He continued, "As a result, I've got a better job, my income has gone up, and my life is better." I congratulated him, shook his hand, and was headed for the door when he said, "Rev, wait. A young couple in my family had a baby that they did not have the means to raise. The baby was headed to foster care. But because I came to the church and some-body cleared my record, I was able to adopt my great-niece." The trajectory of two generations changed in one day.

I am glad. But I am also sad because he had never actually been convicted of anything! He had an arrest record. He was free. Yet for twenty years he had been bound by the massive tentacles of our prison-industrial complex. While helping people like him, it is that fundamental problem that we seek to address in a nation where nearly 30 percent of adults has a record. And now with a faith kit (www.endingmassincarceration.com) and a wonderful documen-tary film put together by our partners at Public Square Media, we are teaching other congregations to do the same. People of faith and moral courage should lead the charge and embrace the challenge of saying to a failed system, "Let my people go."

That is what God told Moses to tell Pharaoh. "Let my people go that they may worship me." Liberate them from human bondage so that they might blossom and live lives of human flourishing, lives that give glory to God rather than to human systems. Moses had a speech impediment. Yet God picked him. Moses had a record. Yet God picked him in spite of his record. Or, maybe God picked him because he had a record. God has a record of using people with a record.

Moses had a record: He slew an Egyptian. He killed a man. God had more in store for him.

Joseph had a record: Long before a Central Park case and a ruthless prosecutor, there was Potiphar's wife. Joseph was thrown in prison, but he held on to his dreams.

The Three Hebrew Boys had a record. And they were sentenced to death for an act of civil disobedience.

Daniel was charged, convicted, and thrown in the lions' den.

John was imprisoned on an island called Patmos, the Rikers Island of that day. There he saw a new heaven and a new earth.

Jesus had a record: Not surprising, given his start. Born in a barrio called Bethlehem. Smuggled as an undocumented immigrant into Egypt. Raised in a ghetto called Nazareth. But he came saying, "The Spirit of the Lord is upon me."

They brought him up on trumped-up charges. Convicted him without the benefit of due process.

Marched him up Golgotha's hill.

Executed him on a Roman cross.

Buried him in a borrowed tomb.

But he was so powerful that he turned the scandal of the cross into an enduring symbol of victory over evil and injustice, and his movement was so contagious that he got off the cross and got in our hearts.

He is my redeemer and liberator, and in his name and in the name of all that is good and just and righteous and true, we must stand together, fight together, walk together, organize together, vote together, pray together, stay together, and say together, "Let my people go!"

Appendix 2

MAIDEN SPEECH ON THE SENATE FLOOR
March 17, 2021

Mr. President, before I begin my formal remarks, I want to pause to condemn the hatred and violence that took eight precious lives last night in metropolitan Atlanta. I grieve with Georgians, with Americans, with people of love all across the world. This unspeakable violence visited largely upon the Asian community is one that causes all of us to recommit ourselves to the way of peace and active peace that prevents these kinds of tragedies from happening in the first place. We pray for these families.

Mr. President, I rise here today as a proud American and as one of the newest members of the Senate—in awe of the journey that has brought me to these hallowed halls and with an abiding sense of reverence and gratitude for the faith and sacrifices of ancestors who paved the way.

I am a proud son of the great state of Georgia, born and raised in Savannah, a coastal city known for its cobblestone streets and verdant town squares. Towering oak trees, centuries old and covered in gray Spanish moss, stretch from one side of the street to the other, bend and beckon the lover of history and horticulture to this city by the sea. I was educated at Morehouse College, and I still serve in the pulpit of the Ebenezer Baptist Church, both in Atlanta, the cradle of the civil rights movement. And so like those oak trees in Savannah, my roots go down deep and they stretch wide in the soil of Waycross, Georgia, and Burke County, and Screven County. In a word, I am Georgia. A living example and embodiment of its history and its hope, of its pain and promise, the brutality and possibility.

Mr. President, at the time of my birth, Georgia's two senators were Richard B. Russell and Herman E. Talmadge, both arch segregationists and unabashed adversaries of the civil rights movement. After the Supreme Court's landmark *Brown v. Board* ruling outlawing school segregation, Talmadge warned that "blood will run in the streets of Atlanta." Senator Talmadge's father, Eugene Talmadge, former governor of our state, had famously declared, "The South loves the Negro in his place, but his place is at the back door." When once asked how he and his supporters might keep Black people away from the polls, he picked up a scrap of paper and wrote a single word on it: "pistols."

Yet there is something in the American covenant—in its charter documents and its Jeffersonian ideals—that bends toward freedom. And led by a preacher and a patriot named King, Americans of all races stood up. History vindicated the movement that sought to bring us closer to our ideals, to lengthen and strengthen the cords of our democracy, and I now hold the seat—the Senate seat— where Herman E. Talmadge sat.

And that's why I love America. I love America because we always have a path to make it better, to build a more perfect union. It is the place where a kid like me who grew up in public housing, first college graduate in my family, can now stand as a United States senator. I had an older father; he was born in 1917. Serving in the army during World War II, he was once asked to give up his seat to a young teenager while wearing his soldier's uniform, they said "making the world safe for democracy." But he was never bitter. And by the time I came along, he had already seen the arc of change in our country. And he maintained his faith in God, and in his family, and in the American promise, and he passed that faith on to his children.

My mother grew up in Waycross, Georgia. You know where that is? It's *way* cross Georgia. And like a lot of Black teenagers in the 1950s, she spent her summers picking somebody else's tobacco and somebody else's cotton. But because this is America, the eighty-two-year-old hands that used to pick somebody else's cotton went to the polls in January and picked her youngest son to be a United States senator. Ours is a land where possibility is born of democracy. A vote, a voice, a chance to help determine the direction of the country and one's own destiny within it. Possibility born of democracy.

That's why this past November and January, my mom and other citizens of Georgia grabbed hold of that possibility and turned out in record numbers, 5 million in November, 4.4 million in January.

Far more than ever in our state's history. Turnout for a typical run-off doubled. And the people of Georgia sent their first African American senator and first Jewish senator, my brother Jon Ossoff, to these hallowed halls.

But then what happened? Some politicians did not approve of the choice made by the majority of voters in a hard-fought election in which each side got the chance to make its case to the voters. And rather than adjusting their agenda, rather than changing their message, they are busy trying to change the rules. We are witnessing right now a massive and unabashed assault on voting rights unlike anything we've ever seen since the Jim Crow era. This is Jim Crow in new clothes.

Since the January election, some 250 voter suppression bills have been introduced by state legislatures all across the country—from Georgia to Arizona, from New Hampshire to Florida—using the Big Lie of voter fraud as a pretext for voter suppression. The same Big Lie that led to a violent insurrection on this very Capitol—the day after my election. Within twenty-four hours, we elected Georgia's first African American and Jewish senators, hours later the Capitol was assaulted. We see in just a few precious hours the tension very much alive in the soul of America. And the question before all of us at every moment is, what will we do to push us in the right direction?

And so politicians driven by that Big Lie aim to severely limit and, in some cases, eliminate automatic and same-day voter registration, mail-in and absentee voting, and early voting and weekend voting. They want to make it easier to purge voters from the voting roll altogether. As a voting rights activist, I've seen up close just how draconian these measures can be. I hail from a state that purged 200,000 voters from the roll one Saturday night—in the middle of the night. We know what's happening here: some people don't want some people to vote.

I was honored on a few occasions to stand with our hero and my parishioner, John Lewis. I was his pastor, but I'm clear he was my mentor. On more than one occasion we boarded buses together after Sunday church services as part of our Souls to the Polls program, encouraging the Ebenezer Church family and communities of faith to participate in the democratic process. Now, just a few months after Congressman Lewis's death, there are those in the Georgia legislature, some who even dared to praise his name, that are now trying to get rid of Sunday Souls to the Polls, making it a crime for people who pray together to get on a bus together in order to vote together. I think that's wrong. Matter of fact, I think that a vote is a kind of prayer for the kind of world we desire for ourselves and for our children. And our prayers are stronger when we pray together.

To be sure, we have seen these kinds of voter suppression tactics before. They are a part of a long and shameful history in Georgia and throughout our nation. But refusing to be denied, Georgia citizens and citizens across our country braved the heat and the cold and the rain, some standing in line for five hours, six hours, ten hours, just to exercise their constitutional right to vote. Young people, old people, sick people, working people, already underpaid, forced to lose wages, to pay a kind of poll tax while standing in line to vote.

And how did some politicians respond? Well, they are trying to make it a crime to give people water and a snack as they wait in lines that are obviously being made longer by their draconian actions. Think about that. Think about that. They are the ones making the lines longer—through these draconian actions. And then they want to make it a crime to bring Grandma some water while she's waiting in a line that they're making longer! Make no mistake. This is democracy in reverse. Rather than voters being able to pick the politicians, the politicians are trying to cherry-pick their voters. I say this cannot stand.

And so I rise, Mr. President, because that sacred and noble idea—one person, one vote—is being threatened right now. Politicians in my home state and all across America, in their craven lust for power, have launched a full-fledged assault on voting rights. They are focused on winning at any cost, even the cost of the democracy itself. And I submit that it is the job of each citizen to stand up for the voting rights of every citizen. And it is the job of this body to do all that it can to defend the viability of our democracy.

That's why I am a proud co-sponsor of the For the People Act, which we introduced today. The For the People Act is a major step in the march toward our democratic ideals, making it easier, not harder, for eligible Americans to vote by instituting commonsense, pro-democracy reforms like

- establishing national automatic voter registration for every eligible citizen, and allowing all Americans to register to vote online and on Election Day;

- requiring states to offer at least two weeks of early voting, including weekends, in federal elections—keeping Souls to the Polls programs alive;
- prohibiting states from restricting a person's ability to vote absentee or by mail;
- and preventing states from purging the voter rolls based solely on unreliable evidence like someone's voting history, something we've seen in Georgia and other states in recent years.

And it would end the dominance of big money in our politics and ensure our public servants are there serving the public.

Amidst these voter suppression laws and tactics, including partisan and racial gerrymandering, and in a system awash in dark money and the dominance of corporatist interests and politicians who do their bidding, the voices of the American people have been increasingly drowned out and crowded out and squeezed out of their own democracy. We must pass For the People so that the people might have a voice. Your vote is your voice, and your voice is your human dignity.

But not only that, we must pass the John Lewis Voting Rights Advancement Act. Voting rights used to be a bipartisan issue. The last time the voting rights bill was reauthorized was 2006. George W. Bush was president, and it passed this chamber 98–0. But then, in 2013, the Supreme Court rejected the successful formula for supervision and preclearance contained in the 1965 Voting Rights Act. They asked Congress to fix it. That was nearly eight years ago, and the American people are still waiting. Stripped of protections, voters in states with a long history of voter discrimination and voters in many other states have been thrown to the winds.

We Americans have noisy and spirited debates about many things. And we should. That's what it means to live in a free country. But access to the ballot ought to be nonpartisan. I submit that there should be one hundred votes in this chamber for policies that will make it easier for Americans to make their voices heard in our democracy. Surely, there ought to be at least sixty in this chamber who believe, as I do, that the four most powerful words uttered in a democracy are "the people have spoken"; therefore, we must ensure that all of the people can speak.

But if not, we must still pass voting rights. The right to vote is preservative of all other rights. It is not just another issue alongside other issues. It is foundational. It is the reason why any of us has the privilege of standing here in the first place. It is about the covenant we have with one another as an American people. *E pluribus unum*, out of many, one. It above all else must be protected.

So let's be clear. I'm not here today to spiral into the procedural argument regarding whether the filibuster in general has merits or has outlived its usefulness. I'm here to say that this issue is bigger than the filibuster. I stand before you saying that this issue—access to voting and preempting politicians' efforts to restrict voting—is so fundamental to our democracy that it is too important to be held hostage by a Senate rule, especially one historically used to restrict the expansion of voting rights. It is a contradiction to say we must protect minority rights in the Senate while refusing to protect minority rights in the society. Colleagues, no Senate rule should overrule the integrity of our democracy, and we must find a way to pass voting rights whether we get rid of the filibuster or not.

And so as I close—and nobody believes a preacher when he says "as I close"—let me say that I, as a man of faith, I believe that democracy is the political enactment of a spiritual idea: the sacred worth of all human beings, the notion that we all have within us a spark of the divine and a right to participate in the shaping of our destiny. Reinhold Niebuhr was right: "[Humanity's] capacity for justice makes democracy possible; but [humanity's] inclination to injustice makes democracy necessary."

John Lewis understood that and was beaten on a bridge defending it. Amelia Boynton, like so many women not mentioned nearly enough, was gassed on that same bridge. A white woman named Viola Liuzzo was killed. Medgar Evers was murdered in his own driveway. Schwerner, Chaney, and Goodman, two Jews and an African American standing up for that sacred idea of democracy, also paid the ultimate price. And we in this body would be stopped and stymied by partisan politics? Short-term political gain? Senate procedure? I say let's get this done no matter what. I urge my colleagues to pass these two bills. Strengthen and lengthen the cords of our democracy, secure our credibility as the premier voice for freedom-loving people and democratic movements all over the world, and win the future for all of our children.

Mr. President, I yield the floor.

Notes

Chapter One: Boys Like Us

2 **ten current and former officers:** Anne Hart, "Mistakes Of Fallen Cops Teach Lessons: The Anniversary of the Arrest of 11 Area Officers Serves as Reminder of the Tests of the Job," *Savannah Morning News*, September 10, 2002, mapinc.org/drugnews/v02/n1699/a05.html.

3 **football at Johnson High School:** "History of Sol C. Johnson High School," Savannah-Chatham Public Schools, https://web.archive.org /web/20090813111235/http://www.savannah.chatham.k12.ga.us /Schools/High+Schools/Johnson+High+School/History+of+Sol+C.+Jo hnson+High+School.htm.

7 **the Harvard University sociologist:** William Julius Wilson, *When Work Disappears: The World of the New Urban Poor* (New York: Alfred A. Knopf, 1996).

8 **The headline screamed:** As per Walter J. Fraser's *Savannah in the New South: From the Civil War to the Twenty-First Century* (Columbia, SC: The University of South Carolina Press, 2018), an article by Keith Paul, "Busted Trust," was published in *Savannah Morning News* on Sept. 11, 1997.

Chapter Two: Close yet So Far

21 **Named for a Confederate officer:** "John Holbrook Estill Indenture and Statement," Georgia Historical Society, accessed Sept. 4, 2021, ghs.ga lileo.usg.edu/ghs/view?docId=ead/MS%200238-ead.xml.

21 **fifty-two miles north:** "Welcome to the Town of Estill," Town of Estill, South Carolina, accessed Sept. 4, 2020, townofestill.sc.gov.

44 **book called *The Spirituals:*** James H. Cone, *The Spirituals and the Blues: An Interpretation* (Maryknoll, NY: Orbis Books, 1991).

44 **book titled *For My People:*** James H. Cone, *For My People: Black Theology and the Black Church* (Maryknoll, NY: Orbis Books, 2012).

44 **a small anthology called *Best Black Sermons:*** William M. Philpot, *Best Black Sermons* (Valley Forge, PA: Judson Press, 1972).

Chapter Three: Becoming a Morehouse Man

54 **King first read Henry David Thoreau's essay:** Martin Luther King Jr., "Morehouse College," in *The Autobiography of Martin Luther King Jr.*, ed. Clayborne Carson (New York: Warner Books, 1998).

54 **"By all measuring rods":** Martin Luther King Jr., "The Purpose of Education," originally published by the *Maroon Tiger* in 1947, reprinted by *The Seattle Times*, 2017, projects.seattletimes.com/mlk /words-education.html.

54 ***Disturbed About Man:*** Benjamin E. Mays, *Disturbed About Man* (Richmond: John Knox Press, 1969).

57 **The student body had jumped:** Jacqueline Trescott, "The Men and the Mystique of Morehouse," *Washington Post*, Nov. 9, 1987.

57 **"Over the heads of her students":** Trescott, "The Men and the Mystique of Morehouse."

58 **Dean Carter, who is also a religion professor:** Carter, interview, Sept. 9, 2020.

61 **Morehouse's first location:** "Our History," Friendship Baptist Church, Atlanta, Georgia, last modified 2019, fbcatlanta.org/who-we-are /about/.

Chapter Four: New York State of Mind

78 **his recently published book:** James H. Cone, *Martin & Malcolm & America: A Dream or a Nightmare* (New York: Orbis Books, 1991).

81 **She was the first female pastor:** "Minister: Rev. Cathlin Baker," First Congregational Church of West Tisbury, accessed Aug. 30, 2020, wtcongregationalchurch.org/staff.

81–82 **in the church's 335-year history:** "First Congregational Church of West Tisbury," Calendar, *Vineyard Gazette*, accessed Aug. 30, 2021, calendar.vineyardgazette.com/first_congregational_church_of_west_tisbury_230#.YdWWNmjMJPY.

83 **story of his grandmother:** Mary E. Goodwin, "Racial Roots and Religion: An Interview with Howard Thurman," genius.com/Mary-e-goodwin-racial-roots-and-religion-an-interview-with-howard-thurman-annotated.

84 **and was found guilty:** These issues ultimately split the UMC. Megan Fowler, "Why Congregations Aren't Waiting to Leave the United Methodist Church," *Christianity Today*, July 16, 2021, christianitytoday.com/news/2021/july/umc-leave-church-methodist-split-lgbt-conference-protocol.html.

85 **Aristide had been a Catholic priest:** "Factbox: Aristide—a Man of Charisma and Controversy," Reuters, Feb. 17, 2011, reuters.com/article/us-haiti-aristide-fb/factbox-aristide-a-man-of-charisma-and-controversy-idUSTRE71G6HP20110217.

88 **one of just two African Americans:** The other African American congressman who served with Powell was William Levi Dawson, representing a Chicago district from 1943 until his death while in office in 1970. "Powell, Adam Clayton, Jr.," History, Art & Archives, U.S. House of Representatives, history.house.gov/People/Listing/P/POWELL,-Adam-Clayton,-Jr--(P000477)/.

90 **The protests spread to other cities:** Mireya Navarro, "Tobacco Companies Find Harlem Wary," *New York Times*, Aug. 8, 1990.

91 **remove liquor and cigarette advertisements:** Stephanie Strom, "Billboard Owners Switching, Not Fighting," *New York Times*, April 4, 1990, nytimes.com/1990/04/04/nyregion/billboard-owners-switching-not-fighting.html.

Chapter Five: Stepping Out on My Own

99 **Reverend Porter's image is immortalized:** "Porter, John Thomas," Martin Luther King Jr. Research and Education Institute, Stanford University, accessed Oct. 5, 2020, kinginstitute.stanford.edu/encyclopedia/porter-john-thomas.

100 **one of his most formative examples:** "Born to Teach, Born to Lead," Profiles in Success, accessed Oct. 5, 2020, profilesinsuccess.com/pro file/freeman-hrabowski.

107 **Douglas Memorial was born in rebellion:** Miss Hale, "Devoted Dissidents: The Black Feminist Founding of Douglas Memorial Community Church, 1925–1948" (master's thesis, Morgan State University, 2002), proquest.com/openview/026d5b4859ac13b8f9f5fdc6cc12ad18/1?pq-origsite=gscholar&cbl=18750&diss=y.

114 **National Black Leadership Commission on AIDS:** "Debra Fraser-Howze," D. Fraser Associates, accessed Oct. 25, 2020, dfraserassociates.com/our-team.

115 **AIDS was the second-leading cause:** Jonathan Bor, "Mayor Declares an AIDS 'State of Emergency,'" *Baltimore Sun*, Dec. 3, 2002, baltimoresun.com/news/bs-xpm-2002-12-03-0212030156-story.html.

115 **O'Malley, declared a state of emergency:** Bor, "Mayor Declares an AIDS 'State of Emergency.'"

CHAPTER SIX: SPIRIT OF THE KINGS

121 **Adam Daniel Williams assumed the pastorate:** "Our History," Ebenezer Baptist Church, accessed Oct. 1, 2021, ebenezeratl.org/our-history/.

121 **The son of slaves:** "Williams, Adam Daniel (A.D.)," Martin Luther King Jr. Research and Education Institute, Stanford University, accessed Oct. 1, 2021, kinginstitute.stanford.edu/encyclopedia/williams-adam-daniel-d.

121 **who was one of the pioneers:** Martin Luther King Jr. Papers Project, Stanford University, accessed Oct. 1, 2021, kinginstitute.stanford.edu/sites/mlk/files/publications/vol1intro.pdf.

121 **Atlanta race riot of 1906:** King Papers Project.

123 **King officially changed his name:** The Reverend Martin Luther King Sr., *Daddy King: An Autobiography* (Boston: Beacon Press, 1980), 78.

124 **In 1939, King senior pushed:** King Papers Project.

125 **"I could see he was confused":** King, *Daddy King*, 99.

126 **"It took courage to call":** Taylor Branch, "How Kennedy Won the Black Vote: A Call to Coretta King Brought Groundswell of Support," *Los Angeles Times*, Dec. 15, 1988.

126–127 **"take off your Nixon buttons":** Branch, "How Kennedy Won the Black Vote."

127 **In the previous presidential election:** Branch, "How Kennedy Won the Black Vote."

128 **It was a regular Sunday morning service:** *Chenault v. State*, 234 Ga. 216 (1975).

129 **A member immediately placed a call:** "Rev. Dr. Joseph L. Roberts," interview by *The Historymakers*, Sept. 14, 2007, video, da.thehistory makers.org/story/633425.

130 **"Now it'll be a dog's breakfast":** Roberts, interview.

130 **"He's not even a Baptist":** Roberts, interview.

131 **"Run for what?" King asked:** King, *Daddy King*, 193.

132 **Carter won the presidency:** "How Groups Voted in 1976," Roper Center for Public Opinion Research, ropercenter.cornell.edu/how-groups -voted-1976.

133 **Johnson, who had served in the Georgia Senate:** Howell Raines, "Revolution in South: Blacks at the Polls and in Office," *New York Times*, April 3, 1978.

CHAPTER SEVEN: PUTTING ON MY OWN SHOES

143 **The historic storm overwhelmed:** "Hurricane Katrina: A Nation Still Unprepared," Special Report of the Committee on Homeland Security and Governmental Affairs, 2006, congress.gov/109/crptsrpt322 /CRPT-109srpt322.pdf.

143 **100,000 of whom had evacuated to Atlanta:** Maria Godoy, "Tracking the Katrina Diaspora: A Tricky Task," NPR, Aug. 2006, legacy.npr .org/news/specials/katrina/oneyearlater/diaspora/index.html.

144 **Before the storm, Black residents:** "Protesters Call for New Orleans Election Delay," NBC News, April 1, 2006, nbcnews.com/id/wbna 12113682.

146 **his final birthday in that room:** Lily Rothman, "See Poignant Footage from Martin Luther King Jr.'s Final Birthday Party," *Time*, updated April 12, 2013, time.com/5221247/martin-luther-king-birthday-1968/.

151 **doctorate at Boston University:** "Boston University," Martin Luther King Jr. Research and Education Institute, Stanford University, accessed Oct. 25, 2020, kinginstitute.stanford.edu/encyclopedia/boston -university.

157 **run for governor in 2010:** "Thurbert E. Baker," *Ballotpedia*, accessed Jan. 4, 2022, ballotpedia.org/Thurbert_E._Baker.

167 **join your voices:** Barack Obama, "Ebenezer Baptist Church Address, Delivered 20 January 2008," American Rhetoric Online Speech Bank, last updated Jan. 6, 2022, americanrhetoric.com/speeches/baracko bama/barackobamaebenezerbaptist.htm.

CHAPTER EIGHT: MAKING HISTORY

176–177 **Since 1975, large southern cities:** Richard Fausset, "Diversity Rises in Georgia, with Whites Making Up Only Half the State," *New York Times*, Aug. 12, 2021, nytimes.com/2021/08/12/us/georgia-white -population.html.

177 **northern cities have continued to see:** Charles Blow, "Chocolate Chip Cities," *New York Times*, Aug. 22, 2021, nytimes.com/2021/08/22 /opinion/black-population-american-cities.html.

182 **Abrams explained that the demographics:** Abrams explained this during a one-on-one conversation with me, but she would discuss and write about it publicly in later years. Here is one example: Stacey Abrams, "Stacey Abrams on the Urgency of Voter Registration and How It Became a Focus of Her Political Career," *Lit Hub*, June 17, 2020, lithub .com/stacey-abrams-on-the-urgency-of-voter-registration/.

184 **register more than 200,000 new voters:** Abrams tweeted, "I led New Georgia Project to register 200,000 voters as part of this effort." Stacey Abrams (@staceyabrams), Twitter, Dec. 14, 2017, 10:32 a.m.

184 **a narrow fifty-five-thousand-vote margin:** Tim Craig and Vanessa Williams, "As Stacey Abrams Enters Governor's Race, Georgia Becomes a Key 2022 Battleground," *Washington Post*, Dec. 4, 2021, wash ingtonpost.com/national/stacey-abrams-brian-kemp-faceoff/2021/12 /04/441de08a-5464-11ec-8927-c396fa861a71_story.html.

189 **the World Health Organization (WHO) declared:** "CDC Museum COVID-19 Timeline," Centers for Disease Control and Prevention, accessed Dec. 15, 2021, cdc.gov/museum/timeline/covid19.html.

193 **Rayshard Brooks was sleeping in his car:** Christina Maxouris, "Rayshard Brooks Was Killed a Day Before He Planned to Celebrate His Daughter's Birthday," CNN, June 15, 2020, cnn.com/2020/06/14/us /rayshard-brooks-atlanta-shooting/index.html.

198 **Former Dream star Angel McCoughtry:** Candace Buckner, "WNBA Players Helped Oust Kelly Loeffler from the Senate. Will She Last in the League?" *Washington Post*, January 7, 2021, washingtonpost .com/sports/2021/01/07/wnba-loeffler-warnock-senate-atlanta -dream/.

Chapter Nine: Fighting for Our Lives

209 **Never forget this day:** "Transcript of Trump's Speech at Rally Before US Capitol Riot," AP News, Jan. 13, 2021, apnews.com/article/election-2020-joe-biden-donald-trump-capitol-siege-media-e79eb516461 3d6718e9f4502eb471f27.

212 **I was among the fifty-seven senators:** "Trump's Second Impeachment: How the Senate Voted," *New York Times*, Feb. 13, 2021, nytimes.com /interactive/2021/02/13/us/politics/senate-impeachment-live-vote .html.

213 **a draconian new voting law:** Faith Karimi, "It's Now Illegal in Georgia to Give Food and Water to Voters in Line," CNN, March 26, 2021, cnn.com/2021/03/26/politics/georgia-voting-law-food-drink-ban-trnd /index.html.

217 **By the end of January 2021:** "National Data: Deaths," COVID Tracking Project at *The Atlantic*, accessed Jan. 3, 2022, covidtracking.com /data/national/deaths.

218 **Their dwindling numbers tell the tale:** "Timeline: Black Farmers and the USDA, 1920 to Present," Environmental Working Group, accessed Jan. 3, 2022, ewg.org/research/black-farmer-usda-timeline/.

Appendix 1: Let My People Go

241 **the ancient biblical stigma "unclean":** See David P. Wright's discussion of "unclean and clean" in the Old Testament and Hans Hübner's discussion of the same topic in the New Testament in *The Anchor Bible Dictionary*, ed. David Noel Freedman (New York: Doubleday, 1992), 6:729–45. Among the many examples of Jesus's radical confrontation with the religion and politics of uncleanness are Mark 2:15–17 and Luke 15:1–2.

241 **some even have reclamation ministries:** See Glorya Askew and Gayraud Wilmore, eds., *Reclamation of Black Prisoners: A Challenge to the African American Church* (Atlanta: ITC Press, 1992).

242 **"one of the most respected people":** Martin Luther King Jr., *Stride Toward Freedom: The Montgomery Story* (San Francisco: Harper & Row, 1958), 44.

244 **the race of the victim:** See Dale S. Recinella, *The Biblical Truth About America's Death Penalty* (Boston: Northeastern University Press, 2004), chapter 18.

244 **By the time I met Troy Davis:** Jen Marlowe and Martina Davis-Correia, *I Am Troy Davis*, with Troy Anthony Davis (Chicago: Haymarket Books, 2013).

Index

Abernathy, Ralph, 66, 126–27
Abrams, Stacey, 181–84, 188–89
Abyssinian Baptist Church, 75,
  87–94, 122
Abyssinian Development Corporation,
  92–93
Affordable Care Act, 220, 221
AIDS Memorial Quilt, 112
Alexander, Michelle, 163, 165
Alford, Lamar, 61
Ali, Muhammad, 134
"The American Dream" speech
  (King), 59
American Rescue Plan,
  217–18
Amico, Sarah Riggs, 200
apartheid, 53
Arbery, Ahmaud, 193
Aristide, Jean-Bertrand, 85
Atlanta department store desegregation
  protests, 125–26
Atlanta Dream, 198–99
Atlanta race riots of 1906, 121
Atlanta Workforce Development
  Agency, 169

Baker, Cathlin, 81–82, 202
Baker, Thurbert, 156–57
Baldwin, Tammy, 221–22
Baltimore, 115–16
Baptists, 40–41, 43, 45
Barber, William, 180
Barr, Bob, 159
Bascom, Marion C., 108, 122
Beasley, Joe, 12
Bell, Lawrence, 174, 175–76, 188
beloved community, 27, 58, 120, 229
Benedict XVI, Pope, 159
Bennett, Lerone, Jr., 57
Benton, Wandetta, 49, 202
B.E.S.T. Academy, 174
Best Black Sermons, 44
Bethany Baptist Church, 74
Biden, Joe, 197, 201, 211
Big Lie, 209
Birth Month Clubs, 127
Bishop, Sanford, 219
Black church freedom movement, 83–84
Black farmers, 217–19
Black Lives Matter movement, 192
Black social gospel, 121

black theology, 44
Bland, Sandra, 193
Blige, Mary J., 201
Bloody Sunday, 70
Bond, Julian, 57, 175
Bonhoeffer, Dietrich, 93–94
Booker, Cory, 228
Boone, Glenda, 146
Boykin, Edward, 128–29
Braun, Carol Moseley, 174
Braxton, Brad, 108
Brinson, Albert, 175
broadband coverage, 219
Brooke, Edward, 174
Brooks, James Alfonso, 29–31
Brooks, Lucinda Armstrong,
    29–31, 154
Brooks, Rayshard, 193–95
Brown v. Board of Education, 50
Bryant, John Hope, 169
Bumpurs, Eleanor, 95
Bush, George W., 197
Butler, Mable, 32
Butts, Calvin O., III, 15, 75, 76, 90–91,
    93, 105, 113, 120, 154, 155, 173
Butts, Patricia, 75–76

Callahan, Leslie D., 81
Calvary Temple, 42
Campbell, Andrew, 63–64
"Caravan of Love" (song), 148
Carter, Harold, A., Jr., 108
Carter, Jason, 178
Carter, Jimmy, 131–32, 159
Carter, Lawrence E., 58–61, 66–67, 154
Casey Family Programs, 169
Center for Working Families, Inc., 169
Chambliss, Saxby, 177
Chapel Assistants, 64–65
Chappelle, Dave, 150
Chenault, Marcus Wayne, Jr., 129
children, investing in, 88–89
Children's Health Insurance
    Program, 221
"Churchmen, Church Martyrs: The
    Activist Ecclesiologies of Dietrich
    Bonhoeffer and Martin Luther
    King Jr." (Warnock), 93–94

"Civil Disobedience" (Thoreau), 54
civil rights movement, 41–42, 70, 99,
    122, 125–27, 175
Clayton, Xernona, 147, 150
Clinton, Bill, 197
Clinton, Hillary, 166, 167
CNN, 204
Cochran, Johnnie, 11, 15–16
Coleman, Frank, 49
Coleman, Jeffrey, 21, 33, 49, 202
Coleman, Keith, 2–4
    Army service of, 5, 8
    arrest and prosecution of, 2, 8–10,
        12–13
    at Johnson High School, 3–4
    in prison, 15–17
    release from prison, 195–96
    sentencing of, 13
Coleman, Leon, 49
Coleman, Robin, 16
Coleman, Terry, 18, 49
Coleman, Zoé, 16
college affordability, 55–56
"Come Sunday" (song), 153
Community Association of the East
    Harlem Triangle, 92
Concord Baptist Church of Christ, 74
Cone, James H., 44, 77–78
Convocation Day speech, 61–62
COVID-19 pandemic, 189–91, 195, 217
crack epidemic, 4, 8
Crawford, Annie, 68
Curry, Michael B., 106–7
Cutler, Jonathan, 82

Davis, Lorie, 222–24
Davis, Ossie, 113
Davis, Troy, 158–62
Davis, Virginia, 160
Davis-Correia, Martina, 160, 162
death penalty
    Davis case and, 158–62
    opening prayer and protests at
        Georgia Senate against, 109–10
debates, Warnock-Loeffler, 200–201
desegregation, 125–26
Diallo, Amadou, 96, 97
Different World, A (TV show), 62–63

disabilities movement, 152
Disturbed About Man (Mays), 54
Do the Right Thing (film), 95
Douglas, Frederick, 107–8
Douglas Memorial Community
    Church, 107, 122
Driver, Tom, 85
drug laws
    mandatory minimum sentencing
        guidelines and, 13
    mass incarceration and (*See* mass
        incarceration)
Dunson, Bernee, 118
Dyson, Michael Eric, 98, 153

Eaton, Kanyere, 81
Ebenezer Baptist Church, 120–33
Edelman, Marian Wright, 14–15
Edenfield, B. Avant, 11
Edmund Pettus Bridge, 70
"Educating Teens for Positive Peer
    Intervention" curriculum
    (Warnock), 56
education funding, 88
Ellington, Duke, 153
Emergency Relief for Farmers of Color
    Act, 218
Engel, Eliot, 98
English, Cynthia, 224
expungement, 164
"Extraordinary Epitaph of an
    Ordinary Man, The" eulogy
    (Warnock), 47–48

faith, 83–84
Farmer, James, 70
farmers, Black, 217–19
Farris, Christine King, 134
Finch, Phillip, 133, 136
Flake, Floyd, 173
Fletcher, Norman, 159
Floyd, George, 192–93, 194–95
Floyd, Virginia, 56
Forbes, James A., Jr., 74
*For My People: Black Theology and
    the Black Church* (Cone), 44
For the People Act, 216
Fraser-Howze, Debra, 114

"Freedom Caravan" commencement
    speech (Warnock), 152–53
Freedom Caravans, 148, 149
Friendship Baptist Church, 61
Frost, Robert, 61

gangsta rap, 91–92
gang warfare, 8
Garner, Eric, 193
gay persons, 84, 111, 152
Genesis 5:22 and 5:24, 47–48
Georgia Department of Human
    Resources, 169
Giffords, Gabby, 185
Giuliani, Rudolph, 98
Goldberg, Whoopi, 207
Goldman, Ron, 11
Goodman, Gwendolyn P., 50–51
Gray, William H., III, 173–74
Griffin, D. Darrell, 148, 202
Griffith, Michael, 95
Guy, Jasmine, 62
Guy, William, 61

Haiti, 85–87
Hall, Joyce Coleman, 18, 29, 46, 49,
    51, 195, 202
Hall, Prathia, 14
Harlem revitalization, 92–93
Harris, Joe Frank, 56
Harris, Kamala, 197, 201, 211
Hawkins, Yusuf, 94–95
Head Start, 28, 88
health insurance, and Medicaid
    expansion, 179–80, 220–24
Henry, Patrick, 152
Herbert Kayton Homes public housing
    project, 4
Hill, Ron, 191
HIV/AIDS virus, 4, 111–15
homophobia, 111
homosexuality, 83, 84
Hostin, Sunny, 207
Hough, Joseph, 154
House Committee on Education and
    Labor, 88
Hrabowski, Freeman A., III, 100
Hurricane Katrina, 143–44

impeachment trial, of Donald Trump, 212–13
infant mortality, 56
integration, 122
"In the Meantime" sermon (Warnock), 105–6
Isakson, Johnny, 184–85, 187
Isley, Isley Jasper, 148
"It's Time I Be About My Father's Business" sermon (Warnock), 36

Jackson, Jesse, 12, 15, 144, 145, 150, 182
Jackson, Maynard, 57
Jackson, Samuel, 175
January 6 riots, 208–10
Jealous, Ben, 159
Jean, Botham, 193
Jefferson, Atatiana, 193
Jenkins, Ron, 56
Jim Crow, 18, 24, 27, 53, 152, 176
Job Training Partnership Act, 39–40
Johnson, Solomon C., 3
Johnson, Francys, 179–80, 183
Johnson, Leroy R., 133–34, 138
Johnson, Lyndon B., 88
Johnson, Robert E., 57
Jones, Shanan, 145, 146
Jones, William Augustus, Jr., 74
Joyner, Tom, 158

Kaine, Tim, 211
Kelly Ingram Park, 99–100
Kemp, Brian, 183–84, 198
Kennedy, John F., 88, 126, 127
King, Alberta Christine, 122–23, 128–29
King, Alfred Daniel, 127–28
King, Coretta Scott, 126, 134, 149–50, 151
King, Lonnie, 175
King, Martin Luther, Jr., 14, 44, 52, 59–60, 69, 124–27, 146–47
    "The American Dream" speech, 59
    assassination of, 127
    Atlanta department store desegregation protests and, 125–26

Cone on, 78
    on death penalty, 162
    as Ebenezer co-pastor, 119–20, 126–27
    "A Knock at Midnight" sermon, 41–42, 67
    Poor People's Campaign and, 146, 153
    released from jail, 126
    on Talmadge and education, 54
    Warnock's thesis on, 93–94
King, Martin Luther, Sr., 122–25, 126, 130–32, 153–54
King, Valencia Warnock, 6–7, 27, 46, 117, 211
Knight, Carolyn Ann, 77, 79–80, 137, 154
"A Knock at Midnight" sermon (King, Jr.), 41–42, 67
Kornegay, Alice Wragg, 92–93
Ku Klux Klan, 121
Kurtz, Jerid, 188

Lain, Shaun, 147
Landrieu, Mitch, 149
Lawry, Steven, 150
Lee, Anthony, 97
Lee, Spike, 57, 62, 95
Legend, John, 145
lesbians, 84, 152
"Let My People Go" mass incarceration summit, 164–65
"Let My People Go: The Scandal of Mass Incarceration in the Land of the Free" lecture, 235–50
Lewis, John, 70, 134, 150, 170–71, 196
liquor industry advertisements, 90–91
"Listen to the Music" sermon (Warnock), 67–68
Lloyd, Marvin, 44
Loeffler, Kelly, 198, 199–200
Loews Express, 147
Louima, Abner, 96
Lowery, Joseph, 12, 14
Luke 4:18, 40

McClellan, Keisha, 61
McCoughtry, Angel, 198
McCoy, Gary, 37–39

McDonald, Timothy, 179–80
McKinney, Samuel Berry, 44
Maiden Speech (Warnock), 215, 251–59
Malcolm X, 78
mandatory minimum sentencing
    guidelines, 13
Mann, Horace, 152
Marble Collegiate Church, 73–74
Maroon Tiger, The, 54
Martin, Trayvon, 193
Martin Luther King, Sr. Community
    Resources Complex, 168–70
*Martin & Malcolm & America: A
    Dream or a Nightmare*
    (Cone), 78
mass incarceration, 17, 163–65
    expungements and, 164
    "Let My People Go" summit,
        164–65
    "Let My People Go: The Scandal of
        Mass Incarceration in the Land
        of the Free" lecture, 235–50
    nonviolent drug offenses and, 163
    racial and class bias in, 163
    Record Restriction Summit and, 164
    William Belden Noble Lecture,
        Harvard Memorial Church,
        235–50
Mays, Benjamin Elijah, 44, 54
Medicaid expansion, 179–80, 220–24
Medicaid Saves Lives Act, 221–22
Middlebrooks, Gwendolyn, 175
Miller, Stephen, 219
Miller, Zell, 176
Mitchell, Jimmie, 129
Montgomery bus boycott, 125
Moral Mondays movement, 180
Morehouse College, 54–60, 154–55
Morse, Christopher, 79
Morton, Paul, 145–46
Moss, Otis, Jr., 14, 44, 175
Multifaith Initiative to End Mass
    Incarceration, 165

Nagin, Ray, 149
National Association for the
    Advancement of Colored People
    (NAACP), 121

National Basketball Association, 190
National Black Leadership Commission
    on AIDS, 114
Ndoye, Oulèye, 185–86
New Frontier, 88
New Georgia Project, 181–84
New Orleans, 143–44
Newsom, Gavin, 211
New York Times Magazine, The,
    133–34
Nixon, Richard, 126
Nunn, Michelle, 178, 187
Nunn, Sam, 178

Obama, Barack, 165–67, 174,
    177–78, 197
O'Malley, Martin, 115
100 Black Men of Atlanta, 169
Operation HOPE, 168–69
Ossoff, Jon, 199, 200, 201, 211,
    221–22

Padilla, Alex, 211
Pathmark, 92
Peale, Norman Vincent, 74
Pell Grants, 28, 55
Pelosi, Nancy, 197
Pentecostals, 40–41
Perdue, David, 187, 199
Perkins, Byron, 202
Phoenix Mercury, 199
Poor People's Campaign, 146, 153
Porter, John Thomas, 67, 69–70,
    99–101, 113, 122
"Poverty and the Faith Community:
    After Katrina" (Dyson), 153
Powell, Adam Clayton, Jr., 87–89,
    122, 173
Powell, Adam Clayton, Sr., 122
Power of Positive Thinking, The
    (Peale), 74
"The Power on the Mountain and
    the Pain in the Valley" sermon
    (Warnock), 137–38
prison-industrial complex, 7
Proctor, Samuel DeWitt, 15,
    89–90
Psalm 137, 67

race card, 10–11
racial stereotyping and discrimination
  criminal justice system encounters
    disparities between whites and
    Blacks, 10–11
  mandatory minimum sentencing
    guidelines and, 13
  mass incarceration and, 17
  racial attacks and killings, in 1980s
    and 1990s New York, 94–98
  selective prosecution and, 10, 11–12
  shoplifting accusations and, 6–7
  Simpson verdict and, 10–11
Raffensperger, Brad, 209–10, 212
Randolph, A. Philip, 70
Rasmussen, Larry, 79
record industry, 91–92
Record Restriction Summit, 164
Reed, Lewis, 134
Reed, Sarah, 134–35
resuscitation, 46–47
Rice, Tamir, 193
Riverside Church, 74
Roberts, Joseph, 129–31, 132–33
Rockefeller, Nelson, 131, 132
Rodney King verdict, 11
Rouché, Maurice, 6
Russell, Richard B., 215

Safir, Howard, 98
Salaam, Yusef, 165
Santana, Raymond, Jr., 165
Savannah State, 51–53
Savannah Tribune, The, 3
"Say Her Name" campaign, 199
School Daze (film), 62
Scroggs, Robin, 79
segregation, 50, 152, 215
selective prosecution, 10, 11–12
Sessions, William, 159
Sharpton, Al, 95, 145, 150
Shelley, Percy, 47–48
shoplifting, 6–7
Simpson, Gary V., 74
Simpson, Nicole Brown, 11
Simpson, O. J., 10–11
Sixteenth Street Baptist Church
  bombing, 78, 100, 122

Sixth Avenue Baptist Church, 66–69,
  71–72, 99–101, 102, 122
slavery, 83–84
Smith, Kelly Miller, 44
"Souls to the Polls" initiative, 196–97
South Africa, 53
Southern Regional Task Force on
  Infant Mortality, 56
spirituals, 83–84
Spirituals and the Blues, The
  (Cone), 44
Stroud, Beth, 82, 84
student loans, 28, 55, 226–28
suffrage movement, 152

Talmadge, Eugene, 54, 215
Talmadge, Herman E., 215
Taylor, Breonna, 193, 199
Taylor, Gardner C., 74–75
Teen Peer Programs, 56
teen pregnancy, 56
Terrell, JoAnne, 80–81
Thompson, Larry, 159
Thoreau, Henry David, 54
three-fifths compromise, 152
Thurgood Marshall Academy for
  Learning and Social Change, 92
Thurman, Howard, 57, 83, 103, 104
Till, Emmett, 193
tobacco industry advertisements, 90–91
Tom Joyner Foundation, 158
transgender persons, 84
Trible, Phyllis, 79
Trump, Donald, 188, 190, 209, 210,
  212–13
Turks, Willie, 95
Tutu, Desmond, 159

Union Theological Seminary, 73–84
Upward Bound Olympics, 52–53
Upward Bound program, 28,
  49–54, 88

Vandiver, Ernest, 126
View, The (TV show), 207
voting rights, 17, 127
  Abrams and New Georgia Project
    voter registration drives, 181–84

federal voting rights legislation,
Warnock's battle for, 213–16
Freedom Caravan and voting in
New Orleans, post–Hurricane
Katrina and, 144–49
"Souls to the Polls" initiative and,
196–97
voter suppression efforts, 213, 215–16

Warnock, Caleb, 186, 225–26
Warnock, Carrie, 23, 31–32
Warnock, Chloé, 186, 225–26
Warnock, Jonathan, 4, 21–28, 40
Army service of, 4, 23
car crash and, 24–25
death of, 46–47
early life of, 23
eulogy for, 47–48
marries Verlene, 26
ministry of, 25–26, 35, 36
ordered to give up seat on bus,
23–24, 28
self-employed junk business of, 4, 24,
34–35
visits with Keith, 21–23, 45–46
Warnock, Jonathan Emmanuel, 49
Warnock, Madison, 23
Warnock, Raphael G.
See also Warnock, Raphael G.:
sermons, speeches, and writings
Abyssinian Church internship of, 76,
87–94
advocacy for brother, 15–17
Antioch College commencement
speech of, 150–53
baptized and ordained to ministry at
Sixth Avenue Baptist Church, 72
birth of, 27
in Chapel Assistants, 65
childhood and early education of,
4–8, 28–29, 32–37
children of, 186, 225–26
college affordability issue and, 55–56
Convocation Day speech of, 61–62
COVID-19 pandemic and, 189–91
Davis case and, 158–62
death penalty prayer and vigil at
statehouse, 109–10

debates Loeffler, 200–201
deliberates running for Congress,
173–78, 185–88
early morning devotional of, 103–4
elected pastor and ministry at
Douglas Memorial Community
Church, 107–18
elected Senator, 18, 204–6
falsely accused of shoplifting, 6–7
father's eulogy given by, 47–48
federally financed education
programs and, 28–29
federal voting rights legislation and,
213–16
on Floyd and Brooks killings, 193–95
Haitian trip of, 85–87
high school years of, 37–45, 50–54
HIV/AIDS fight and, 111–15
installation ceremonies, for
Ebenezer's pastorship, 153–55
interviews and elected pastor at
Ebenezer Baptist Church,
119–20, 133–41
interviews and rejection for
pastorship at Sixth Avenue
Baptist Church, 100–105
joins Diallo killing protests and
arrested, 98
King Jr. as inspiration for, 14, 41–42,
52, 120
leaders who inspired, 14–15,
41–42, 44
marriage of, 186
Martin Luther King, Sr. Community
Resources Complex and, 168–70
master's thesis of, 93–94
Medicaid expansion issue and,
179–80
ministry of, at Ebenezer Baptist
Church, 143–71
ministry studies of, 13–14, 40–42
at Morehouse College, 54–72
organizes Freedom Caravan for
voting in New Orleans post–
Hurricane Katrina, 144–49
as peer counselor, 39–40
priorities as Senator, 213–30
religious upbringing of, 34, 35–36

Warnock, Raphael G. (*cont.*)
  runoff election against Loeffler, 197–203
  on sanctions against South Africa's apartheid regime, 53
  Senate campaign of, 186–91
  sermons and preaching of, 42–45
  Sixth Avenue Baptist Church internship of, 66–69
  social justice issues, and Church's mission, 43, 44, 45
  social life of, 63, 70–71, 80–82
  "Souls to the Polls" voting initiative and, 196–97
  on Southern Regional Task Force on Infant Mortality, 56
  swearing-in ceremony, as Senator, 211–12
  Teen Peer Program work of, 56
  Trump impeachment and, 212–13
  at Union Theological Seminary, 73–87
  Upward Bound program and, 28, 49–54
  visits with Coretta Scott King, 149–50
  voter registration work with Abrams and New Georgia project, 181–84
  Wilson case and, 155–58
Warnock, Raphael G.: sermons, speeches, and writings
  "Churchmen, Church Martyrs: The Activist Ecclesiologies of Dietrich Bonhoeffer and Martin Luther King Jr.," 93–94
  "Educating Teens for Positive Peer Intervention" curriculum, 56
  "Extraordinary Epitaph of an Ordinary Man, The" eulogy, 47–48
  "Freedom Caravan" commencement speech, 152–53
  "In the Meantime" sermon, 105–6
  "It's Time I Be About My Father's Business" sermon, 36
  "Let My People Go: The Scandal of Mass Incarceration in the Land of the Free" lecture, 235–50
  "Listen to the Music" sermon, 67–68
  Maiden Speech, 215, 251–59
  "The Power on the Mountain and the Pain in the Valley" sermon, 137–38
Warnock, Samuel, 23, 31
Warnock, Verlene, 34
  early life of, 25–26
  informs Raphael of Keith's arrest, 1–2
  learns son has become Senator, 18–19
  marries Jonathan, 26
  as preacher, 40–41
  visits with Keith, 21–22
War on Poverty, 88
Washington, James Melvin, 77
Watkins, Angela Farris, 153–54
Weathers, Doug, 40
Weathers, Norma, 40
West, Cornel, 76
When They See Us (TV show), 165
White, Aunetta, 49
Wilkins, Roy, 70
Williams, Adam Daniel, 121, 122
Williams, Alberta Christine. *See* King, Alberta Christine
Williams, Delores S., 76–77
Wilson, Genarlow, 155–58
Wilson, William Julius, 7
Wimbush, Vincent, 77
Winfrey, Oprah, 149–50
Wire, The (TV show), 116
womanist theology, 76
women
  churches and denominations excluding women from pulpit, 40–41
  suffrage movement, 152
"Work That" (song), 201
World Health Organization, 189

Young, Andrew, 147, 150, 153, 170, 176
Young, Whitney, 70

Zechariah 4:6, 109